OUTCOMES

UPPER INTERMEDIATE

STUDENT'S BOOK

HUGH DELLAR

ANDREW WALKLEY

Contents **3**

Contents **5**

1

ENTERTAINMENT

IN THIS UNIT YOU LEARN HOW TO:

- talk about habits
- describe films, books and music
- politely disagree with opinions
- talk about pictures and art
- tell stories and discuss plots

SPEAKING

1 Work in pairs. Look at the photo and discuss the questions.

- Where do you think the place is? Would you want to read in a place like this? Why? / Why not?
- Do you usually take a book with you when you're travelling or do you prefer e-book readers?
- What's the nicest or most unusual place you've spent time reading?

2 Change partners. Tell each other about your other interests and how you spend your free time. Think about TV, music, films, sport and hobbies. Find five things that you have in common.

A QUESTION OF TASTE

LISTENING

1 ▶ 1 Listen to the answers to eight questions such as *Do you read much?* or *Do you watch TV much?* Listen and decide which *Do you … much?* questions were asked.

GRAMMAR

Habits

We use the present and past simple and a number of different structures such as *tend to* and *used to* to talk about habits. We use words and phrases such as *rarely*, *all the time* and *not as much as I'd like to* to show how often.

2 ▶ 2 Listen and complete the sentences with the expressions and structures used to talk about habits.

1 I don't _____ during the week, though.
2 Yeah _____ ! My headphones are glued to my ears.
3 Not as much _____ , because I really love it.
4 _____ , to be honest. I guess I might in the summer.
5 I don't pay much attention to it most of the time. _____ a big game, if there's one on.
6 Yeah, I guess so. I usually play football on a Wednesday and I go running _____ .
7 No, _____ . I tend to watch films on demand through my TV at home.
8 Not as much as I _____ . I was addicted to this online game, until my parents banned me. I _____ sometimes play for five hours a day!

3 In Exercise 2, find:

1 two ways we talk about a past habit.
2 one verb that describes a current habit – it means *usually* or *generally*.
3 two other structures we use to talk about current habits.
4 phrases that mean *always*, *(not) normally*, *sometimes* and *almost never*.

G Check your ideas on page 166 and do Exercise 1.

4 Complete the sentences about your own leisure interests. Then find out about your partner. How much do you have in common?

1 I … all the time.
2 I don't … as much as I used to because …
3 I tend to … at the weekends and now and again I …
4 As a rule, I don't … , but I will if …
5 I used to … a lot. I'd …

G For further practice, see page 166 and do Exercise 2.

5 Write five *Do you … much?* questions about other areas.

Think about:

• work
• study
• holiday
• eating
• family

Then find out about your partner. Use some of the structures from Exercise 2 in your answer.

VOCABULARY Describing films, music and books

When we describe things, we often use pairs of adjectives that have similar meanings to emphasise what we mean. We sometimes repeat the same adverb with each adjective.

It's very **moving** – just very, very **sad**.

It's **great**, absolutely **amazing**.

6 Complete the sentences with these words.

awful	disturbing	hilarious	uplifting
catchy	dull	over-the-top	weird
commercial	gripping		

1 It does nothing for me. It's quite boring, quite _____ .

2 It's one of those tunes that's very easy to remember – very _____ .

3 It's _____ – just really, really funny.

4 It didn't do much for me. It's typical big-budget Hollywood – very _____ .

5 I can't explain it. It's really strange – really _____ .

6 It's just too much for my liking – really _____ .

7 You can't stop reading. It's so exciting, so _____ !

8 It's good, but it's quite upsetting – quite _____ .

9 It's a really inspiring story, really _____ .

10 Don't go and see it! It's dreadful, absolutely _____ .

PRONUNCIATION

7 ▶ **3** Listen to the sentences from Exercise 6. Notice when you stress the adverb. Repeat the sentences.

8 Write at least two words or phrases that you associate with each adjective in the box in Exercise 6.

awful – leave before the end / hate / waste of money

9 Tell a partner the words you thought of. Your partner should guess the adjective.

LISTENING

10 ▶ **4** Listen to two people talking about films and decide which statement is true.

1 They agree on everything.

2 They agree on most things.

3 They don't agree on very much.

4 They don't agree on anything.

11 ▶ **4** Take notes about the two speakers to answer these questions. Listen again to check.

1 Do they go to the cinema much?

2 What kind of films are they mainly into?

3 Have they seen any films recently?

4 What did they think of them?

DEVELOPING CONVERSATIONS

Disagreeing politely

You heard the speakers disagree with viewpoints like this:

Yeah, I guess, but, **to be honest**, **I'm not that keen on** action movies.

It was all **a bit too weird for my liking**.

As I say, it's **not really my kind of thing**.

The Hunger Games was well-made / not bad, **I suppose, but ...**

When disagreeing with someone's tastes, instead of saying directly I don't like it or it's really weird, we often soften our responses by using phrases such as I'm not that keen on, I guess, I suppose, to be honest, for my liking, etc. We also use a bit to soften negative adjectives.

12 Look at three short conversations. Soften B's responses using some of the ideas above.

1 A: I'm really into 60s music. The Beatles, The Stones, stuff like that.

 B: Yeah? I don't like it. It's the kind of stuff my dad listens to.

2 A: Do you like Tarantino? I love his films.

 B: He's all right, but I'm not keen on his films. They're very over-the-top.

3 A: Have you ever read any Paulo Coelho? His books are fantastic.

 B: I've read one. It was OK, but it didn't do much for me.

PRONUNCIATION

13 ▶ **5** Listen to the example conversations. Notice the stress and intonation. Repeat them.

14 Write some responses to these sentences, disagreeing politely. Practise them in pairs.

1 I love Harry Potter and stuff like that.

2 I'm really into opera. It's fantastic.

3 I love any reality TV show.

CONVERSATION PRACTICE

15 Work in pairs. Have conversations about your habits using the guide below. Then swap roles.

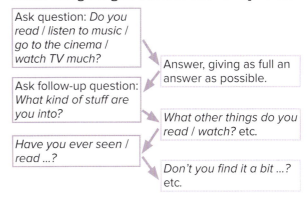

Ask question: Do you read / listen to music / go to the cinema / watch TV much?

Answer, giving as full an answer as possible.

Ask follow-up question: What kind of stuff are you into?

What other things do you read / watch? etc.

Have you ever seen / read ...?

Don't you find it a bit ...? etc.

▶ 1 To watch the video and do the activities, see the DVD-ROM.

IN THE PICTURE

SPEAKING

1 Read the quotations about art. Then discuss in pairs what you think each quotation means. How far do you agree with each one? Explain why.

' Art is the lie that enables us to realise the truth. '

' Modern art = I could do that + Yeah, but you didn't. '

' Advertising is the greatest art form of the 20th century. '

' Art is what you can get away with. '

' The urge to destroy is also a creative urge. '

' The more minimal the art, the longer the explanation. '

' Art never responds to the wish to make it democratic; it is not for everybody; it is only for those who are willing to undergo the effort needed to understand it. '

VOCABULARY Talking about pictures

2 Look at the painting below. With a partner, discuss who the character might be and what you think is happening.

3 Read the definitions. Discuss which adjectives could describe the painting above.

1 **Bold** colours are very bright, strong and clear, whereas **subtle** colours are not strong or bright. They're softer and more delicate.

2 If a painting is **conventional**, it's traditional and not new or different in any way.

3 If a painting is **dramatic**, it contains a lot of exciting action.

4 If it's **atmospheric**, a painting creates a special mood – such as a feeling of romance or mystery.

5 **Abstract** paintings show an artist's feelings or thoughts, whereas **realistic** paintings show real objects or events.

6 If it's **ambiguous**, the meaning of the work isn't clear – it's **open to interpretation**.

7 An **intimate** painting shows private moments in someone's life.

4 Which of these sentences about the painting do you agree with?

1 The main character has his back to the viewer, which **creates** a feeling of mystery.

2 He **looks as if** he's thinking about killing himself.

3 He's **obviously** a sad and lonely man.

4 He **seems to** be the most important thing in the painting.

5 He **appears to** be looking for something better than what he has.

6 He **looks** very proud. I **get the impression** he feels very pleased with himself.

7 He **looks like** a very wealthy man.

8 It **must** be somewhere in Europe. It **could well** be France.

5 Cover Exercise 4. Complete the sentences about other paintings using words and phrases from Exercise 4.

1 I think it could _____ be Spain or Italy in this picture.

2 Everyone looks _____ they're having a really good time in this picture.

3 I get the _____ she's been crying. She _____ really upset.

4 They've _____ just moved in and are redecorating the whole flat, from the look of it.

5 They _____ all be students. That looks _____ a university canteen to me.

6 Everyone in this picture _____ to be queuing or waiting for something.

LISTENING

6 Work in pairs. Use language from Exercises 3 and 4 to discuss the following questions.

• What do you think the portraits on page 11 show?

• Who do you think the people in the two paintings might be?

• How do you think they're feeling – and why?

• What might the connection between the two works be?

7 ▶ 6 Listen to a guide in a gallery telling visitors about the two paintings on page 11. Which five adjectives from Exercise 3 does the guide use?

8 ▶ 6 Listen again. Answer the questions.

1 Where was the artist from?

2 Was he well known when he was alive?

3 In what way are the two paintings connected?

4 In what way might the viewer's first impression of the paintings be wrong?

5 Why did the painter include the globe and the Turkish rug?

6 Why did the painter include the two paintings within these paintings?

GRAMMAR

9 Look at these examples from the talk in Exercise 7. Then work in pairs to complete the rules below.

Adjectives and adverbs

Adjectives

a symbol of the difficult, stormy nature of love

she looks calm and content

Adverbs

Look carefully and you'll notice that ...

These may look like fairly conventional, fairly realistic pieces,

Sadly, though, he died at the age of 37.

1 Adjectives are often used *before / after* nouns. Adjectives are also often used *before / after* the verbs *be, look, become, seem, get, taste*, etc. to describe the subject of the verb.

2 Most adverbs are formed by adding _____ to the adjective, but some have the same form as the adjective: *fast, hard* and *later*. Adverbs can be used to modify verbs, _____ , other adverbs and whole clauses or sentences.

G Check your ideas on page 166 and do Exercise 1.

10 Complete the sentences using the adjectives in brackets. Change the adjectives into adverbs where necessary.

1 _____ , van Gogh sliced his ear off while suffering from _____ depression. (severe / famous)

2 The painting was _____ damaged in a fire and, _____ , it couldn't be restored. (severe / unfortunate)

3 This _____ landscape is by the British artist, Kieron Williamson. _____ , he was only nine when he painted this. (amazing / lovely)

4 _____ , some people will just think it's _____ , but _____ some will like it and it may even change the way they think. (obvious / hopeful / weird)

5 _____ , Picasso's work was quite realistic, but it soon changed and _____ became more and more _____ . (experimental / gradual / initial)

6 There is a _____ debate about these _____ Chinese prints, because, well, _____ , they were stolen before they were donated to the museum. (frank / heated / amazing)

PRONUNCIATION

11 ▶ **7** Listen and notice the stress on the adverbs and the slight pause that follows. Repeat the sentences.

G For further practice, see Exercises 2–4 on page 167.

SPEAKING

12 Work in pairs.

Student A: look at the painting in File 1 on page 184.

Student B: look at the painting in File 17 on page 192.

Make notes on the following:

- what's happening in the painting

- the impression and feelings you have about it

- information about the painter and/or people in the picture (you can invent this if you want)

- additional comments you want to make about the painter and/or the painting. Start some comments with adverbs such as *Interestingly, Sadly, Actually*, etc.

Now present the picture to your partner.

TELLING TALES

READING

1 Work in pairs. Discuss the questions.

- Have you read a book or seen a film recently where the ending was quite predictable? What happens in the story?
- How did you know what was going to happen?
- Did you still enjoy the story? Why? / Why not?

2 Read the first part of a review of a book about why we tell stories. Answer the questions.

1 Why does the writer claim we often find films predictable?

2 Does the author think this is a problem or not? Why?

3 For one of the 'overcoming the monster' stories mentioned, think about:

a what or who is the monster or baddie?

b what community is threatened?

c what challenge does the monster present?

d what special weapon does the hero have?

e does the monster have a fatal flaw?

f how or where is the hero trapped and how does he escape?

g what is the final reward?

3 Look at the names of four of the other plots. Check the words in bold in a dictionary. Then discuss which sentences might go with which plot.

- Comedy
- Rags to riches
- Voyage and Return
- Tragedy

1 The central character is destroyed by committing suicide or by a relative of the victim **seeking revenge**.

2 People **disguise** themselves (including men as women and vice versa) or **pretend** to be someone different.

3 The hero is living in **poverty** or being bullied by a baddie.

4 The hero **encounters** a problem which **reveals** a dark side to the new world.

5 The couple are **bound to** get together but can't see it.

6 The baddie **asserts** their power or society presents an **obstacle** preventing the hero becoming successful.

7 Back in the normal world, the hero has gained a new **insight** that makes them a better person.

8 The hero **gets away with** the **bad deed** and enjoys the rewards.

4 Work in pairs. You will each read about two plots. Check your ideas from Exercise 3 and tell your partner.

Student A: read the text in File 2 on page 185.

Student B: read the text in File 7 on page 186.

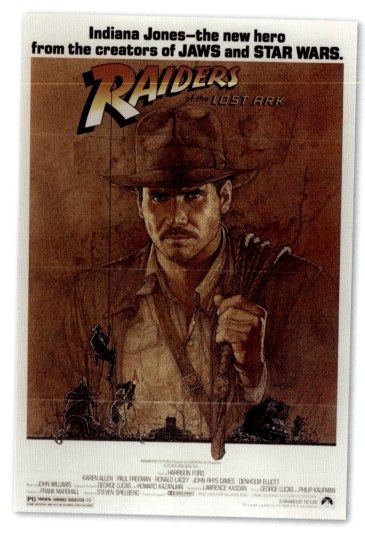

Indiana Jones—the new hero from the creators of JAWS and STAR WARS.

RAIDERS of the LOST ARK

PARAMOUNT PICTURES Presents A LUCASFILM LTD Production A STEVEN SPIELBERG Film

HARRISON FORD

KAREN ALLEN · PAUL FREEMAN · RONALD LACEY · JOHN RHYS-DAVIES · DENHOLM ELLIOTT

Music by JOHN WILLIAMS Executive Producers GEORGE LUCAS and HOWARD KAZANJIAN Screenplay by LAWRENCE KASDAN Story by GEORGE LUCAS and PHILIP KAUFMAN

Produced by FRANK MARSHALL Directed by STEVEN SPIELBERG

PG PARENTAL GUIDANCE SUGGESTED A PARAMOUNT PICTURE

5 Explain each plot you read without looking at the texts. Your partner should say the name of a story with that plot.

6 Work in pairs. Discuss the questions.

1 The two other plots Christopher Booker describes are called *Quest* and *Rebirth*. What do you think they might involve?

2 Do you agree with Booker that the best stories follow the basic plots? Why? / Why not?

3 Can you think of any stories that don't follow these plots? What do you think of those stories?

LISTENING

7 ▶ **8** Listen to someone explaining a story. Try to decide what plot it fits.

8 Think of a book, film or other story you like which might fit one of the plots. Explain the story. Your partner should ask questions to help you. When you have finished, your partner should guess the name of the story and/or the kind of plot.

HEARD IT ALL BEFORE

Ever been watching a film or reading a book and had the feeling you've heard it all before? You know the boy's going to get the girl, the baddie – the bad guy – is going to lose or be killed, or the team will win their last game. What's really surprising is that we don't have this feeling more often, because, according to Christopher Booker's brilliant book *Why We Tell Stories*, nearly all stories are based around just seven basic plots and in each plot we see the same character types and the same typical events over and over again.

Take the first plot, which Booker calls *Overcoming the Monster*. Stories of this kind all have several common features.

1   A community is threatened by a monster or 'baddie' and a hero is called to save it. The hero prepares to meet the monster and is either given a special weapon or learns about a particular weakness that the monster has – its fatal flaw.

2   The hero approaches the monster and initially everything goes according to plan.

3   The hero confronts the monster for the first time and is frustrated. They realise the huge challenge that the monster presents.

4   There is a nightmare stage. The hero is trapped and faces death.

5   Finally, the hero makes an amazing escape, succeeds in destroying the monster usually with the help of their special weapon or by exploiting the monster's only weakness. They are rewarded and order is restored.

You can see these features in ancient myths like Perseus killing Medusa or George and the Dragon, religious stories like David defeating the giant Goliath, modern tales like *Dracula* or *Harry Potter*, and films such as *Jaws*, *Star Wars* or in *James Bond* movies. Booker argues that we don't tire of these plots because they fulfil a deep psychological need for love and moral order. Indeed, where stories don't follow these plots, we may find them unsatisfying or they may reveal issues in the author and society that produced them.

2

SIGHTSEEING

IN THIS UNIT YOU LEARN HOW TO:

- describe buildings and areas in more detail
- agree using synonyms
- show people around your town or city
- talk about festivals and carnivals
- talk about future events in a variety of ways

SPEAKING

1 **Work in pairs. Discuss the questions.**

- Do you know where this photo was taken?
- What do you think of the photo? Is there anything that surprises you about it?

2 **Change partners. Discuss the questions.**

- What's the most famous place you've been to? Did it live up to your expectations? Why? / Why not?
- Where would you most like to visit? Why? What would you do there?
- Do you think the place where you live is a good tourist destination? Why? / Why not?

ABOUT TOWN

VOCABULARY Buildings and areas

1 Check any new words in bold in a dictionary. Work in pairs. Discuss the questions.

1 What kind of buildings and other things might you see in an **affluent** area?

2 What kind of buildings are usually described as **grand**?

3 What might you want to do to a **hideous** building or monument?

4 Can you think of a place with a lot of **high-rise** buildings?

5 What might the government do to an **historic** area or building? Why?

6 What do you call the opposite of a **deprived** area?

7 What do you find in a **residential** area?

8 Would you recommend a tourist to visit a **rough** area? Why? / Why not?

9 What might a local government do to a **run-down** building or area?

10 What do you call the opposite of a **stunning** building?

11 What might you find in a **trendy** area? And what kind of people might live there?

12 What's usually happening in an **up-and-coming** area?

2 Which of the words in bold could you use to describe the area in the photo?

3 Complete the sentences with the correct form of these verbs.

base	dominate	knock down	soar
date back	house	renovate	steer clear

1 I hate that building – it's hideous. If you ask me, it should be _____ .

2 The whole area's really run-down. It really needs to be _____ and given some investment.

3 It's quite a rough part of town. I'd _____ of it after dark if you don't want to be stabbed!

4 Some of the buildings in the historic centre _____ over 600 years.

5 It's an up-and-coming area. Lots of businesses are relocating there so property prices have _____ .

6 That grand building over there was previously a palace, but now _____ the national gallery.

7 It's the most affluent part of town. All the embassies are _____ there.

8 They built this huge skyscraper a few years ago. It really _____ the city.

PRONUNCIATION

4 ▶ **9** Listen to and repeat some key words from Exercises 1 and 3. Notice the stress.

5 Work in groups. How many adjectives and verbs from Exercises 1 and 3 can your group use to describe buildings and areas where you live?

LISTENING

6 ▶ **10** Listen to a Serbian woman, Ivana, and her friend, May, as they drive through Belgrade. Take notes on what you hear about each place. Work in pairs to compare your ideas.

New Belgrade	
the Arena	Big concerts / sports events held there. One of the biggest entertainment venues in Europe.
the Ada Bridge	
Manakova Kuca	
St Mark's Church	Built late 1930s – on site of older church. Contains tomb of a great Serbian emperor.
Kalemegdan Fortress	
the Victor Monument	
Dedinje	

GRAMMAR

7 Look at the sentences from the conversation in Exercise 6. Then work in pairs to discuss the questions below.

Relative clauses

We use relative clauses to add information about nouns or previous clauses.

a *Over to the right is the Arena, <u>which is where all the big concerts and sports events are held</u>.*

b *It contains the tomb of Stefan Dusan, <u>who was perhaps the greatest Serbian emperor ever</u>.*

c *You might've seen it on TV – it's <u>the place they held the Eurovision Song contest</u>.*

d *There's the Victor Monument up there as well, <u>which was erected after the First World War</u>.*

1 Which sentences have a comma?

2 If you removed the underlined relative clauses, which sentences would still make sense?

3 Do we need a comma before adding a) essential or b) non-essential information?

4 Apart from *which* and *who*, do you know any other relative pronouns?

5 Do you always need a relative pronoun to add information after the noun?

G Check your ideas on page 167 and do Exercise 1.

8 Rewrite each of the pairs of sentences below as one sentence using a relative clause.

1 That statue is of our first president, Vaclav Havel. He was also a famous writer.

That statue is of our first president, Vaclav Havel, who was also a famous writer.

2 We're coming up to Dedinje. Dedinje is one of the more affluent parts of the city.

3 Just behind us, over to the right, is Santa Catalina Cathedral. I was actually married in there.

4 And that building over there is the Courts of Justice. I got divorced there!

5 This shop on the left is run by my friend Zora. Her son plays professional football in Turkey now.

6 I started working in that office over there in 2003. Even then, the area was already starting to boom.

7 They produce tiles in that factory. They export most of them to northern Europe.

G For further practice, see page 168 and do Exercises 2 and 3.

DEVELOPING CONVERSATIONS

Agreeing using synonyms

In the conversation in Exercise 6, you heard this exchange:

A: *The houses certainly do look very **grand**.*

B: *Yeah, they're **amazing**.*

We often use some kind of synonym (a word with a similar meaning) to show we agree.

9 Work in pairs. Take turns saying and agreeing with the opinions below. Use synonyms to agree.

1 That's a really hideous building!

2 All the houses round here are amazing, aren't they?

3 That church is incredible!

4 The river looks wonderful, doesn't it?

5 This is pretty run-down, isn't it?

6 This seems like quite a wealthy area.

CONVERSATION PRACTICE

10 Imagine you are going to drive a friend round your hometown, the city you are in now, or round a city you know well. Write the names of four or five places you will pass through. Think of details about the places, what you think of them and if you'd recommend visiting them.

11 Now roleplay the conversation. Follow the guide below. Continue as long as you can. Then swap roles.

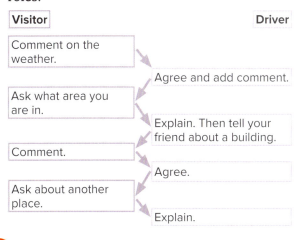

Visitor	Driver
Comment on the weather.	
	Agree and add comment.
Ask what area you are in.	
	Explain. Then tell your friend about a building.
Comment.	
	Agree.
Ask about another place.	
	Explain.

2 To watch the video and do the activities, see the DVD-ROM.

A CARNIVAL ATMOSPHERE

VOCABULARY Festivals and carnivals

1 Look at the photo above. In pairs, discuss the following questions:

- Where do you think it was taken?
- What do you think is going on?
- What might the event be celebrating?

2 Which of these words can you see in the photo?

a band	a costume	a mask
a bonfire	a fireworks display	a parade
confetti	a float	a sound system

3 Match the nouns above with the groups of words they go with.

1 make your own ~ / wear a ~ / hide behind a ~
2 build a ~ / ride on a ~ / a ~ in the shape of a fish
3 set up a ~ / a really loud ~ / hire a ~
4 dress up in a ~ / a very ornate ~ / wear national ~
5 make a ~ / sit round a ~ / throw wood on a ~
6 listen to a ~ / form a ~ / play in a ~ / book a ~
7 watch a ~ / a spectacular ~ / cancel a ~ / miss a ~
8 hold a ~ / take part in a ~ / a ~ through town
9 throw ~ / be showered with ~ / sweep up all the ~ afterwards

4 Work in pairs. For each of the nouns in Exercise 2 choose one of the collocations in Exercise 3. Think of an example from your own life. Tell your partner your example. Find out if your partner has had similar experiences.

A: *I went to a fancy dress party last year and **wore a** scary monster **mask**.*

B: *Really? I've never been to a fancy dress party.*

READING

5 Before you read, discuss the question in groups.

- What do you know about Venice? Can you say ten things about its history, location, sights or carnival?

6 Read the email about the Venice Carnival. Add the relative clauses (a–j) in the spaces (1–10) in the email.

a which are very ornate and beautiful
b during which time people fasted
c which I hope you enjoy
d which would've been almost impossible
e which can give you a real shock
f which are these pastry things full of cream and stuff
g where they hold the big costume parade
h which is great fun
i who I'm sure you remember
j who used to look after the dead and dying

7 Decide if these sentences about the email are true (T) or false (F). Then look back at the email and underline the sentences that support your decisions.

1 Chiaki, Kyeong Jin and Nina all studied together.
2 Hotels are a bit more expensive during carnival.
3 Chiaki preferred the modern costumes.
4 Carnival celebrates the end of Lent.
5 Traditionally, people ate a lot less during Lent.
6 Chiaki sprayed some strangers.
7 She was shocked at the way people behaved.
8 Chiaki plans to send more photos.

8 Find words in the email that mean the same as the words in italics.

1 It was very kind of Nina to *let me stay at her house for free*.

2 The city was completely *full of* tourists.

3 It's *not surprising* most costumes look so good.

4 The locals generally *continue with* traditional costumes.

5 The Plague Doctor costume is quite scary and *threatening and evil*.

6 The food is delicious, but *high in calories*.

7 Venice is completely *changed in a good way* during carnival.

8 People *light and explode* fireworks all the time.

9 Work in pairs. Discuss the questions.

• Do you have a carnival or festival in your town, city or area?

• Do you usually go to it?

• What does it involve? Use some words from Exercises 2 and 3 to describe what happens.

• Have you ever been to any other carnivals or festivals? Where? When? What were they like?

To   KyeongJin@hotmail.ml
Subject   Re: Hello there

Hi Kyeong Jin,

I hope this finds you well. I'm really sorry I haven't written for so long, but the beginning of the year was really busy for me – and then I went off to Venice for the carnival. In fact, I only got back to Boston last night!

Venice was absolutely amazing. You would've loved it. I stayed with Nina, [1]_____ from uni. It was really kind of her to put me up – and it meant I didn't have to struggle with trying to find a hotel, [2]_____ . The city was completely packed with tourists for the whole ten days, and prices really shoot up.

Nina lives with her family, about ten minutes' walk from the main square, [3]_____ on the first day of the carnival. Some of the costumes were just incredible – people spend months and months preparing, so it's no wonder they look so good, really. Lots of tourists were dressed up in all kinds of crazy outfits – giant rabbits, pirates, even hot dogs – but the locals tend to stick to traditional costumes, [4]_____ and they all wear masks as well. My favourite costume is called the Plague Doctor. It's really scary and sinister and I was told it's based on real doctors, [5]_____ when the plague hit Venice.

Apparently, carnevale, the word the Italians use, comes from Latin and means 'farewell to meat'. Traditionally, the carnival took place in the week leading up to Lent, the 40 days before Easter, [6]_____ . That's why food is really important during carnival, and I ate lots and lots of *frittelle*, [7]_____ – fattening, but really delicious!

Venice is as beautiful as everyone says: very romantic and atmospheric. All through the carnival, though, it's transformed as they have big fireworks displays, bonfires, parties and so on, and all the kids throw confetti and spray shaving foam and stuff everywhere, [8]_____ – unless it lands on you! Mind you, we ended up buying a few cans and joining in ourselves! Attack is the best form of defence, right? People also set off fireworks all the time, [9]_____ if you're not expecting it. I nearly had a heart attack a couple of times.

I've attached a few photos, [10]_____ . I was going to send more, but I didn't want to make your computer crash like I managed to last time! I've uploaded loads more onto my website, if you fancy having a look.

Anyway, hope to hear from you soon.

All the best,

Chiaki

WORTH A VISIT

SPEAKING

1 Look at these different places to visit when on holiday. Rank them from 1 (like visiting most) to 8 (like least). Explain your choices to your partner.

amusement parks	monuments	street markets
galleries	museums	zoos
historic buildings	sports stadiums	

LISTENING

2 ▶ **11** Listen to five extracts. Match each with one of the places above.

3 ▶ **11** Listen again. Match the extracts (1–5) with the situations (a–e). Then discuss the questions (in brackets) with a partner.

a   Protesting about a proposal. (What's the proposal and why is there opposition to it?)

b   Promoting something. (What is it?)

c   Using their powers of persuasion. (How? Why?)

d   Talking about a forthcoming trip. (Where to? When?)

e   Feeling unwell. (Why?)

4 Work in pairs. Discuss the questions.

• Do you think galleries and museums should be free to get in to? Why? / Why not?

• Have you ever been to any unusual museums or exhibitions? When? What were they like?

• What do you think the most innovative architecture in your town or city is?

• Have there been any campaigns against tourist developments in your area or country?

GRAMMAR Talking about the future

There is no future tense in English. Instead, there are different ways of talking about the future such as *going to* + infinitive (without *to*), *will* + infinitive (without *to*), the present simple and the present continuous.

5 ▶ **12** Listen to these different ways of expressing the future from Exercise 2. Complete the sentences.

1   This year we _____ a new wing dedicated exclusively to Asian art.

2   The kids _____ it.

3   It _____ at ten.

4   I _____ down there tomorrow morning and have a look at that.

5   I think I _____ faint.

6   I _____ and get you a glass of water.

6 Match the explanations with the sentences in Exercise 5.

a   This is a fixed timetable.

b   This is an offer to do something – made at the moment of speaking.

c   This is a decision about the future that someone has made on their own.

d   This is a prediction made at the moment of speaking.

e   This has already been arranged and organised with others.

f   This is a prediction based on what you can see, feel, etc.

G Check your ideas on page 169 and do Exercise 1.

For certain meanings, we prefer one particular form. However, in many cases, more than one form can be used with little or no change of meaning. For instance, we prefer the present continuous to talk about arrangements, but we can also use *going to* + infinitive (without *to*).

*I'm **having** dinner with a client tonight.*

*I'm **going to have** dinner with a client tonight.*

7 In sentences 1–6, either one or two of the three options are incorrect when talking about the future. In pairs, discuss your choices.

1 a The move will improve things in the future.
  b The move is improving things in the future.
  c The move is going to improve things in the future.

2 a We're going to meet some friends later.
  b We're meeting some friends later.
  c We meet some friends later.

3 a I think I'll faint.
  b I think I'm going to faint.
  c I'm fainting.

4 a It's going to cause problems at some point.
  b It causes problems at some point.
  c It'll cause problems at some point.

5 a What are you doing over the holidays? Any plans?
  b What will you do over the holidays? Any plans?
  c What are you going to do over the holidays? Any plans?

6 a I'll carry that for you. It looks heavy.
  b I carry that for you. It looks heavy.
  c I'm going to carry that for you. It looks heavy.

We often use adjectives to talk about the future. In the extracts, you heard:

a *Officially, it's* **due to** *open in a couple of months.*

b *That's not* **likely to** *happen.*

c *Any expansion is* **bound to** *worsen the situation.*

8 Match the explanations 1–3 with the examples (a–c) above.

1 this is almost certain not to happen

2 this is almost certain to happen; it's seen as highly probable by the speaker

3 the action should happen at a particular time; it's expected to happen then

G Check your ideas on page 169 and do Exercise 2.

9 Choose the correct option.

1 There are *due to / bound to* be problems when the new system is introduced.

2 I think we're *due to / bound to* arrive at something like twenty to ten.

3 If he keeps doing things like that, something bad is *due to / bound to* happen sooner or later.

4 He is *due to / bound to* appear in court on the 31st of the month.

5 Your mum's *due to / bound to* worry about you while you're away. It's only natural.

6 She can't travel at the moment as she's *due to / bound to* give birth any day now.

7 It is technically possible to get a visa to travel there, but it's *due to / not likely to* be easy.

PRONUNCIATION

10 ▶ **13** Listen and check your answers. Notice the pronunciation of the adjectives for talking about the future. Then practise saying the sentences.

SPEAKING

11 Work in pairs. Discuss how important 1–6 below are for the future of the area you live in.

1 jobs for young people

2 attracting investment

3 schools and education

4 affordable housing

5 leisure facilities

6 protecting the environment

12 Read the proposal below and decide if you support it or are against it. Write ideas about the effect it will have on 1–6 in Exercise 11, using future forms. Then work in groups to discuss your opinions. Try to persuade anyone who disagrees with you or suggest changes.

> A LOCAL BUSINESSMAN IS CURRENTLY APPLYING FOR PLANNING PERMISSION TO BUILD ONE OF THE COUNTRY'S BIGGEST HOTELS AND LEISURE COMPLEXES NEAR WHERE YOU LIVE. IF PERMISSION IS GRANTED, THE COMPLEX WILL INCLUDE A TWENTY-FIVE STOREY HOTEL, THREE GOLF COURSES, A SPA, A CASINO AND A WATER PARK.

VIDEO 1

A CHINESE ARTIST IN HARLEM

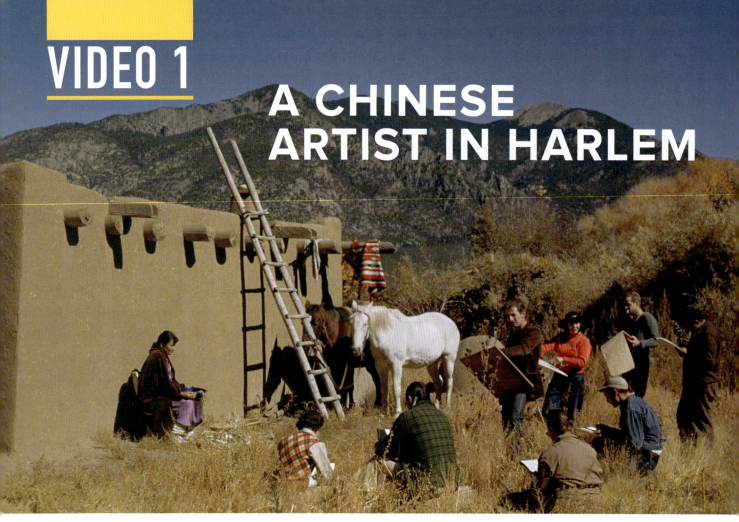

1 **Look at the photo. Work in pairs. Discuss the questions.**

- Have you ever had any art lessons?
- What did you do in the lessons? Did you enjoy them? Why? / Why not?
- Do you think art is a good subject to study at college or university? Why? / Why not?
- What do you think art students go on to do once they've graduated?

2 ▶3 Watch the first part of a video about a Chinese artist, Ming Liang Lu. Find out about his life. Compare what you understood with a partner.

3 Before watching the next part, discuss how his current work might be important to the children in Harlem. Watch and see if your ideas were mentioned.

4 ▶3 In pairs, discuss how you think these extracts from the video continued. Watch again to check the actual words used in the video.

1 Sometimes this diversity results in clashes between cultures. Other times …

2 At a very young age, he learned about calligraphy and painting from his father and …

3 Ming set up his easel and drew and painted portraits of tourists in order to survive. But …

4 Ming [...] began to work for the New York Chinese Cultural Center. Through them …

5 You cannot teach solely by the book, paper and pencil. They …

6 The children view Ming as their teacher from China, but Ming sees beyond ethnicity. He just …

7 Even though New York is already established as a diverse international city, ….

8 What we don't want to do to our students is to ….

9 Ming is also serving as a kind of cultural ambassador for his country. In the long run, …

5 **Work in groups. Discuss the questions.**

- What is your impression of Ming and the work he does? What do you think of his art?
- What do you see as the benefits and problems of the project in Harlem? Explain your ideas.
- Did you meet people from other countries when you were growing up? Who?
- Would you be a good cultural ambassador for your country? Why? / Why not?

UNDERSTANDING FAST SPEECH

6 **Look at this extract from the video. To help you, groups of words are marked with / and stressed sounds are in CAPITALS. Pauses are marked //. Practise saying the sentence.**

AS we all KNOW / a LOT of Artists / ARE // not emPLOYED // BEing ARtists // SO / i'm HOPing that what WE do / IS / to provide them this opporTUnity / to really PRActise // UM / in the FIELD that they've been TRAINED for // .

7 ▶4 Listen to how Amy said this sentence. Now you have a go! Practise saying the extract again fast.

REVIEW 1

GRAMMAR

1 Complete the text with one word in each space.

I'm a big football fan. I've been going to watch my local club for nearly twenty years. I [1] _____ to go with my grandad, [2] _____ was a fan all his life. He [3] _____ usually pick me up early and take me for a burger before the game, so it was a real day out. My dad came with us now and [4] _____ but he isn't that keen [5] _____ football, to be honest.
[6] _____ , my grandad died a couple of years ago, so now I [7] _____ to go on my own and meet friends [8] _____ have made at the club.

The club has decided it's [9] _____ to move to a new stadium because it [10] _____ have a bigger capacity than the current one and they hope to host some matches in the tournament [11] _____ will be held here next year. The old stadium is going [12] _____ be knocked down and replaced with flats, some [13] _____ which will be available at a cheaper price. I've applied to buy one and they have said that, I'm highly [14] _____ to get one, [15] _____ is great.

2 Complete the second sentence so that it has a similar meaning to the first sentence, using the word given. Do not change the word given. You must use between three and five words, including the word given.

1 100,000 people built the Great Pyramid. There were a few slaves.

   The Great Pyramid was built by 100,000 people, only _____ were slaves. **OF**

2 He said it's possible he'll be late, so start without him.

   He said to start without him as _____ late. **MIGHT**

3 There has been a gradual change in the city over the last ten years.

   The city _____ over the last ten years. **CHANGED**

4 They'll definitely change their minds about it.

   They _____ their minds about it, as usual. **BOUND**

5 I don't tend to go out much on a weekday.

   _____ at home during the week. **RULE**

3 Choose the correct word or form.

1 Don't worry about it. *I / I'll* sort it out later.

2 *Apparent / Apparently*, it's quite a rough area.

3 As a rule, Monet *was painting / painted* outside.

4 This guy was looking at me *strange / strangely*. I felt really *uncomfortable / uncomfortably*.

5 The main character looks very *weird / weirdly* when he's in his disguise.

6 We wandered round the city till two o'clock, *when / by which time* we were starving.

7 Just to say, the traffic's pretty bad here, so *I am arriving / I might arrive* late.

8 This film, *who / whose* writer died shortly after it opened, has won a number of awards.

4 ▶ **14** Listen. Write the six sentences you hear.

VOCABULARY

5 Match the verbs (1–10) with the collocates (a–j).

1 It houses
2 It dominates
3 It dates back to
4 It fulfils
5 The hero seeks
6 The hero encounters
7 They cancelled
8 The baddies assert
9 They should knock down
10 The report has finally revealed

a revenge for his father's death.
b that hideous building.
c the firework display.
d a number of problems along the way.
e the whole skyline.
f a huge collection of art.
g the sixth century.
h a psychological need.
i their power and strength.
j the cause of the accident.

6 Decide if these adjectives describe a building, an area, a film or a song.

catchy	grand	high-rise	up-and-coming
disturbing	gripping	residential	uplifting

7 Complete the text with one word in each space. The first letters are given.

You may know Notting Hill from the film of that name but perhaps you'd be surprised to know that it used to be quite a [1] de_____ and run-down area of London. Over the last 40 years, though, people have gradually bought houses and [2] re_____ them. As a result, prices have [3] so_____ and it has become the affluent area you see in the film. Notting Hill is also famous for its carnival, which is held every year in August. Each day people take part in a [4] pa_____ through the streets, many of whom wear masks or incredible ornate [5] co_____ . There are also [6] fl_____ carrying musicians, which are beautifully decorated or built in the [7] sh_____ of all kinds of different things. In the side streets local people [8] s_____ up sound systems playing reggae music.

8 Complete the sentences. Use the word in brackets to form a word that fits in the space.

1 The main character is living in _____ at the beginning of the film. (poor)

2 I love the photo of the shadow of the pyramid. It's so _____ . (drama)

3 The meaning is open to _____ . (interpret)

4 It's quite an _____ scene in some ways. (upset)

5 They're building an _____ park near there. (amuse)

6 There have been a number of protests against the _____ . (propose)

7 The city undergoes a huge _____ during the carnival. (transform)

8 I shouldn't eat any more of these *frittelle*. They're so _____ . (fat)

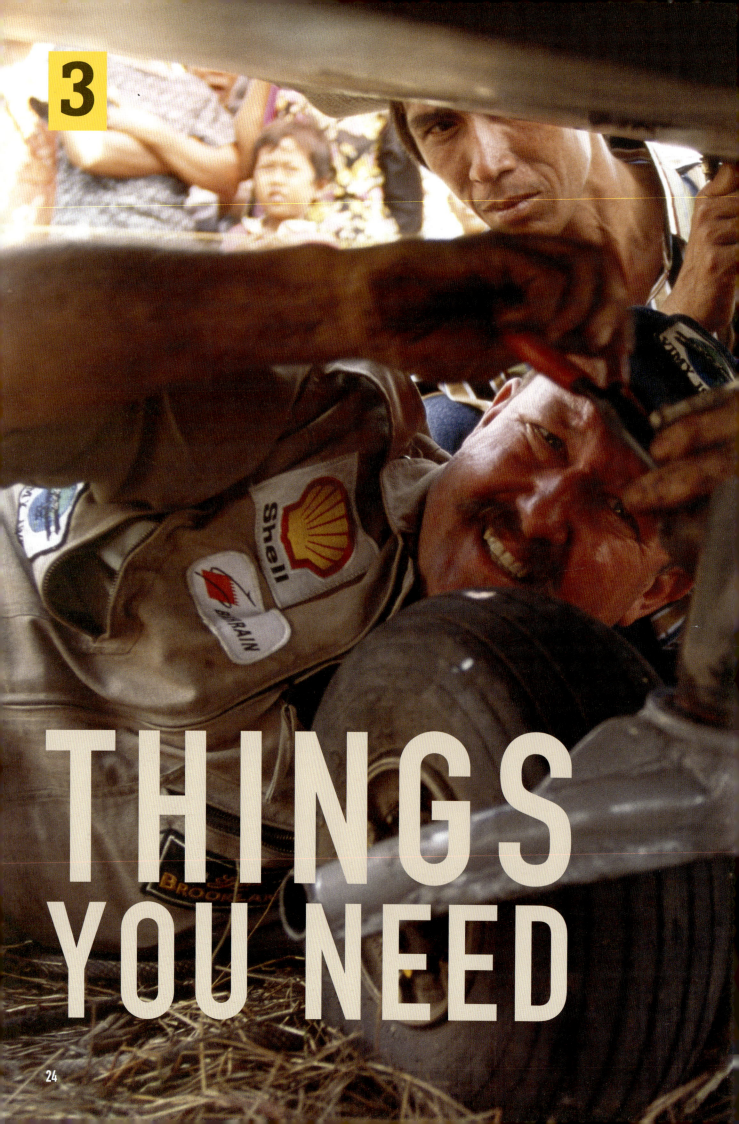

THINGS YOU NEED

IN THIS UNIT YOU LEARN HOW TO:

- talk about a wide range of objects
- describe what things are for
- check you understand what people mean
- use suffixes and prefixes better
- describe problems with things
- give advice and express regrets

SPEAKING

1 **Work in pairs. Discuss the questions.**

- What do you think the men in the photo are trying to fix? Why? How?
- Are you any good at fixing things?
- Can you remember what you fixed most recently?
- What problems connected with the things below do you know how to fix?

| cars | computers | bicycles | houses or flats |

- What tools have you used? How well did you handle them?
- Have you ever tried to fix something only for it to all go terribly wrong? When? What happened?

MAKING DO

VOCABULARY Useful things

1 Look at the pictures in File 11 on page 188 and discuss the questions.

- Are there any things you've never used? Why? / Why not?
- Which of the objects do you use: all the time / regularly / now and again / hardly ever?
- Do you have any of these things on you now? Which of the things do you have at home?
- Which of the things did you NOT know in English before?

2 In groups, add as many of the things on page 188 as you can to the categories below without looking at the pictures. Which group can remember the most words?

- the office / study: _____
- the kitchen: _____
- clothes: _____
- DIY: _____
- first aid: _____

3 Work in pairs. Take turns to test each other on the vocabulary from page 188 by asking the questions below.

Student A: look at File 11 on page 188.

Student B: keep your book closed.

Student A: ask: *What do you need …*

- to tie things together?
- to put up a poster or a notice?
- to wash and hang up your clothes to dry?
- if there's a crack in your roof and it's leaking?
- so you can mend a rip in your clothing?

Student B: look at File 11 on page 188.

Student A: keep your book closed.

Student B: ask: *What do you need …*

- to keep papers together?
- to put up a picture on the wall?
- to make holes in the wall?
- if you knock over a cup and it smashes on the floor?
- so you can see better in dark places?

GRAMMAR Explaining purpose using *so, if* and *to*

4 Look back at Exercise 3. Notice how *so, if* and *to* were used when explaining purpose. Which was followed by:

– an infinitive (without *to*)?

– a subject plus verb?

– the problem you want to solve?

Then complete these sentences:

---

a I need some tape _____ put up a poster on the wall.

b Can I have a cloth _____ I can wipe the table?

c It's a thing you can put on your heel _____ your shoes rubbing.

G Check your ideas on page 169 and do Exercise 1.

5 Why would you use or need the following things? Think of one common and one less common purpose for each.

---

a bandage   a bucket   a lighter   a nail   a needle

For example: a cloth

You use it to wipe the table after you've had dinner.

If you can't open the top of a jar, you can put a cloth over the top so you can grip it better.

G For further practice, see Exercise 2 on page 170.

DEVELOPING CONVERSATIONS

6 ▶ **15** Listen to two conversations. Which of the things in the picture below are they talking about?

7 Think of four things you don't know the name of in English. Use some of the language in the box below to explain them to a partner. Your partner should check they have understood and draw what you have explained.

Explaining and checking

Look at the ways the speakers explained things:

A: That **stuff** – it's **a bit like** chewing gum **or something**.

A: They have **a sort of** clip **thing** that opens and shuts.

You can check you understand by using these patterns:

B: What? **You mean** Blu-Tack?

B: What? **You mean the thing you use to** connect yourself to the rope?

LISTENING

8 ▶ **16** Listen to a man asking for something. Answer the questions.

1 What does he want?

2 What for?

3 What does he use instead?

4 What else does he need – and why?

9 ▶ **16** Work in pairs. Try to complete the sentences you heard. Then listen again to check your ideas.

a I don't think there's one here. _____ use a knife?

b You need a stick _____ to push it down.

c Would a pencil _____ ?

d It wouldn't be _____ .

e What about a wooden spoon? _____ the handle.

f Yeah, _____ do.

g Don't worry about it. These _____ .

h You might want to rub some salt into that shirt or it'll _____ .

SPEAKING

10 Work in groups. Discuss the questions.

- Can you think of a situation where you didn't have the things you needed and you had to improvise or make do?

- Do you know any ways of removing these kinds of stains?

coffee	grass	oil	paint	wax

CONVERSATION PRACTICE

11 You are going to take turns to ask for different things and to solve different problems.

Student A: look at File 18 on page 191.

Student B: look at File 14 on page 189.

Then use this guide for each conversation.

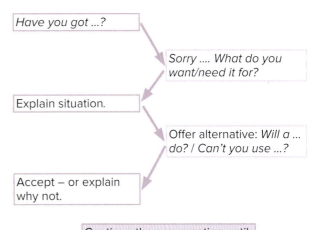

Have you got ...?

Sorry .... What do you want/need it for?

Explain situation.

Offer alternative: Will a ... do? / Can't you use ...?

Accept – or explain why not.

Continue the conversation until you find a good solution.

🎥 5 To watch the video and do the activities, see the DVD-ROM.

FULL HOUSE

SPEAKING

1 Write six questions you could ask the person who collected the cameras in the photo.

How did you get into collecting them?

2 Think about something you collect or used to collect. Take turns to find out about your partner's collection. If you've never collected anything, imagine you're the owner of the collection in the picture!

READING

3 Read the blog post about a man called Mr Trebus and answer the questions.

1 What did Mr Trebus collect?

2 How does the blogger say he is similar to Trebus?

3 What reasons are given for Trebus and the blogger keeping things?

4 Are you at all similar to Trebus and the blogger?

4 Correct these sentences about Mr Trebus. Look at the blog post again if you need to.

a His house became a fire hazard.

b He was a veteran of the Vietnam War.

c He was a navy commander.

d The trauma of his father's death caused his obsession.

e He settled in Birmingham after the war.

f He sorted the junk into piles of different colours.

g He acquired a number of valuable paintings.

h The neighbours complained about infestations of cockroaches.

i He resisted arrest by the police.

5 Write at least two words or phrases that you associate with each of the corrected sentences in Exercise 4.

*His house became a **health hazard**: rats, spread disease, smell awful*

6 Work in pairs. Compare your ideas and discuss how each of your words or phrases are connected to the sentences.

UNDERSTANDING VOCABULARY

Word families

Suffixes – word endings – often indicate a particular word form. For example, the suffix *-er* often indicates a noun: *a tank commander, a writer, a teacher*. All these kinds of jobs have connected verbs: *command, write, teach*. When you learn connected word forms, try to also learn the collocations that go with these words.

7 In groups, think of words ending with these suffixes and then answer the questions below.

-al	-ious	-ism	-less	-ness
-ion	-ise	-ity	-ment	-y

1 Which of these suffixes normally form nouns?

2 What kinds of words do these other suffixes form?

8 Look at the underlined words and find the noun forms in the blog post. Complete 1–8.

1 he's <u>obsessed</u>	have an _____
2 They tried to <u>evict</u> him	face _____
3 he's <u>cautious</u>	show great _____
4 I'm <u>afraid</u>	overcome my _____ of flying
5 he's well-<u>intentioned</u>	have good _____
6 I'm very <u>optimistic</u>	be full of _____
7 he's really <u>mean</u>	it's pure _____
8 he's <u>pessimistic</u>	despite the _____

9 In what ways are Mr Trebus and/or the blogger:

1 obsessive? 4 pessimistic?

2 optimistic? 5 cautious?

3 well-intentioned? 6 mean?

10 Do you – or does anyone you know – have the characteristics in Exercise 9? How do these characteristics affect your behaviour? Give examples.

My brother has an obsessive personality. He gets really obsessed with things quite easily. Recently, it's been this online computer game he's discovered. He stays up all night playing it sometimes!

SPEAKING

11 Read the comments on the blog post. Decide how far you agree with each point – and which you like or agree with most. Discuss your ideas with a partner.

SEARCH BLOG   FLAG BLOG   NEXT BLOG

I AM ... MR TREBUS

Some years ago, an 80-year-old Polish war veteran hit the headlines when the local council tried to force him out of his own house in London because it had become a health hazard. Mr Trebus, who'd had to leave his hometown in Poland after Germany invaded at the beginning of the Second World War, later served as a tank commander in the British army. Perhaps it was the trauma of what he lost when he left Poland that caused his obsession – who knows? – but after he settled in London, he began collecting all kinds of things. He would tour the local neighbourhood recovering things from bins that others had seen as mere rubbish. He then took this junk home and sorted it into piles of similar things: a room packed with vacuum cleaners, a corner for old doors, another for windows. He also managed to acquire practically every record Elvis Presley ever made.

However, as he filled his house, his wife left him and the neighbours increasingly complained about rat infestations. By the time the council came to evict the old man, he had just a tiny space in his kitchen to live in, surrounded by stacks of old newspapers and children's toys. Yet he resisted eviction, accusing the local council of acting like dictators and arguing that everything he kept was useful.

He was clearly over-the-top, but let's face it, there's a bit of Mr Trebus in most of us. How many collectors do you know? Personally, I have boxes of old comics in the attic, which I don't read, but can't get rid of. Who hasn't made some impulse purchase, which has then been left lying in some cupboard for years? How many of you have a drawer like mine in the kitchen: a drawer full of caution and fear, stuffed with good intentions (albeit unfulfilled); packed with optimism and meanness and, of course, all rubbish? In my drawer, there are a number of instructions and guarantees for things I've bought over the years, just in case they break down or I forget how to use them. Considering one of these was for a chair, that shows a good deal of pessimism – I mean, what can go wrong with a chair? There are also a large number of dead batteries which I've been meaning to take to the recycling centre and a number of leaflets – one about a local gym I still haven't joined, THREE about sponsoring a child in a developing country and several advertising a local takeaway which has now closed down. There are various odd screws, nails and pins (I'd have to buy new packs if I didn't keep them), a broken cup (I must buy some glue to stick it back together), and finally a large number of foreign coins, quite a few preceding the introduction of the euro (they might be collector's items one day, they might be valuable!).

I AM...

... Barack Obama
... Frankenstein
... that man talking to a tree
... an estate agent
... the man at a customer call centre
... Mark Zuckerberg
... Cristiano Ronaldo
... a petty criminal

COMMENTS

Redyellowblue	Come on! Get a life! Just throw it all out!
Dani79	Nice post. On top of my cupboard, there's a box of stuff I did when I was at primary school. I read your blog and I thought 'what do I need it for?' But then I looked at those cute drawings, my funny handwriting and ... I couldn't get rid of it and put the box away again. Don't feel guilty about it!
TimR1975	So we're all a bit like Trebus, but it's difficult to sympathise when you live with someone like my flatmate, who has 300 pairs of shoes. Are you suggesting I should just put up with it?
Proshrink	I am a psychologist and I read your post with interest. I think you're very brave to admit that you have something in common with Mr Trebus, and I hope your admission helps a few more people think about the issue. Actually, around one in twenty people has a problem like this. Research suggests it's at least partly genetic, but if we're honest, we're all potential hoarders. We all want to keep things we think we may one day need – and we all want things to stay as we remember them too. It's a very fine line.
Greengoddess	Trebus showed how wasteful human beings are! He's a hero!

FINDING FAULT

VOCABULARY How things go wrong

1 Match these items with the problems in bold in the sentences below.

| a desk | jeans | shoes | a top |
| face cream | a kettle | a tablet | a watch |

1 When it arrived and I put it on, it **didn't fit.**

2 When I took it out of the box, I found the screen **was scratched**.

3 When I tried to put it together, I realised it had **a bit missing**.

4 It was supposed to be for sensitive skin, but it **gave me spots**.

5 When I filled it the first time, I realised it **had a leak**.

6 I only wore it for a week and the strap **came off**.

7 They **fell apart** after a month. The soles came off!

8 When I got home and tried them on I realised the back pocket **was ripped**.

PRONUNCIATION

2 ▶ **17** Listen to the sentences and repeat them. Notice how words can link around pronouns.

3 Take turns to think of two more items that can have one of the problems in Exercise 1. Tell your partner the items you are thinking of. Can your partner guess the problem they might have?

A: *A boat and a pipe can have this problem.*

B: *OK. They can both have a leak.*

LISTENING

4 ▶ **18** Listen to part of a radio show about consumer rights and a problem a listener had. Answer the questions.

1 What problem did Fei have?

2 Which of the following happened when he complained about the problem?

  a They didn't believe him.

  b They said it was his fault.

  c They gave him a refund.

  d They gave him a replacement.

  e He had to go back more than once.

  f They offered a gift as compensation.

  g They sorted it out eventually.

  h He had to talk to several people.

3 Why do you think Fei left a comment on the programme's website?

5 Work in pairs. Discuss the questions.

- Do you think Fei did the right thing? What about the company and its employees?

- Do you think Fei was treated differently because he was a visitor? Why? / Why not?

- What advice would you give to the company as an expert on Customer Care? Why?

6 ▶ **19** Listen to the second part of the radio show. Find out how John Squire from the Institute of Customer Care would answer the questions in Exercise 5.

GRAMMAR

10 Look at these sentences from the radio show. Then work in pairs to answer the questions below.

should and *should have (should've)*

a He **should have checked** the shoes at the point of sale.

b Clearly, Fei **shouldn't have been treated** like that.

c You **should start** from the view that they do have a valid point.

d All companies **should see** complaints in this way – as a gift.

1 Which of the sentences give general advice or suggestions?

2 Which show a criticism or regret about a past action?

3 How are the two forms different?

G Check your ideas on page 170 and do Exercise 1.

11 Work in pairs. Use *should / should've* to say what advice you would give to:

1 Fei.

2 the shoe company.

3 assistants working in a shoe shop.

12 Use *should / should've* to add criticism, advice or suggestions to sentences 1–5.

It's your birthday today? You should have told me earlier. We should go out and celebrate!

1 You're never going to get anyone to buy that car.

2 We were stupid to have moved here!

3 It's your fault we haven't got any money.

4 Don't blame me for the fact your life is a disaster!

5 The country's a mess!

G For further practice, see Exercises 2 and 3 on 170.

SPEAKING

13 Make some notes about a time when:

• you bought or had something that went wrong.

• you took something back to a shop.

• you complained about something.

Decide the following:

• Was anyone at fault?

• Why? / Why not?

• Were you satisfied with the result?

14 Work in pairs. Use language from the Vocabulary and Grammar sections to explain what happened.

---

7 ▶ 19 Listen again and complete the extracts with three words in each space.

1 … given _____ , the company hasn't achieved anything by *it*.

2 … we also know that *this* can be because of a _____ the company.

3 *That* then stops the assistant listening to the issue and thinking _____ .

4 Your institute's produced _____ on *this* recently.

5 Well, I think *that*'s an _____ .

6 In Japan, *they* are often made in _____ improving a service rather than seeking compensation.

7 *They* are _____ and reveal how you can improve products and services.

8 … *they* may have additionally _____ their language abilities.

8 Work in pairs. Discuss what you think the pronouns in Exercise 7 in italics refer to.

9 Work in pairs. Discuss the questions.

• What do you think of John Squire's advice? Is there anything else he could have said?

• What's customer care like in your country? Does everyone get the same treatment? Why? / Why not?

• Which companies have good or bad reputations for customer care? Why?

• Do you ever have to deal with complaints? Who from? What about? How do you deal with them?

4

SOCIETY

IN THIS UNIT YOU LEARN HOW TO:

- talk about the government and their policies
- talk about how the economy is doing
- respond to complaints
- discuss social issues
- comment on news stories
- describe correlations

SPEAKING

1 **Look at the photo. Work in pairs. Discuss the questions.**

- Where do you think this photo was taken? What do you think it shows?
- What do you think might have caused this situation? And what might the results be?
- What do you think it says about the society?

THE STATE OF THE NATION

VOCABULARY The government, economics and society

1   Match the words in bold in sentences 1–10 with the meanings a–j below.

1   The government's **made a** huge **difference** since they came to power. They've done a lot to help the poor.

2   There's too much **bureaucracy**. Businesses spend half their time dealing with official paperwork!

3   There's a **recession**. The economy's in a total mess.

4   The government is **soft** on drugs. They should introduce stricter penalties.

5   A lot of companies have **gone bankrupt** recently, so unemployment's going up.

6   The economy's **booming**. Lots of new businesses are starting up and plenty of new jobs are being created.

7   With so little rain, there are a lot of water **shortages**.

8   The government's policies for the protection of the environment have **boosted** our reputation in the world.

9   Their policies are **undermining** national unity. They've created divisions and made society less stable.

10 People are really **struggling** because wages are so low and the cost of living's so high.

a   not tough enough

b   trying really hard to do something very difficult

c   lost all their money and cannot pay their debts

d   had a positive effect

e   doing very well

f   making something become less successful or effective

g   helped increase

h   a complicated and annoying system of rules and ways of doing things

i   a time when industry and businesses are not doing well

j   there's not enough of something you want or need

2   Work in groups. Discuss whether you think the sentences in Exercise 1 are true or false for your country. Explain why.

Number 1 isn't true in my country. Actually, the opposite is true. The government hasn't made any difference to most people's lives. They've done a lot for the rich – and nothing for the poor.

LISTENING

3   ▶ **20** Listen to two students talking about their countries. Take notes on the political and economic situation in each country. Whose country sounds like it's in a better situation – the man's or the woman's? Why?

4   ▶ **20** Try to complete the sentences you heard with the missing prepositions. Listen again to check your answers.

1   Whenever I see him _____ TV, he comes across as being fairly well-intentioned.

2   He's done nothing _____ people like me. In fact, he's just put up tuition fees for students.

3   Tell me _____ it! I'm going to be so far _____ debt by the time I graduate, I'll be paying it back for years.

4   They've been so concerned _____ supposedly 'green' laws …

5   Can't you vote _____ them?

6   The opposition are so busy fighting _____ themselves …

7   I know what you mean, but there must be someone worth voting _____ .

8   … our government has done a few controversial things – stuff I didn't agree _____ .

9   They've actually done a lot to cut back _____ bureaucracy too.

5 Work in pairs. Discuss the questions.

- Have you ever voted? What did you vote in?
- Why do you think people choose not to vote in elections? What could be done to encourage them?
- Do you know of any recent election controversies?
- How bureaucratic is your country? Give some examples.
- Have you heard of anyone who has had problems with bureaucracy and administration?

GRAMMAR

6 Look at these examples from the conversation in Exercise 3. Complete the rules below.

so and such

So and *such* are often used to link cause and result.

*The opposition are **so** busy fighting among themselves, they're not going to make any difference.*

*There's **such** a skills shortage that companies are paying really good money now.*

1 Use *so / such* before an adjective, adverb or words like *much* or *many*.

2 Use *so / such* before a noun or adjective + noun.

3 You *have to / don't have to* start the result clause with *that* – especially in spoken English.

G Check your ideas on page 170 and do Exercise 1.

7 Complete each sentence starter with *so* or *such*.

1 The government is _____ worried about its falling popularity …

2 Food prices have gone up _____ quickly …

3 Most people have to work _____ long hours …

4 The police made _____ a mess of the investigation …

5 The area ended up being _____ polluted … .

6 The government minister was involved in _____ a terrible public scandal …

8 Work in pairs. Write a possible ending for each sentence in Exercise 7. Compare your ideas with another group.

9 Have you heard any news stories similar to the ones in Exercise 7? What happened in the end?

G For further practice, see Exercise 2 on page 171.

DEVELOPING CONVERSATIONS

Showing understanding

To show we agree and understand when someone is talking about problems, we can use expressions such as:

I know!   ***Tell me about it!***

and then add a comment.

If we disagree or don't feel sympathy, we often soften our response:

I know what you mean, but …   ***Yeah, I guess. Mind you …***

10 Match the problems 1–6 with the responses a–f.

1 I don't know how people can make ends meet.

2 The job market is so competitive at the moment.

3 The pace of life is so fast here.

4 There's so much crime, you can't go out at night!

5 They haven't done anything to boost tourism.

6 This country is so bureaucratic!

a I know! It's exhausting. I feel like I spend my life just rushing around.

b Tell me about it! I can only just get by and I've got a good job.

c Tell me about it! I had to fill in four forms in three different places to get a work permit!

d I know what you mean, but if you're prepared to be flexible there's plenty of work.

e Yeah, maybe. Mind you, it's not like that everywhere. If you avoid certain areas, it's perfectly safe.

f Yeah, I know what you mean. Mind you, look what they've done to improve poor areas. That's great.

PRONUNCIATION

11 ▶ **21** Listen and check. Notice the intonation of the phrases showing understanding of problems. In pairs, repeat the conversations.

12 Respond to the sentences below.

1 They're destroying the environment!

2 It's so expensive to travel abroad at the moment.

3 All politicians are corrupt.

4 The government's soft on terrorism.

5 They're doing nothing to improve state schools.

6 The government is undermining democracy.

CONVERSATION PRACTICE

13 Work in pairs. Look at the role cards below. Choose your roles and then follow the instructions.

Student A You think:
- The government is incompetent.
- They are soft on crime.
- The president is a bit corrupt.
- The opposition have some good ideas, but their leader is a bit weak.

OR you really don't like the opposition leader.

You think:
- The government is doing a lot to improve education.
- They have made some mistakes.
- Some parts of the economy are doing badly.

Student B You think:
- Your president has a good image on TV and in the world.
- The economy is fine.
- The government's given too much power to different regions.

OR you don't really like the government's foreign policy.

You don't really trust the president.

You think:
- It's good that the opposition wants to cuts taxes.
- You're personally doing well and live in a nice area.

 **6** To watch the video and do the activities, see the DVD-ROM.

BIG ISSUES

SPEAKING

1 Rank these social issues from 1 (most important) to 10 (least important) in your society.

a gender discrimination

b homelessness

c family size

d domestic violence

e bullying in schools

f school dropout rates

g the destruction of the environment

h drug and alcohol abuse

i family breakdown

j racism

2 Work in pairs. Find out what your partner thinks and explain your own choices.

LISTENING

3 ▶ **22** Listen to five short news stories. Decide which of the issues from Exercise 1 is discussed in each one.

4 ▶ **22** Work in pairs. Decide which of the five stories mention a–e below. Then listen again to check your ideas.

a someone being assaulted

b people welcoming some news

c people being at risk

d someone winning damages

e someone being prevented from carrying out major development work

5 Add these verbs to the nouns they were used with in the news stories. Then look at the audio script on page 197 to check.

become	conduct	launch	uphold
claim	be denied	suffer	win

1 _____ a new initiative

2 _____ her case

3 _____ promotion

4 _____ investigations

5 _____ several broken bones

6 _____ victory

7 _____ a claim

8 _____ a grandmother

DEVELOPING CONVERSATIONS

Commenting on news stories

When we talk about news stories people often use quite fixed phrases to comment on them, such as those in Exercise 8 below. We might use the same phrases to talk about different news stories.

8 ▶ **23** Look at the examples of different ways of commenting on news stories. Which three were used in the conversation? Listen again to check.

1 It was shocking what happened to her.

2 It just seems a bit excessive.

3 Mind you, it was a lot of money.

4 It makes you wonder what's gone wrong with the world.

5 It was such typical double standards!

6 That's good news for a change!

7 I don't know how they manage.

8 At least they're doing something about it at last!

9 You can't have everything in life, can you?

10 It's a bit of a worry.

11 It's lucky it was caught on film.

12 That kind of thing shouldn't be tolerated.

PRONUNCIATION

9 ▶ **24** Listen to the sentences in Exercise 8. Mark the main stress, or stresses, in each sentence. Then repeat the sentences.

10 Which of the sentences in Exercise 8 could be used to talk about the other four news stories?

SPEAKING

11 Work in pairs. Choose one of the other four news stories from Exercise 3 to discuss. Note some comments you want to make about it. Choose at least one sentence from Exercise 8.

12 Have a conversation about the story. Use the guide below. Continue as long as you can. Then swap roles.

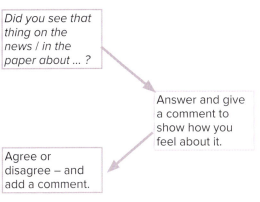

Did you see that thing on the news / in the paper about ... ?

Answer and give a comment to show how you feel about it.

Agree or disagree – and add a comment.

6 Work in pairs. Discuss the questions.

- Have you heard any similar stories about social issues to those mentioned in the news stories?

- Do you know any people with big families? How would you feel about growing up as part of a very large family? What would be difficult about it? What would be good?

- Are security cameras used widely in your country? Should there be more or fewer? Why?

- Can you think of any initiatives that your government or other authorities have launched recently?

- Can you think of any investigations that are being conducted at the moment? What do you think they'll find?

- What do you think the root causes of homelessness are? And what's the best way to tackle it?

7 ▶ **23** Listen to a conversation about one of the news stories from Exercise 3. Answer these questions.

1 Which story do they talk about?

2 What do they agree on?

3 What do they disagree about?

4 Who do you agree with more? Why?

MAKE A DIFFERENCE

READING

1 Work in pairs. Discuss the questions.

1 Do you think the future of the world is *bleak* or *bright*? Why?

2 Do you think the following are global problems? Why? / Why not?
- rising population
- extreme poverty
- hunger
- conflict
- child mortality
- AIDS and malaria

3 How could these problems be solved – and how easily?

2 Read an article which discusses these issues, based on a book by the academic Jeffrey Sachs. How would Jeffrey Sachs answer the questions in Exercise 1? Explain the title of the report.

3 Work in pairs. Discuss the questions.

1 How is **extreme poverty** defined and how many people suffer from it?

2 What does Jeffrey Sachs describe as **relatively straightforward**?

3 What two things does he see as **interconnected**?

4 What is the first step to **reverse the downward spiral**?

5 What truly **makes a difference**?

6 What *three* things lead to better **harvests**?

7 What has been **successfully implemented**? Where?

8 What **target** has been **met** by five countries?

9 What is $700 billion and what does the writer **compare** it **to**?

4 Work in groups. Discuss the questions.

- Do you think Sachs is right to be optimistic? Why? / Why not?
- What problems might there be with Sachs's solutions?
- Do you think your country should meet the 0.7% target? Why? / Why not?
- How do you think Sachs might suggest the problem of conflict be resolved?

GRAMMAR

5 Look at these examples from the article. Then work in pairs to answer the questions below.

1 Can you match each of the sentences in the Grammar box to one of the two graphs below?

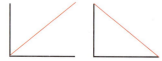

2 What kinds of words can follow each comparative?

Comparatives with *the ..., the ...*

We can show how two or more things change at the same time using a pattern with *the* + a comparative.

a **The higher** the child mortality rate is, **the higher** the birth rate.

b **The more** secure parents feel, **the fewer** children they have.

c **The longer** we wait, ... **the larger** the long-term costs.

G Check your ideas on page 171 and do Exercise 1.

6 Choose three sentence starters and complete them with your own ideas. Tell a partner.

1 The more aid we give to underdeveloped countries, ...

2 The more globalised the world becomes, ...

3 The less we spend on weapons, ...

4 The more coffee you drink, ...

5 The more I work, ...

7 Work in pairs. Choose one of your sentences from Exercise 6. Make a chain of effects. Start each new sentence with the second half of the previous.

A: *The more I work, the less free time I have.*

B: *The less free time I have, the less exercise I do.*

A: *The less exercise I do, ...*

G For further practice, see page 171 and do Exercise 2.

SPEAKING

8 Read some ideas for ways to raise money for aid. Then work in pairs to discuss questions 1 and 2.

- hold an auction or sale
- hold a party
- skip a meal and donate the money you save
- make food to sell in a market
- get sponsored to run a marathon
- run an online campaign
- organise a bingo event and charge a fee
- do some paintings and sell them at a craft fair

1 Decide if you would take part in each event and explain why / why not.

2 Agree on which are the two best ideas and try to think of one more idea. Explain your choices.

ONLY CONNECT

Pia Mendelson reflects on 'The Common Wealth', a book by Jeffrey Sachs, Director of the Earth Institute at Columbia University and special advisor to the UN secretary general.

In summarising the state of the planet – rising population, widespread conflict, one-sixth of the planet suffering extreme poverty and hunger, global warming, deaths from AIDS and malaria – Jeffrey Sachs can paint a bleak picture. However, he's an optimist and believes that all of these problems can be overcome in relatively straightforward ways and at relatively little cost. That's because the root causes are interconnected and essentially man-made.

Take child mortality. Perhaps surprisingly, the higher the child mortality rate is, the higher the birth rate. This leads to a booming population which puts a greater strain on already scarce resources, so farmers have to work harder to produce enough food for all, which means children are often put to work in the fields or at home. This, in turn, stops children getting the education which will allow them to learn, among other things, about better farming techniques to boost crop yields and provide more food to eat and sell. Sachs argues that the simple solution of providing every child in poverty with an anti-mosquito bed net is a major first step. Malaria is a huge cause of death in children and the bed nets massively reduce infections. The fewer children that die of malaria, the more secure parents feel about their children surviving. The more secure parents feel, the fewer children they have, and so on, reversing the downward spiral just described.

However, it is adopting a combination of measures at the same time which truly makes a difference: free school meals boost school attendance and improve health; supplying fertilisers to improve soil and better seeds provides even better harvests; access to family planning further controls the birth rate; basic health care and clean water supplies prevent more lethal diseases.

These ideas are already being successfully implemented in over 100 African villages in deprived regions. The cost of the project is just $110 per person per year, of which $50 comes from donors and the rest from a mixture of local and national governments and the villagers themselves.

So if it's so simple why hasn't it been done before? What about all the aid that has been given to Africa and the underdeveloped countries of the world? Has it been lost to corruption? Sachs argues that the real problem is not corruption, but the fact that rich governments have promised such a lot, but actually given so little. They agreed to give 0.7% of national income in aid, but only five countries have met that target. He suggests current aid is $24 billion per year, which translates as just ten dollars per person – not nearly enough to implement the combined measures. He compares that to military spending, which in the USA alone has reached $700 billion in some years.

So while Sachs sees an unprecedented opportunity to end poverty forever, he also raises an alarm that this could be the last chance we have, 'The longer we wait, the greater is the suffering and the larger the long-term costs.'

VIDEO 2

WOOD-POWERED CAR

1 Look at the photo. Work in pairs. Discuss:
- where you think the picture was taken – and what it shows
- what the causes of this situation might be
- whether anything similar has happened anywhere that you know
- how possible it is that this could happen in your country in future

2 ▶7 Watch the first part of a video about two Americans who are preparing for the collapse of the economy. Why are the following mentioned?
1 supermarkets
2 six or seven thousand dollars
3 canned goods
4 toilet paper

3 Compare your ideas with a partner.

4 You are now going to watch Scott describe his own preparations in more detail. Tell a partner three things you expect he will talk about.

5 ▶7 Watch the rest of the video. Are the sentences true (T) or false (F)?
1 Scott has very recently started growing wheat, corn and vegetables.
2 It takes his daughter about ten minutes to grind enough flour for one day.
3 To make beef jerky, Scott dries the meat using hot water, a heat exchanger and an old oven.
4 He believes that helping with the preparations makes his kids feel safe and protected.
5 Humans cannot survive more than two weeks without water.
6 He's using energy from the sun to help pump water out of a spring.
7 Scott has invented his own way of using wood to power his car.

6 Work in pairs. Discuss the questions.
- What is your impression of the two men and their lifestyle? Give reasons for your opinions.
- Are there any other things you'd need to get or do if you were preparing for the future in this way?
- Who's the most self-sufficient person you know? In what way?

UNDERSTANDING FAST SPEECH

7 Look at this extract from the video. To help you, groups of words are marked with / and stressed sounds are in CAPITALS. Pauses are marked //. Practise saying the sentence.

It's a LOT of WORK to HAND grind. / It's a lot EAsier to / um / PEdal it with a BIcycle // and SO we're GRINding THIS / toDAY / and we're gonna make BREAD from IT toMOrrow.

8 ▶8 Listen to how Scott said this sentence. Now you have a go! Practise saying the extract again fast.

REVIEW 2

1 Complete the text with one word in each space.

The Spirit Level by Richard Wilkinson and Kate Pickett argues that [1]_____ more equal a society is, the healthier it is and the [2]_____ social problems it has. Inequality in places such as the USA has increased [3]_____ rapidly over the last decades that people have started to feel alienated from society and there is more violence and addiction than in more equal societies. The authors suggest that governments should [4]_____ done more during the boom years [5]_____ reduce the wealth gap because there is [6]_____ a lot of unemployment now, it is more difficult to reverse the situation. Nevertheless, the authors believe that change can happen. The government should [7]_____ more money on education and increase the minimum wage [8]_____ everyone feels valued for the job they do.

2 Complete the second sentence so that it has a similar meaning to the first sentence, using the word given. Do not change the word given. You must use between two and four words, including the word given.

1 Have you tried using a knife to open it?

Maybe _____ a knife to open it. **SHOULD**

2 What do you call that stuff you use if you've got a stain on your clothes?

What do you call the stuff you use _____ your clothes. **REMOVE**

3 The investigation was so poor, the chief of police had to resign.

The police _____ of the investigation that the chief of police had to resign. **MESS**

4 As the economy improves, we will see youth unemployment fall.

The better the economy performs, _____ will be for young people. **JOBS**

5 It was a mistake to invest so much in the Olympics.

I don't think the government _____ much in the Olympics. **SHOULD**

6 There's a positive correlation between practice and performance.

It's simple: the more you _____ get at something. **BETTER**

3 Complete the sentences with your own ideas.

1 I need a cloth to _____ .

2 Have you got a screwdriver so _____ .

3 There's such a shortage of housing, _____ .

4 When I was younger, I should _____ .

5 The more money I have, the _____ .

6 The more I study English, the _____ .

4 ▶ **25** Listen. Write the six sentences you hear.

5 Match the verbs (1–10) with the collocates (a–j).

1	undermine	a	our reputation / crop yields
2	overcome	b	victory / she was discriminated against
3	claim	c	national unity / my confidence
4	uphold	d	my embarrassment / my fear of flying
5	acquire	e	the claim / the decision in court
6	meet	f	a target / the goal to end poverty
7	boost	g	valuable paintings / new skills
8	provide	h	a huge difference / do with what we've got
9	make	i	discrimination / a broken leg
10	suffer	j	feedback / children with food

6 Complete the text with one word in each space. The first letters are given.

In times when the economy is in [1]re_____ people often can't afford to buy new things or pay for repairs because they are [2]str_____ on low incomes. Many would like to turn to DIY or making their own stuff. That's easy enough if a strap has come off a bag or your shirt or trousers are [3]r_____ as most people have a [4]n_____ and thread. But what if it's a bigger repair like your roof has a leak or a desk has [5]f_____ [6]a_____ ? Not everyone has the tools they need and they're expensive to buy. Well, one solution is visiting one of our network of tool libraries that have started up all around the country. You can borrow a [7]l_____ to climb up on the roof or a saw and [8]dr_____ to make a new desk and, just like a normal library, it's free. To find out more, visit our website. If you would like to [9]d_____ any tools, contact us on the number below. We will accept any that are [10]sc_____ or otherwise slightly damaged, but we do ask that they have no parts [11]m_____ and are in working order. We'd also love to hear from you, if you are interested in joining our network and [12]l_____ your own library.

7 Complete the sentences. Use the word in brackets to form a word that fits in the space.

1 My boyfriend is _____ with his new phone. (obsess)

2 I'm _____ about the future, despite some of the problems we're facing. (optimism)

3 When I was younger I used to be a stamp _____ . I'd go to lots of stamp fairs. (collect)

4 I know he did it with good _____ , but it didn't help. (intend)

5 I'm very _____ when it comes to buying stuff online. (caution)

6 The incident caused considerable _____ to the company. (embarrass)

7 The government has launched an _____ into the causes of the riots this summer. (investigate)

8 The government has _____ implemented a number of initiatives to combat poverty. (success)

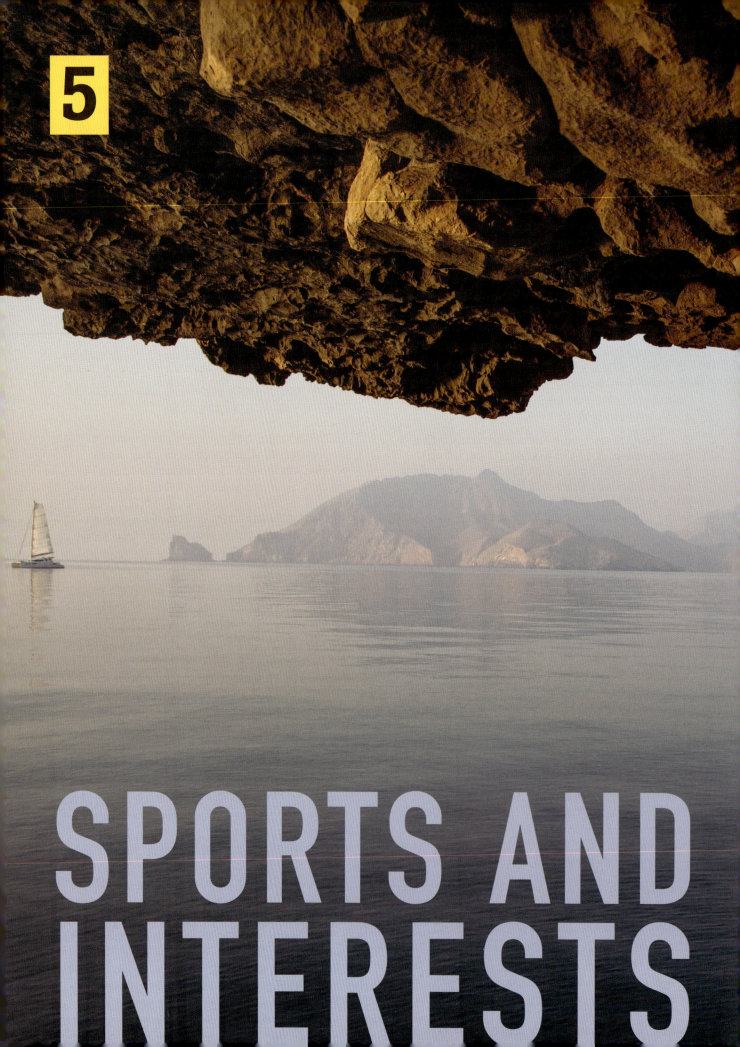

5

SPORTS AND
INTERESTS

IN THIS UNIT YOU LEARN HOW TO:

- talk about what you do in your free time
- talk about how fit you are
- check you heard things correctly
- talk about sport
- comment on past events
- describe accidents and injuries

SPEAKING

1 **Work in pairs. Discuss the questions.**

- What do you think the woman in this photo is doing?
- Have you ever done anything like this? If yes, then when? If not, would you like to? Why? / Why not?

2 **Work in groups. Discuss which statements are true for you or people you know.**

- I enjoy sports with a bit of a risk.
- I like outdoor pursuits – walking, camping, that kind of thing.
- I'm a member of a sports club.
- I take part in a music or drama group.
- I do volunteer work for a charity.
- I go to dance classes to keep fit.
- I like wandering round flea markets and junk shops.
- I love doing puzzles – crosswords, Sudoku, stuff like that.
- I like sewing and knitting. I make my own clothes.
- I spend a lot of time on Facebook and other social media.
- At the weekend, I lie in bed till lunchtime and then just chill out at home.

TIME OUT

LISTENING

1 ▶ **26** Listen to three conversations about free-time activities. Answer the following questions for each conversation:

1 What's the second speaker going to do?

2 How long have they been doing this activity?

3 How did they first get interested in it?

4 Is the other person interested in doing the activity?

2 ▶ **26** Listen again. Choose the correct option.

1 What are you *up to / on to* later?

2 You've got a lovely *figure / fixture*.

3 It took me about ten minutes to get my *breath / bread* back!

4 It's like a *master / faster* class with this top Russian fencer.

5 I'm going to have a wander round the *free / flea* market.

6 I'm just going to have a *lie-in / light in*.

7 *Fair enough / Very tough*. Just the thought of doing that kind of exercise makes me sweat!

8 I took *that top / it up* because I was giving up smoking.

9 She said it'd give me something to *fit well / fiddle with*.

10 *Is it / Isn't it* just full of old women, this group?

3 Work in pairs. Discuss the questions.

- Do you know anyone who has an unusual hobby – or have you ever discovered that someone had a hidden talent for doing something?

- How long have they been doing it?

- How did they first get interested in it?

VOCABULARY Health and fitness

4 Match the fitness words 1–6 with sentences a–f.

1 flexibility

2 hand-eye coordination

3 healthy lifestyle

4 speed

5 stamina

6 strength

a She swims around 60 lengths every day.

b He can do the 100 metres in under twelve seconds.

c She can touch the back of her head with her leg!

d He can lift 50 kilos.

e She's really good at racket sports.

f He doesn't drink, doesn't smoke, doesn't stay out late.

5 Complete the sentences with these words.

breath	junk	sweat
demanding	shape	uncoordinated

1 He's really unfit. He works up a _____ just running for the bus! It's awful to see!

2 She gets out of _____ just walking up the stairs.

3 He's really out of _____ . He does absolutely no exercise whatsoever. He doesn't even walk!

4 I went to an aerobics class for a while, but it was too _____ . I couldn't keep up with the others in the class.

5 I'm so unfit. I really need to stop eating so much _____ food. I'm getting fat – look at that flab!

6 I'm totally _____ – really clumsy. I'm always tripping over and bumping into things.

6 Work in pairs. Use vocabulary from Exercises 4 and 5 to discuss the questions.

1 How fit and healthy are you in terms of lifestyle, speed, stamina, strength, etc? Give examples.

2 What's the best way to improve your:
• coordination?
• flexibility?
• stamina?
• speed?
• strength?
• general health?

3 Have you tried any of these methods? How did it go?

4 Who is the fittest or least fit person you know? How do you know? What makes them so fit or unfit?

5 What sports and activities are you good or bad at? Why?

DEVELOPING CONVERSATIONS

Checking what you heard

If we are surprised by what someone tells us and we want to check information, we often repeat part of the statement and add a question word.

A: *I've got my knitting group tonight.*

B: **You've got what?**

A: *I'm going to a fencing workshop all day.*

B: **You're going where?**

7 Complete the mini-conversations with similar questions to those in the box.

1 A: I usually run about ten kilometres most days.
   B: _____ ?
   A: Ten kilometres. I'm not that fast, though.

2 A: I do capoeira on Wednesday nights.
   B: _____ ?
   A: Capoeira. A kind of Brazilian dance thing.

3 A: I went to a comic fair at the weekend.
   B: _____ ?
   A: A comic fair. They had all these old Spiderman comics there. It was great.

4 A: My mum's really into embroidery.
   B: _____ ?
   A: Embroidery. It's like sewing, but you use thread to make pictures or patterns on the cloth.

5 A: Well, I didn't get up till three on Saturday.
   B: _____ ?
   A: Three o'clock. I'd had a heavy week. I needed a lie-in!

PRONUNCIATION

8 ▶ **27** Listen to the checking questions and notice how the intonation goes up. Which questions sound more surprised? Listen again and repeat.

9 Work in pairs. Practise reading the conversations in Exercise 7.

CONVERSATION PRACTICE

10 Think about an unusual or surprising hobby – and a future arrangement you have that is connected to it. Decide: where you're doing it, who with, and so on. It can be true or not.

Write three questions people might ask you and answers you would give. Then work in pairs and have similar conversations to those you heard in Exercise 1. Use the guide below to help you. Then swap roles.

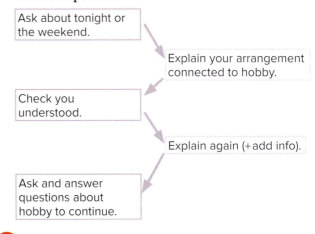

Ask about tonight or the weekend.

Explain your arrangement connected to hobby.

Check you understood.

Explain again (+ add info).

Ask and answer questions about hobby to continue.

🎥 **9 To watch the video and do the exercises see the DVD-ROM.**

YOU SHOULD'VE BEEN THERE

SPEAKING

1 Work in groups. Discuss the questions.

- Do you know anyone who is a big sports fan? In what way? What team(s) do they support?
- What are the most popular sports in your country? Why do you think they are so popular? Do you like them? Why? / Why not?
- What do you think the most popular sports in the world are? Why?

VOCABULARY Sport

2 Check any words in bold that you don't understand in a dictionary. Then discuss in pairs which sports each sentence describes.

1 She hit a powerful **drive** and made a hole in one.
2 He came off the **track**. He was trying to **overtake** on a corner and lost control of the car.
3 They almost scored – they hit a **post** and the **bar** twice.
4 They were losing so they called **a time-out** to discuss **tactics**.
5 They got **promoted** to the top **division** last season.
6 Oh no! That's the third double **fault** I've **served**.
7 I was **tackled** – just as I was about to **shoot**!
8 He ran from the halfway line to score that **try**. It was incredible!
9 I came on as a **substitute** after a player got injured.
10 He got **a red card** for a bad tackle.
11 She lost five first-round matches in a row so she **sacked** her **coach**.
12 If you ask me, the fight was **fixed**. The **judges** made some really dubious decisions.

3 Work in pairs. Which other sports can you use the words in bold from Exercise 2 to describe?

'Drive' could be for cricket – when a batsman hits the ball a long way.

4 Change partners. Discuss the questions.

- Have you heard of anyone being sacked recently? Do you know why?
- Have you heard of anyone – or any team – who's been promoted recently?
- Do you know any competitions that you think were fixed?
- Can you think of any unpopular decisions that judges have made?
- Have you done or experienced any of the things in Exercise 2 when playing sport?

READING

5 Write four possible benefits of doing or watching sport. Think about both individuals and society. Then compare your ideas with a partner.

6 Read the article. Find out if it mentions any of the benefits you thought of.

7 Which of these statements do you think the writer would agree with? Underline the parts of the text that support your answers.

1 If you did more exercise, you'd be more positive.
2 Forcing kids to compete undermines their confidence.
3 We shouldn't encourage people to read.
4 The most important thing is to win.
5 Sports clubs keep young people out of trouble.
6 It's OK for players to pretend to be injured.
7 I work long hours to give my family the best.
8 Seeing great sportsmen in action is uplifting.

GRAMMAR

8 Look at these examples from the article. Then work in pairs to complete the rules.

> ### should(n't) have, could(n't) have, would(n't) have
>
> a I **shouldn't have stuck** to the rules! Then **I would have won**.
>
> b I **should have worked** more. I **could have bought** a better car.
>
> To show we think something in the past was a good idea but didn't happen, use [1] _____ + past participle. To show we think something that happened wasn't a good idea, use [2]_____ + past participle. We can add comments to show our thoughts about the result. [3]_____ + past participle shows a certain past result and [4]_____ + past participle shows a possible past result.

G Check your ideas on page 171 and do Exercise 1.

9 Complete the sentences with the correct modal verb and the correct form of the verb in brackets. You may need to use negative forms.

1 It was a close game. We _____ (try) any harder and there's no shame in losing to such a good team, but I still think we _____ (draw) with them at least.
   could should

2 I don't know what I was thinking! I _____ never _____ (study) Art. Something like History _____ (be) much better for me.
   should would

3 She _____ (think) before using Twitter. All of the trouble she then got into _____ (be) avoided.
   could should

4 I guess it was my own fault really. I probably _____ (read) her personal emails. Then I _____ (find out) all the stuff she'd been saying about me.
   should would

G For further practice, see page 171 and do Exercise 2.

SPORT – YOU'VE GOT TO LOVE IT

Record levels of people do no sport at all, while others will not even watch it. Jerry Travis explains what they're missing.

HEALTHY BODY, HEALTHY MIND

It's maybe obvious, but worth repeating: sport keeps you in shape. Moreover, people who are physically fit are, on average, happier. In fact, the British health service has recently experimented with giving people suffering from mild depression a course of exercise instead of drugs; gym membership rather than therapy.

PREPARATION FOR LIFE

I'm not talking about those weird non-competitive sports that some schools insist on: no winners, no losers and everyone gets a prize. Not only are such games dull and pointless for children, but life is simply not like that. Competitive sport teaches us to cope with losing and disappointments. Sure, we're not all naturally sporty, but then I'm rubbish at crosswords. You just have to find your own level and learn to enjoy your own performance. You can feel the same sense of achievement as Real Madrid winning a game, by beating an opponent who is at a slightly higher (though still low!) level than you. Similarly, I'm happy completing a puzzle others would find easy.

SOCIAL AND FUN

What would we do without sport? Read? Play computer games? Hang around on the street? Obviously, these aren't necessarily all bad things – reading in particular brings many benefits – but the first two are hardly social, and the last not that interesting or purposeful. Playing sports helps to build relationships and teaches the importance of supporting each other whether you win or lose. I'm reminded of a lovely, funny scene in a film called *Gregory's Girl*, where two teenage characters compare injuries they've had after a bad game. Likewise, sports fans often enjoy sharing the pain of their team losing almost as much as the joy of winning.

CRIME AND MORALITY

Just going back to hanging around on the streets, if you need proof that it's not that fun, why do so many of those kids end up committing crime? It's simply out of boredom – something which sport can often replace. So making sport more widely available is good for society. It also benefits society by showing children the importance of rules and moral choices. Of course people cheat and perhaps you've been denied the chance to win something as a result. You think 'I shouldn't have stuck to the rules! Then I would've won'. However, the rules are the sport and you know if everyone starts cheating, the game falls apart and stops being fun. That's how we learn about making the correct moral decisions in sport, but we also learn why, in life, cheats are looked down on or excluded.

SPORT IS LIFE

But sport isn't just learning about life. It IS life. I play tennis; I'm basically fairly hopeless, regularly serving double faults or weakly hitting the ball into the net. However, there are moments when somehow everything comes together and I hit a great shot down the line or serve a clean ace. I suddenly feel like a world-beater and it's a great feeling, even if the next ball flies miles out. Isn't life all about having those feelings? And sport – playing or watching – provides many of them. No-one looks back at the end of their life and says, 'I should've worked more. I could've bought a better car' or 'I'll never forget that time my kids watched TV'. No, what we remember are things like Usain Bolt smashing the world 100-metre record in Beijing – beating everyone else so easily that he could actually slow down in order to start celebrating ten metres before he crossed the line. And we're more likely to think 'I should've played with my kids more' or 'I wish I'd done more sport'.

PRONUNCIATION

10 ▶ 28 Listen and write down the six sentences you hear. Check your sentences by looking at the audio script on page 198. Then practise saying the sentences.

SPEAKING

11 Choose one of the topics below and take turns to tell your partner about it. Give details using vocabulary from this unit and *should(n't) have / could(n't) have / would(n't) have*. Then swap roles.

- a sporting event where something went wrong
- something you regret doing – or not doing
- something a famous person has done wrong

A BIT EXTREME

LISTENING

1 Work in pairs. Look at these activities. Then discuss the questions. Use the sentence frames below to explain your reasons.

ballroom dancing	ice-skating	tai chi
handstands	parachuting	windsurfing
hang-gliding	shooting	yoga

- Have you ever done any of these activities? When?
- Would you like to try any of them in the future? Why? / Why not?

I think it'd be fun / amazing / really exciting.

I think I'd really enjoy it because I like other similar kinds of things.

I don't have the hand-eye coordination.

I'm not flexible **enough**.

I'd be scared of break**ing** my leg.

I'd worry about mak**ing** a fool of myself.

I wouldn't be able to stand up.

2 ▶ 29 Listen to a conversation between three people – Chloe, Molly and Kyle. They talk about Molly's uncle, a health and fitness fanatic. Find out which of the activities in Exercise 1 he has done. Then compare your answers with a partner.

3 ▶ 29 Work in pairs. Decide if the sentences about Molly's uncle are true (T) or false (F). Then listen and check.

1 He taught Chloe and Kyle how to do handstands at his home.

2 He stopped ice-skating after an hour because Molly and Kyle were bored.

3 He used to go hang-gliding three or four times a month.

4 He gave up hang-gliding because he badly injured his neck.

5 He's only taken up windsurfing recently.

6 He lives by the sea now.

7 He drinks lemon juice every day because he thinks it's good for him.

8 Kyle admits Molly's uncle can be fun – but only for very short periods of time.

4 Discuss these questions with your partner.

- Does Molly's uncle sound mad to you? Why? / Why not?
- Do you know anyone who's unusual for their age? In what way?
- Do you know anyone who's only OK in small doses? Why?
- Do you know any other things (like lemons) that are supposedly good for your skin, feet, hair, eyesight, etc.? Do you think it's true?
- Do you know anyone who had a lucky escape? What happened?

VOCABULARY Injuries and accidents

5 Work in pairs. Discuss which of the problems you think is worse in each case.

1 He had some cuts and bruises.
  He broke his leg.

2 I tore my knee ligaments.
  I bruised my knee.

3 She knocked herself out.
  She banged her head.

4 I twisted my ankle.
  I broke my ankle.

5 She lost consciousness.
  She drowned.

6 He lost an arm.
  He was killed.

6 Practise the vocabulary in Exercise 5 by having conversations like this.

A: *Was he OK?*
B: *Well, he had some cuts and bruises.*
A: *Really? That's bad / terrible!*
B: *I know. It could've been worse, though. He could've broken his leg.*

7 Work in pairs. Tell each other about an accident you know about that had one of the results in Exercise 5. Was the person who had the accident lucky or unlucky? Do you think the accident or result could have been avoided? Why?

GRAMMAR

8 Look at these sentences from the unit. Then work in pairs to answer the questions below.

> ### The present perfect continuous and simple
>
> a *I've put on* five kilos since January.
> b *I've been doing* knitting for six months now.
> c That's the third double fault *I've served*.
> d The last few years he*'s been* really into windsurfing.
> e For the last few months he*'s been rubbing* lemon in his hair every day.
> f *I've been meaning* to go round and see him, because he's not been well, but Kyle's a bit reluctant.

1 Which sentences (a–f) in the box are present perfect continuous and which are present perfect simple? How do you know?

2 Which sentences describe something that has finished before now and which show something that is possibly unfinished?

G Check your ideas on page 172 and do Exercise 1.

9 Complete the conversations using the words in brackets and the present perfect continuous or simple.

1 A: _____ to buy the tickets for the game yet?
   (you / manage)

   B: No. _____ all morning, but I can't get through.
   (I / call)

2 A: _____ *The End of the Day* yet?
   (you / see)

   B: No. _____ to for ages now, but _____ the chance. Is it still on?
   (I / mean, I / just / not / have)

3 A: So why _____ to leave? It's a bit sudden, isn't it?
   (Wayne / decide)

   B: Not really. _____ about it for a while, but _____ the right job – and now he _____ it.
   (he / think, he / look for, he / find)

4 A: I played tennis with her yesterday. She's really good, considering _____ a few times.
   (she / only / play)

   B: I can imagine. _____ good at sports. She's just got that natural fitness and coordination.
   (she / always / be)

PRONUNCIATION

10 ▶ **30** Listen to examples of the present perfect simple and continuous from Exercise 9. Notice the weak forms of *have* and *been*. Then repeat the sentences.

11 Work in pairs. Practise the conversations in Exercise 9. Try to continue them for as long as you can.

12 Complete these sentences using *because* or *but* and the present perfect continuous or simple. Then share your ideas with a partner.

I'm getting quite good at tennis now, because I've been practising three times a week.

I'm getting quite good at tennis now, but I still haven't beaten my brother!

1 I'm getting quite good at tennis now …
2 I've always wanted to do parachuting …
3 I've never been abroad …
4 I know Maria quite well …
5 The company is doing a lot better now …
6 The government's changing its policy on education …
7 I should really go to the doctor about it …

G For further practice, see page 172 and do Exercise 2.

6

ACCOMMODATION

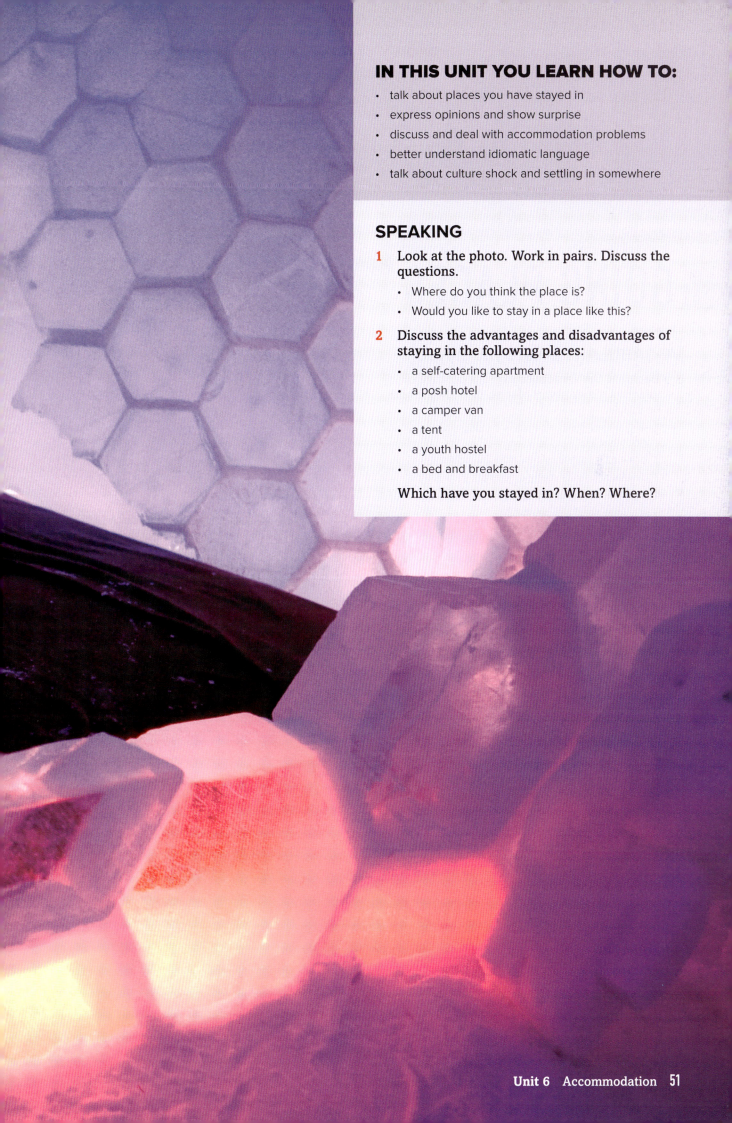

IN THIS UNIT YOU LEARN HOW TO:

- talk about places you have stayed in
- express opinions and show surprise
- discuss and deal with accommodation problems
- better understand idiomatic language
- talk about culture shock and settling in somewhere

SPEAKING

1 **Look at the photo. Work in pairs. Discuss the questions.**
  - Where do you think the place is?
  - Would you like to stay in a place like this?

2 **Discuss the advantages and disadvantages of staying in the following places:**
  - a self-catering apartment
  - a posh hotel
  - a camper van
  - a tent
  - a youth hostel
  - a bed and breakfast

  Which have you stayed in? When? Where?

GOING PLACES

VOCABULARY Where you stayed

1 Decide if the sentences express positive or negative views about places, or if they could be either.

1 The whole place was really muddy and everything got filthy.
2 We had a stunning view from our room.
3 The service was really efficient.
4 The weather was just unbearably hot.
5 It overlooked a building site.
6 People were so welcoming, it was quite overwhelming.
7 The place was a bit of a dump, to be honest.
8 The facilities were absolutely incredible.
9 It was quite isolated – basically, in the middle of nowhere.
10 The beach was deserted so we had the whole place to ourselves.

2 Work in pairs. Use the vocabulary in Exercise 1 and your own ideas to describe the photos.

3 Think of three places you have stayed. Use the language from Exercise 1 and tell a partner about each place.

LISTENING

4 ▶ 31 Listen to two conversations about places that people have stayed in. Answer the questions.

1 Where did they stay?
2 In what ways did they have a good time?
3 What problems did they have?

5 ▶ 31 Listen again. Complete the phrases with three words in each space.

1 It _____ this island in the middle of the Danube.
2 It _____ while we were there.
3 They _____ for a couple of nights.
4 We had a great time _____ the weather.
5 In August? _____ a bit hot?
6 Look _____ . That's stunning!
7 It was a bit annoying, but _____ the place was, you couldn't complain.
8 It was a bit of a struggle climbing back up, but it was _____ .

6 Work in pairs. Discuss the questions.

- Have you ever been to a music festival? If yes, which one? What was it like?
- If not, would you like to go to one? Why? / Why not?
- Has anyone ever put you up? When? Where?
- What's the best sunset you've seen? Where? What were you doing?

GRAMMAR

7 Read the Grammar box, then look at the corrections of common mistakes below. Work in pairs. Discuss why you think the original sentences were wrong.

Modifiers

Modifiers make adjectives, adverbs, verbs or nouns stronger or weaker.

Adjectives and adverbs can be made stronger with *very, really, absolutely, completely*.

Adjectives and adverbs can be made weaker with *a bit, quite, fairly, pretty*.

Nouns can be modified by *complete, real, a bit of, hardly any, almost no*.

Verbs can be modified by *really, absolutely, hardly (ever)*.

1 We got ~~very~~ **absolutely** soaked. (or **very / really wet**)
2 It was ~~absolutely~~ **really** hot. (or **absolutely boiling**)
3 Oh it was ~~too~~ **really** incredible. I loved it. (or **absolutely incredible**)
4 It was ~~quite~~ **a bit too** hot for my liking.
5 The food was ~~a bit~~ **quite** nice, but maybe a bit bland.
6 It was ~~completely a~~ **a complete** waste of time.
7 It was a bit **of a** nightmare.
8 It was a bit dull. There were hardly **any** facilities.
9 We ~~hardly~~ did **almost nothing** all day apart from lie on the beach.

G Check your ideas on page 172 and do Exercise 1.

DEVELOPING CONVERSATIONS

Negative questions

You can use negative questions to express your opinion or show that you find something surprising.

Couldn't you stay somewhere else?

Wasn't that a pain, having to rely on the bus?

Didn't they run more often than that?

11 Complete the questions with negative forms.

1 A: _____ it a bit noisy?

B: Yeah, really noisy. The bar opposite had really loud music playing all night.

2 A: _____ you find it annoying, the way the sand gets everywhere?

B: Yeah, a bit, but stony beaches are just really uncomfortable. They're no good for sunbathing.

3 A: _____ you ever heard of it? It's very well known.

B: Not in Asia, it's not!

4 A: I couldn't go diving. _____ you scared?

B: Not at all. I loved it. I'm thinking of taking it up.

5 A: _____ it really uncomfortable, camping?

B: It can be a bit, yeah, but we've got mattresses and chairs and stuff, so it won't be too bad.

12 Ask negative questions about these sentences using the words in brackets. Then have conversations using your ideas.

1 We stayed in a big five-star hotel in Cairo. (expensive)

2 Eight of us are going to share a room in a youth hostel. (crowded)

3 The area's quite rough, but the rent's really low. (scary)

4 I had to share a room with my boyfriend's mother. (feel awkward)

CONVERSATION PRACTICE

13 With a new partner, have a conversation about places you've been to. If you haven't been anywhere recently, use the photos for ideas. Begin by using the guide below. Continue the conversation with comments, questions and responses. Then swap roles.

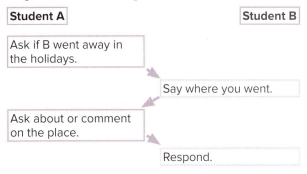

8 Match each of these modifiers with a group of words (1–7). Which two groups of words can be used with more than one modifier?

a bit	absolutely	fairly	really
a bit of a	almost	hardly	very

1 pain / tourist trap / waste of money / dump / struggle

2 no-one there / nothing to do / missed the bus / cried

3 cold / amazing / boiling / interesting / loved it

4 isolated / noisy / rough / too cold / overwhelming

5 posh / welcoming / efficient / dull / warm

6 filthy / amazing / gorgeous / deserted / enormous

7 anywhere to eat / anything to do / slept / noticed

PRONUNCIATION

With *a bit*, *quite*, *fairly*, *pretty*, we usually stress the adjective that follows, but we sometimes stress the modifier to emphasise that we are making the adjective weaker.

9 ▶ **32** Underline which of the two words in italics you think is stressed in each sentence. Then listen and check.

1a It was *quite near* the beach, which was good.

1b It was *quite near* the beach but I was expecting it to be nearer.

2a The beach was a *bit crowded* so we didn't go there much.

2b The beach was a *bit crowded* but there was still enough room to relax in.

3a The surrounding area's *fairly nice*. It's very green and it's nice to hire a bike.

3b The surrounding area's *fairly nice*. There are a few factories, which kind of spoil it.

4a The food was *pretty good*, which I wasn't expecting.

4b The food was *pretty good*, although it was a bit too oily for my liking.

10 Use some of the language in Exercises 8 and 9 to talk about places in your town or city.

G For further practice, see page 173 and do Exercise 2.

10 To watch the video and do the activities, see the DVD-ROM.

SORTED!

LISTENING

1 Work in pairs. Think of three common problems that people have in each of the following situations:

- staying in a hotel
- renting a flat or a house
- sharing a flat or house

2 What's the worst problem? Why?

3 ▶ 33 Listen to four conversations about accommodation. Decide what kind of place is discussed in each conversation and what the main problem is.

4 ▶ 33 Listen again. Match two statements with each conversation.

1 Someone didn't know what was supposed to happen.
2 The place is dirty.
3 There's no way to change the temperature in the room.
4 Someone is sarcastic at the end of the conversation.
5 The heating system was dangerous.
6 Someone is refusing to pay money.
7 The person repeats their complaint in stronger language.
8 Someone was paid to sort out a problem.

5 Discuss what you would do in each situation.

> A: **What would you do** in the first conversation?
>
> B: **I'd ask** to see the manager.
>
> A: **How would that help?**

SPEAKING

6 Read the situations below. With a partner, choose two that you would like to roleplay.

- You rent a house. The bath has leaked and flooded the house. Your landlord wants you to pay for the damage.

- You recently started university. You're sharing a flat with three other students, all from different countries. You realise you're the tidiest person in the flat. You're always tidying up after everyone else – and it annoys you. You decide to try and talk to the person you think is messiest – an English student.

- The room in your hotel is too hot and so you complain to the receptionist.

- You're fairly sure you left your camera and laptop in your hostel room when you went out this morning, but now you can't find them. You think a member of staff might have stolen them.

- You are staying in a hotel. You need to get up early for an important meeting tomorrow. There's a huge wedding party going on downstairs. You decide to go and ask them to keep the noise down.

- You have been having serious problems with your neighbours. They make a lot of noise: they have loud arguments, and they have a large dog that barks at night. Recently, they've started throwing rubbish into your garden. You've had enough.

7 Choose your roles. Before you start, look through audio script 33 on pages 199–200 and underline any expressions you think will be useful.

8 Write the full conversations you want to have. Then try to remember what you wrote.

9 Roleplay the conversations. Try not to look at what you have written.

GRAMMAR

10 Look at this sentence from Exercise 3. Then complete the rules.

> ### have/get something done
>
> *You were right to have it checked and to get it repaired.*
>
> a *get* or *have* + object + past participle is *an active / a passive* construction.
>
> b We use this structure when the person who does the action is *unknown or unimportant / known and important*.
>
> c The structure *only focuses on the object of the verb / focuses on both the object of the verb and the person that the object belongs to.*

G Check your ideas on page 173 and do Exercise 1.

11 Work in pairs. How many different ways can you complete each of these sentences?

You ought to get your arm seen by a doctor.

You ought to have your arm X-rayed.

1 You ought _____ your arm _____ .

2 You should _____ that picture _____ .

3 I should _____ this coat _____ .

4 She has _____ a tooth _____ .

5 I've just _____ my passport _____ .

6 I need _____ my computer _____ .

7 We _____ the house _____ last month.

8 I'm going _____ my hair _____ .

12 Use the ideas in Exercise 11 to talk about things:

- you've had/got done recently.
- you need to have/get done.
- you'd never have/get done.

**G** For further practice, see Exercise 2 on page 173.

UNDERSTANDING VOCABULARY

> ### Idioms
>
> In Exercise 3, you heard these two idioms:
>
> *You're taking the mickey* and *I'm completely out of pocket.*
>
> An idiom is a group of words that means something different to the meaning of the individual words. You can sometimes work out the meaning of an idiom from the words and the context. If you look up the idiom in a dictionary, it's usually listed under the entry for the noun.

13 Replace the idioms in italics in sentences 1–8 with these definitions.

> been very expensive
>
> for very short periods of time
>
> getting used to things
>
> have enough money to pay for everything needed
>
> in an overly optimistic way
>
> it's his turn to react and do something
>
> making fun of
>
> short of money

1 We shared a flat for a year and then one day she just left without paying her share of the bills, leaving me really badly *out of pocket*.

2 Our old place really wasn't that great! I think you're looking back at it *through rose-coloured glasses*.

3 Don't get me wrong. My roommate is great *in small doses*. It's just that after too much of him, I have an overwhelming desire to fall asleep!

4 I've told my landlord I'm not going to pay any more rent until he gets the heating fixed, so now *the ball is in his court*.

5 They pay a lot in rent, so they must be struggling to *make ends meet* now she's lost her job.

6 I don't know how they can afford a place like that, considering what they earn. It must have *cost an arm and a leg*.

7 They were all *taking the mickey out of* me because of my haircut. I didn't find it very funny though.

8 I only moved here a few months ago. It was really hard to begin with, but bit by bit I'm *finding my feet*.

14 Choose three idioms from Exercise 13 and think of a situation for each. Tell a partner about them.

I took my old landlord to court and even though I won the case and got some compensation, I still ended up out of pocket because of all the legal fees.

A SHOCK TO THE SYSTEM

READING

1 Look at the photos of Ben's hometown in England – and where he has moved to: Hong Kong. Discuss the questions in pairs.

- What do you think Ben's life in England was like? Think about: social life, social circle, places to eat, nightlife, things to do in your free time, and so on.
- How easy do you think he will find moving to Hong Kong? Why?
- What things do you think Ben will have to get used to?
- How would someone find moving the opposite way, from Hong Kong to a small village?
- Which place would you rather live in? Why?

2 Read an email from Ben to a friend back home. Which things you thought of does he mention? Are you surprised by his reaction? Why? / Why not?

3 Work in pairs. Discuss what changes might have happened in Ben's life over his first few weeks in Hong Kong. Then read Ben's second email and find out if you were correct.

1

To   Jacksonjane@shotmail.ml

Subject   Greetings from HK

Hi Jane,

Just a quick email to say I've arrived and am slowly finding my feet. It's been an absolutely mad few days. Got off the plane and was immediately hit by the heat – just unbearably hot and humid. I was picked up at the airport by Tony, who works for the company. He was taking the mickey a bit in the taxi because he said I looked like some little boy who'd just arrived from the countryside. I suppose I probably did as I sat there gazing out of the window with my mouth hanging open. I mean, it's SO different. It's a bit overwhelming – but in a good way.

Anyway, after a couple of days getting over my jet lag and orientating myself a bit, I started at work. Mind you, I haven't exactly been slaving away at my desk. I seem to have spent most of my time being taken out for lunch, meeting people and partying! It's been pretty wild. I'd better start doing some proper work soon or the company will wonder what they're paying me for!

Anyway, they've already sorted out an apartment for me – 15th floor, stunning view – so that's all gone very smoothly. I already know I'm going to love it here.

How are things with you?

Ben

2

To   Jacksonjane@shotmail.ml

Subject   Too little time!

Hi Jane,

Sorry it's been a while. Things have settled down a bit since I last wrote. In fact, I've been working fairly long hours. People just don't seem to stop here. When I used to travel into London from the country, I thought the pace of life there was pretty fast, but here it's completely ridiculous! Then there's the noise – people seem to scream at each other all the time, they have the TV on full, and constantly sound their horns in the car. At the same time, I'm getting really frustrated in the office because, when I ask about things, most of the time I can't get a straight answer out of anyone.

Fortunately, I've made friends with this guy who joined around the same time as me and we go out and have a moan about things and just generally share our frustrations. Tony calls us The Moaning Twins, but he really is an idiot! To be honest, I'm already thinking of leaving. I honestly can't bear it! I never thought I'd miss home so much! Skype me sometime soon.

4 Work in pairs. Discuss the questions.

- Have you ever been homesick? When? Why?
- What kind of things do you moan about in terms of school, work, family? Who do you moan to?
- What kind of things do you think a foreigner might find difficult about your country?

5 Read Ben's third email below and answer the questions.

1 What has Ben been doing since he last wrote to Jane?
2 How has his attitude to both Hong Kong and the UK changed?
3 What do you think has caused the change?

3

To   Jacksonjane@shotmail.ml
Subject   Why go back when you can go forwards?

Hey Jane,

I know I said I was going to be back in England over Easter, but then I thought why go back to the miserable weather, rubbish food and dull conversation? In the end, I sold my plane tickets online and used the money to travel round here a bit. There are some amazing places to visit and I've now been onto the Chinese mainland quite a bit. The people are so much more in touch with their culture here. It's made me realise that back home, people just aren't interested anymore. It's all reality TV and celebrities.

Have you ever thought of coming out here? There's a lot to be said for it. Life's a lot easier here. I have all my laundry done through a service in my block; a maid comes and sorts out my flat every day. It's not like the poor service you get in England – it's far more efficient. People just take more pride in what they do here. And as for the food – honestly, I don't know how you lot eat the bland rubbish that gets served up there. Hong Kong is miles better. Anyway, I must dash – I've got my Chinese lesson in ten minutes.

Ben

6 Before you read Ben's final email – written over a year later – discuss the questions. Then read his final email in File 5 on page 185 to see if you guessed correctly.

- What do you think it will say?
- Why do you think there has been such a gap between emails?
- Where do you think he's living and how is he feeling?

7 Match the verbs from the four emails with the words they were used with.

1	pick up	a	my apartment
2	gaze	b	pride in what they do
3	get over	c	out of the window
4	slave away	d	very smoothly
5	sort out	e	at my desk
6	go	f	Ben at the airport
7	sound	g	my jet lag
8	take	h	their horns

LISTENING

8 Work in pairs. Discuss the questions.

- What do you understand by culture shock?
- When might you experience it?
- What might it involve?

9 ▶ **34** Listen to an extract from a radio programme on the topic. Take notes on what is said about the three questions in Exercise 8.

10 ▶ **34** Listen again and answer the questions.

1 What two misconceptions about culture shock are mentioned?
2 What is acculturation?
3 What four stages do people go through?
4 What happens in each phase?
5 Why might it be a problem if you don't complete the cycle?

11 Look back at the four emails and find examples of the following things mentioned in the extract:

1 wonder and joy
2 settling into a routine
3 swinging from one extreme to another
4 looking critically at your previous existence and its culture
5 insulting someone
6 refusing to mix with people
7 getting stuck in a phase

12 Has what you heard in Exercise 9 changed the way you feel about Ben? Why? / Why not?

SPEAKING

13 Think of a time when you experienced culture shock and had to adapt to new ways of doing things (in another country, when changing schools, starting university, beginning a new job, etc.)

Spend five minutes thinking about the following:

- what was strange for you
- the different feelings you went through
- how well you adapted
- any things you just couldn't get used to

Decide which language from this unit you want to use. Then share your experiences in groups.

CAPOEIRA –
THE FIGHTING DANCE

1 Look at the photo of people doing capoeira. Work in pairs. Discuss what you know about the questions below – or guess using the picture.

1 What exactly are they doing?

2 Where does it originate?

3 How did it originate?

4 Who does it now?

5 How is it used to benefit young people now?

2 ▶ **11** Now watch the video and answer the questions in Exercise 1.

3 Tell a partner what you thought of the video. Use some of these sentence starters.

> What did you think of ...?
>
> You were right about ...
>
> I hadn't realised that ...
>
> I didn't really understand the bit about ...
>
> I've heard of a similar kind of project in ...

4 Complete the summary of the video with a noun form of the words below.

Capoeira is a [1]_____ of dance and martial art which was developed by slaves in the early 1800s. The slaves used capoeira as a way of opposing their owners without the owners realising that they were practising fighting moves. After [2]_____ was abolished it became popular as a form of [3]_____ and as a way to raise [4]_____ of ex-slaves' identity. In more modern times it has been used to work with kids who are at risk because of [5]_____ . In Brazil, there are considerable numbers of homeless children, who are often involved in [6]_____ , crime and drugs, and have disappeared from official records. Organisations such as Project Axe find foster homes for the kids and then provide

combine

slave

amuse
aware

homeless

beg

education and social [7]_____ through capoeira. Capoeira not only allows the kids to develop their [8]_____ and stamina, it encourages self-control and respect for others by teaching [9]_____ , rules and limits within the capoeira 'circle'. Many children have had their lives changed as a result and sometimes may go on to give [10]_____ and become masters themselves.

develop

strong

normal

perform

5 Work in pairs. Discuss the questions.

- Would you be any good at capoeira? Why? / Why not?

- What sport(s) originated in your country? What do you know about its history?

- How do people become homeless? How could homelessness be solved?

- Think of a person who has been saved from problems because of sport or some other passion. What happened?

- What organisations help young people in your country? What do they do?

UNDERSTANDING FAST SPEECH

6 Look at this extract from the video. To help you, groups of words are marked with / and stressed sounds are in CAPITALS. Pauses are marked //. Practise saying the sentences.

BAsically // I TAKE what they HAVE to OFFer // their BOdy strength and their ENergy // and MOULD it / by INtegrating them into the GROUP. // ONCE they're in the CIRcle, / which is the most SAcred MOment of the CApoeira PROcess // I SHOW them that there are NORMS // RULES / and LImits / withIN yourself // AND with OTHers / that NEED to be FOllowed.

7 ▶ **12** Listen to how Mario said these sentences. Now you have a go! Practise saying the extract again fast.

REVIEW 3

GRAMMAR

1 Complete the second sentence so that it has a similar meaning to the first sentence, using the word given. Do not change the word given. You must use between two and five words, including the word given.

1 She took up golf around ten years ago.

She _____ about ten years now. **GOLF**

2 There was absolutely nothing worth seeing at the music festival.

Unfortunately, the music festival was _____ time. **COMPLETE**

3 He was incredibly lucky that he didn't kill himself.

Honestly, he _____ . He was lucky really. **DIED**

4 I knew the lock was broken and now we have been burgled.

I _____ fixed. We might not have been burgled. **SHOULD**

5 I wanted to go and see that game. Why didn't you tell me you were going?

You should've told me you were going. I _____ you. **WOULD**

6 The house is in chaos at the moment because it's being painted.

We _____ , so it's a bit chaotic at the moment. **REDECORATED**

7 It's not been a sudden decision to move to the country.

We _____ of moving to the country for a while. **HAVE**

8 He weighs eight kilos more than he did before he injured his leg.

He has _____ he got injured. **SINCE**

2 Choose all the correct words or forms in italics.

A: How was your holiday?

B: ¹*Absolutely / Very / Really* fantastic.

A: Oh great. What did you do?

B: ²*Hardly / Almost / Nearly* anything to be honest. We just went to the beach most days.

A: Don't you find that ³*a bit / really / absolutely* boring?

B: No, not at all. I read and swim and play with the kids and being from the city it's just a ⁴*really / real / bit of a* change. Do you know the east coast of Spain?

A: Not really – but ⁵*I've visited / I've been visiting* the big theme park near there a couple of times. Did you go?

B: No, we were told it's always ⁶*a bit / really / very* packed and you have to queue too long for the rides.

A: I know what you mean, but you ⁷*could've / should've / would've* gone. It's worth it even with the queues.

B: Well, ⁸*we've already talked / we've been talking* about going back there next year, so maybe we'll go then.

3 ▶ 35 Listen. Write the six sentences you hear.

4 Write a sentence before and after the sentences from Exercise 3 to create a short conversation.

VOCABULARY

5 Match the verbs (1–10) with the collocates (a–j).

1 I get out of	a us quite out of pocket.
2 We worked up	b tactics beforehand.
3 They hit	c the main square.
4 They sacked	d the mickey.
5 We didn't discuss	e a bit of a sweat.
6 I tore	f the coach after six games.
7 The place overlooked	g breath very quickly.
8 They got promoted	h the post twice.
9 It left	i to the top division last year.
10 They're just taking	j a ligament in my ankle.

6 Decide if these words are connected to sport or accommodation and in what way.

a boiler	tackle	a leak	a substitute	a dump
overtake	a landlord	isolated	time-out	a track

7 Complete the email with one word in each space. The first letters are given.

Dear Juan

Just a quick email to tell you how I'm getting on here in Tokyo. Sorry I haven't written sooner but it took me a week to ¹get o_____ my jet lag and then, what with the new job and ²s_____ o_____ somewhere to live, I'm only just beginning to find my ³f_____ . I've finally found a flat – it's cost me an ⁴a_____ and a l_____ to rent, but it's very central and I have a ⁵st_____ view across the city. It really is amazing. People here have been very ⁶we_____ and I've been out a few times with people from the company. The food is amazing. I think I'm going to love it here. Mind you, I've started reading that book you gave me about acculturation so I'm trying not to look at everything through ⁷r_____-coloured glasses. That way, maybe then I won't be disappointed and ⁸sw_____ to the other extreme.

Asher

8 Complete the sentences. Use the word in brackets to form a word that fits in the space.

1 I'm hopeless at racket sports. I have no hand-eye _____ . (coordinate)

2 He banged his head quite badly, but he didn't lose _____ . (conscious)

3 Sport stops kids getting into trouble out of _____ . (bored)

4 I've twisted my ankle several times and I've lost some _____ in it. (flexible)

5 I've tried climbing but I never took it up seriously. I don't have the _____ to do it well. (strong)

6 After initial feelings of elation, people typically go through a period of _____ . (resist)

7 My flatmate is OK in small doses, but after a while I get an _____ desire to fall asleep. (overwhelm)

7

NATURE

IN THIS UNIT YOU LEARN HOW TO:

- talk about your experiences of different weather
- talk about natural disasters
- make stories more dramatic
- talk about issues connected to animals and plants
- talk about trends
- use context to understand different meanings of words

SPEAKING

1 Imagine you are the man in the photo. What happened? Think about these questions:

- Where do you live?
- When did the bad weather start?
- What effect did it have on your life?
- Did you sort out the problems? How?

2 Work in pairs. Tell the story to a partner. Your partner should sympathise and ask extra questions. Then change roles.

WEATHER THE STORM

VOCABULARY Weather

1 Match these different kinds of weather with the descriptions below.

cold fog rain snow storm sun/heat wind

1 I woke up in the middle of the night because the thunder was so loud and then there were these incredible flashes of lightning. It was quite scary.

2 We were driving along the motorway and suddenly we just hit it. It was really thick and you could hardly see the car in front. We had to come off the motorway and wait for it to lift.

3 It was boiling and really humid and there was no air conditioning on the bus. It was unbearable. I thought I was going to pass out!

4 I lost all feeling in my fingers and my lips turned blue. I thought I was going to freeze to death!

5 I got absolutely soaked on the way. When we left it was fine, but then the clouds came in and it suddenly started pouring down, and of course I hadn't brought an umbrella or anything.

6 It blew down a tree and it hit our house. It did quite a lot of damage.

7 It was pouring down and then it turned to hail. It was incredible. In the end, we had to pull over until it all eased off.

8 The ferry couldn't sail because it was so strong, but it eased off after a couple of hours.

9 Honestly, we had to slow right down because it started to settle and I was afraid of skidding. Apparently, there were lots of crashes and some people got stuck in their cars overnight.

10 It continued non-stop for about a week! The whole place was flooded. It was miserable.

PRONUNCIATION

2 ▶ 36 Listen to phrases from Exercise 1 that contain the word *was*. Notice how the sound of the word changes in fast speech. Then listen again and repeat the phrases.

3 Underline any new expressions or collocations in 1–10 in Exercise 1. Compare what you underline with a partner.

4 Have you ever experienced anything like any of the situations in Exercise 1? Tell your partner.

LISTENING

5 ▶ 37 Listen to two people sharing experiences of extreme weather. Answer the questions.

1 Where were the two people when they experienced extreme weather?

2 What kind of weather did each person experience?

3 How did they feel?

4 What did they do as a result of the weather?

GRAMMAR

6 Read the Grammar box on page 63. Then work in pairs to answer the questions below.

1 Find an example of the past perfect simple and of the past continuous in the Grammar box.

2 Which tense shows an action was at the same time as another, but was unfinished or interrupted?

3 Which tense shows an action finished before a previously mentioned action or before the story began?

8 Choose one of the sentences below and use it as part of a story about weather. Imagine what happened before and afterwards. Plan how you will describe the experience. Use the past continuous and past perfect at least once.

1 We were absolutely soaked by the end of it.

2 The roads were really icy.

3 We couldn't see a thing.

4 The wind was so strong it nearly blew me over.

9 Tell your story to a partner.

DEVELOPING CONVERSATIONS

Making stories more dramatic

Look at three patterns you heard in Exercise 5 that make the story more dramatic.

a *They were **as** big **as** golf balls.*
   (*as* + adj + *as* to make comparisons)

b *Honestly, they were hitting the car **so** hard they nearly broke the windscreen.*
   (*so* + adv + result)

c *I poured **something like** a litre of water out of my shoes.*
   (*something like* + number)

10 Write five sentences using the patterns in the box about the things below. Share your ideas with a partner.

- how hot / cold / wet / windy, etc. the weather is
- how big / small / dirty / clean, etc. someone's flat is
- how lazy / hard-working / fat / thin / tall, etc. someone is
- how posh / dangerous, etc. an area is
- how good / bad, etc. a film or book is

CONVERSATION PRACTICE

11 Think of a time when you experienced really extreme weather. Plan how to tell your story. Decide when you could use the past continuous or past perfect and make the story dramatic.

12 Work in pairs. Tell your stories. Describe where you were, what you were doing and what happened. When listening to other stories, show interest and ask questions. You might also try to respond by talking about a similar experience. Use some of the phrases in the box below.

Do you know what happened to me last night?

I had this really scary experience when I was on holiday ...

Really? What happened?

Actually, that reminds me of ...

■ 13 To watch the video and do the activities, see the DVD-ROM.

Narrative tenses

When we tell stories, we usually describe the main events in the order they happened and we use the past simple to do this. For example: in the story you heard, '*One moment we **were** in sunshine, the next we **saw** like a line on the road ahead and we **drove** through it and it **was** hail!*'

Sometimes we have to use the past perfect and past continuous to show background information and causes.

Read this summary of the story:

When they **were driving** to Rome, it started to hail. It was terrifying because they were the biggest hailstones they**'d ever seen**, so they pulled over and waited for it to stop.

G Check your ideas on page 174 and do Exercise 1.

7 Complete this summary of the second story you heard by putting the verbs in brackets into the correct tense.

We were in Sardinia and we ¹_____ (visit) this little village somewhere. It ²_____ (be) boiling all day and in the evening we ³_____ (take) a walk along the beach when suddenly we ⁴_____ (see) this incredible forked lightning. It ⁵_____ (start) spitting and then just two seconds later, it started pouring down. As we ⁶_____ (not bring) an umbrella, we just ⁷_____ (run) to the nearest café we ⁸_____ (can) find. It can't have been more than a minute, but we got absolutely soaked. I must have emptied something like a litre of water out of my shoes.

ANIMALS MAKING HEADLINES

SPEAKING

1 Work with a partner. Which ideas do you agree with most or least? Why?

> The true sign of a civilised country is the way it treats its animals.

> If everyone became vegetarian, we would all be healthier and happier – and it'd be much better for the long-term future of the world.

> The only animals in the world that you really need to be scared of are humans!

> Wearing fur is indefensible!

> Time spent with cats is never wasted.

> Vivisection – carrying out experiments on animals – is morally wrong. It may be true that it helps advance our knowledge, but it also damages the soul, the human spirit.

READING

2 Work in pairs. Look at the phrases from four articles. Discuss which pairs of phrases might go together and what each story might be about.

1 the will is being contested
2 try them for a dare
3 intimidation of laboratory staff
4 reverse a ban

a spark a heated debate
b research will provide invaluable insights
c her rightful inheritance
d fried maggots

3 Work in two groups.

Group A: read the two articles on page 65.

Group B: read the articles in File 10 on page 187.

Then, discuss what you understood with a partner from your group.

4 Change partners. Work with a student from the other group. Without looking at your articles, summarise what you read. Share your opinions about each story. Now read the two other articles. Is there anything your new partner forgot to mention?

5 Continue working with your partner from the other group. Decide in which article:

1 a contract was cancelled.
2 business is booming.
3 someone got a nasty surprise.
4 people's privacy has been violated.
5 a change was highly controversial.
6 a cultural taboo has been broken.
7 there may well be a court case.
8 people are struggling to make ends meet.

6 Work in pairs. Discuss the following:

1 Put the stories in order of interest from 1 (= most interesting) to 4. Explain your choice.

2 Tell your partner any similar stories to the four you read. Use some of these phrases.

> Did you see that thing in the news / on TV about ...?
>
> Someone was telling me about ...
>
> I read this amazing thing online about ...
>
> I read a great article in the paper the other day about ...

GRAMMAR

7 Look at these sentences from two of the articles. Then answer the questions below.

Participle clauses

We can sometimes shorten relative clauses by using a past or present participle instead of a full relative clause. This is more common in written English. In the articles, you read:

a *Since adding a range of dishes **featuring** the insects to their menu, Espitas restaurant claims to have been almost constantly fully booked.*

b *The £18-million centre was intended to allow experiments **aimed at** combating illnesses such as cancer, heart disease and diabetes to be carried out.*

1 Is the verb in each clause active or passive?

2 How would you say these sentences using a full relative clause in place of the participle clause in bold?

G Check your ideas on page 174 and do Exercise 1.

8 Choose the correct option.

1 the number of animals *abandoning / abandoned* by their owners
2 the number of people *living / lived* together before marriage
3 the number of people *moving / moved* abroad
4 the number of young people *suffering / suffered* from depression
5 the number of people *studying / studied* at university
6 the amount of organic food *selling / sold* last year
7 the amount of money *donating / donated* to charities
8 the amount of food *throwing / thrown* out by the average family

9 Think of two trends you know about. Decide how you can use some of the phrases in the box below to describe the trends over recent years. Then explain your ideas to a partner.

> I think the number / amount of ... has gone up / down sharply / slightly in recent years, because ...
>
> I think it's mostly because of / a result of ...
>
> This has led to / resulted in ...

a

THE SPORT THAT REFUSES TO DIE

The Spanish government's 2012 decision to reverse a ban on showing live bullfighting on the state-run channel Televisión Española sparked a heated debate about the sport and its role in Spanish culture.

The initial ban came in 2006 amidst claims that the rights to show fights were too expensive, and that bullfighting was too violent for children who could be watching. However, the conservative Popular Party sees the sport as an art with deep roots in Spanish history and has given the industry tax breaks and ensured low ticket prices.

To fans, bullfighting is full of drama, risk and bravery. Opponents, though, insist the sport is cruel and the region of Catalonia, which includes the city of Barcelona, has completely banned all fights. Increasingly, younger Spaniards seem uninterested. In a recent opinion poll, over 70% claimed to have no interest in watching the sport at all.

In addition, bull breeders are finding it increasingly hard to make a profit. This is partly down to the rising costs of food, but also due to increased competition from the growing number of rich breeders involved in the business mainly as a hobby. Many now only survive thanks to European Union subsidies of around €200 per bull per year.

b

ANIMAL CHARITY'S GAIN IS DOCTOR'S LOSS

A woman who gave up a career as a university lecturer in order to help her parents run their farm was shocked to discover that they had left everything they owned to the RSPCA – the Royal Society for the Prevention of Cruelty to Animals – the main animal-protection charity in the UK.

Dr Christine Gill spent much of the last ten years looking after her ageing parents and working on the farm. However, on his death, her father asked for his entire estate – worth around £1.5 million – to be given to the charity. His will is now being contested as Dr Gill struggles to win back what she sees as her rightful inheritance.

The RSPCA has said that it hopes the matter can be settled 'without the need for legal proceedings'. Founded in 1824 (over 60 years before the NSPCC – the National Society for the Prevention of Cruelty to Children), the organisation is left over £40 million a year and is one of Britain's biggest charities.

The group has recently come in for criticism for what many see as its involvement in politics after it supported calls for a ban on fox hunting.

PLANT LIFE

LISTENING

1 ▶ **38** Work in groups. Discuss the questions. Then listen to five conversations related to plants and find out what answers are given to these questions.

1 Look at the photo. What else kills plants or trees?

2 How can plants or trees cause problems?

3 Why might you give or receive flowers or a plant?

4 What food can you get for free near where you live?

5 What are some different uses of herbs?

2 ▶ **38** Listen again and match one of the statements a–f with each conversation 1–5. One statement isn't used.

a a speaker talks about a misunderstanding

b a speaker expresses concern about dying

c a speaker gives a probable explanation

d a speaker complains about a plant

e a speaker expresses thanks

f a speaker offers a cure

3 In which conversation was each of the words in the box used? Do you remember what was said?

awkward	gather	lethal	rots	swears by
cheer up	get rid of	native	settle	thank you

4 ▶ **38** Listen again and read the audio script on page 201. Underline the part of the sentence each word or phrase is used in.

5 Work in pairs. Discuss the questions connected to the conversations in Exercise 1.

1 How connected to nature are you? In what way?

2 Do you have any plants in your house? Why? / Why not?

3 Are there any invasive plants (or animals) in your country? What's the effect? What's being done about it?

4 Are any flowers or plants connected to particular festivals or events in your country?

5 The grandmother of one of the speakers swears by lemon and honey for a cold. What things do you swear by?

UNDERSTANDING VOCABULARY

The different meanings of words

You will know the word *water* as in *drink some water*, but in one of the conversations in Exercise 1 you heard this:

*I've been **watering** [the plants] every day.*

Most words have more than one meaning. Sometimes you can tell a word is being used in a different sense because the form of the word is different (here, *water* is a verb in the present perfect continuous). Sometimes the word has a connected meaning as here (*give water to plants*), but sometimes it is less clear, and you need to look at the words around it to work out the meaning in this context, as in these examples in this unit.

*The snow's beginning to **settle**.* (= it's something snow does)

*It'll really **settle** your stomach.* (= it's something you do to your stomach)

If you think of words as often being part of collocations and phrases, you will also start to notice other vocabulary connected to them. This will boost your understanding of how words work.

6 Work in pairs. Match the seven words related to nature with the photos.

blossom   flood   plant   root   seed   stem   stormy

7 ▶ **39** Listen to seven pairs of sentences. Decide if the words in each sentence have the same (*S*) meaning as in Exercise 6 or different (*D*). Use the word forms and other words in the sentences to help you.

8 Work in pairs. Discuss the questions.

- Do you know anyone who has a stormy relationship? In what way is it stormy?
- Public and private debt has increased in many countries. What do you think the root cause is?
- Can you think of anything that has prompted floods of complaints? Why?
- Can you think of anyone whose career is blossoming?
- What problem in your town, city or country most annoys you? What do you think it stems from?

a
b
c
d
e
f
g

8

CRIME AND PUNISHMENT

IN THIS UNIT YOU LEARN HOW TO:

- talk about crimes and what they involve
- make comments and ask follow-up questions
- express varying degrees of certainty
- talk about prison and punishment
- talk about trends and statistics

SPEAKING

1   **Work in pairs. Look at the photo. Discuss the questions.**

- What crime do you think the photo shows?
- Where do you think it is taking place?
- Why do crimes like this occur?
- What punishment do you think the seller and/or buyers should get? Why?
- Have you ever heard of any similar crimes where you live?

CAUGHT IN THE ACT

VOCABULARY Crimes

1 Complete sentences 1–9 with the pairs of verbs. You may need to reverse the order of the words.

beaten – found	raided – seized
doing – caught	set – smashed
~~got hold of – gone~~	stolen – broken into
grabbed – came up to	vanished – came back
killed – went off	

1 I got a phone call from the bank saying I'd ___*gone*___ $1000 overdrawn. Someone must've *got hold of* my details somehow and used my card number.

2 I was _____ on camera and had to pay a €100 fine. I was only _____ about 65!

3 A local businessman was _____ dead in a park. Apparently, he'd been attacked and then _____ to death.

4 She went out to the shops and never _____ . She just completely _____ .

5 They made such a mess. They _____ shop windows, threw rocks at police and _____ fire to cars.

6 When we got back, we found the house had been _____ . Fortunately, they hadn't _____ much.

7 I was standing outside the cathedral and this guy _____ me, _____ my bag and ran off.

8 Apparently, the police _____ this café near us and _____ 5 million dollars worth of ivory.

9 Luckily, there weren't many people around when the device _____ so no-one was _____ , but it did a lot of damage.

2 Work in pairs. Match these crimes with the descriptions in Exercise 1.

a bombing	fraud	smuggling
a burglary	murder	speeding
a disappearance	a riot	a street robbery

3 Spend two minutes memorising the language in Exercises 1 and 2. Test each other.
Student A says the crime.
Student B says the example from Exercise 1.

4 Think of real examples for four of the crimes in Exercise 2. Explain what happened using some of the new vocabulary in Exercise 1.

LISTENING

5 ▶ **40** Listen to three conversations and answer the questions.

1 What crime from Exercise 2 do they talk about?

2 How do the speakers know about the crime?

3 What happened?

6 ▶ **40** Work in pairs. Decide which conversation each group of words comes from and how each word was used. Then listen again and check.

1 swipe / trainers / relief

2 stuffed / shock / drugged

3 directions / fortunately / spoil

7 Which of the three crimes is most serious? Explain your reasons.

DEVELOPING CONVERSATIONS

Comments and questions

When listening to stories, we often make a comment and then follow it with a question.

Oh you're joking! What happened?

That's terrible! Did it have much in it?

We often use modal verbs (*must, can't, might* or *could*) to show degrees of certainty when we are giving opinions and speculating about what's true.

a It **can't have been** very nice.

b Someone **must have got hold** of my card details.

c **It could have been** when I bought those new trainers on the internet, but then again it **might** equally **have been** in the local supermarket.

d That **must be** a relief.

1 Which two modals show the speaker is uncertain about what happened?

2 Which two modals show the speaker is almost certain about what happened?

3 How does the speaker show they're referring to a past event or feeling rather than the present?

G Check your ideas on page 174 and do Exercise 1.

8 Put the words in order to make comments and questions. Add exclamation and question marks.

1 Was dreadful killed That's anyone

That's dreadful! Was anyone killed?

2 been must've That you awful Were OK

3 anything no valuable they Oh take Did very

4 parents What thinking were dreadful That's the

5 insured a What shame you Were

6 police Did you That's terrible report to the it

7 did joking they know Do who it You're

8 must It's What awful through his going family be

PRONUNCIATION

9 ▶ **41** Listen to the comments and questions in Exercise 8 and notice the intonation. Repeat them.

10 Work in pairs. Using the prompts below, take turns to start conversations. Respond to each prompt with a comment and a question. Continue each conversation for as long as you can, adding extra comments and questions.

1 I had my camera stolen while I was on holiday.

2 We got caught in the middle of a riot.

3 We had our house broken into last night.

4 I had my bag snatched in the street.

5 Did you hear there's been a bombing in town?

6 Did you read about that guy who was murdered near here?

GRAMMAR

11 Look at the sentences in the Grammar box. Then answer questions 1–3 below the box.

12 Look at the situation below. Complete sentences 1–6 with an appropriate verb.

A 17-year-old boy has disappeared after having an argument with his parents. He's been gone three days and they've just reported it to the police.

1 They must ___have had___ a very serious argument for him to run away like that.

2 It can't _____ the first time it's happened or they would've reported him missing sooner.

3 His parents must _____ really worried, but they should've said something earlier.

4 He might _____ to a friend's house and he's too angry to get in touch.

5 Or he might _____ too embarrassed to phone because he thinks he's in trouble.

6 He might _____ . The police should _____ .

13 Work in pairs. Use *might / must / can't / should* + past and present infinitives to make similar comments to those in Exercise 12 about 1 and 2 below.

1 Your neighbours have been buying a lot of expensive things recently. You've seen a man acting suspiciously outside their house.

2 A 43-year-old man is in hospital after being shot at his home. A woman is in custody.

G For further practice, see page 175 and do Exercise 2.

CONVERSATION PRACTICE

14 Think of a crime you have heard about. Write down five key words. Swap them with a partner. They should think of two comments and questions such as those in Exercise 8. Then have the conversations together.

🎥 14 To watch the video and do the activities, see the DVD-ROM.

BEHIND BARS

VOCABULARY Crime and punishment

1 Complete the sentences with these words.

appeal	convicted	cells
fine	got	offence
rehabilitation	released	served
treated		

1 Prisoners *share / have tiny / are let out of their / are locked in* their _____ .

2 He was _____ of *fraud / murder / robbery / assault.*

3 He was _____ *early / for good behaviour / after an appeal.*

4 They need to *place more emphasis on / undergo / try new approaches to* _____ .

5 The prisoners are _____ *well / very harshly / with respect / like animals.*

6 He _____ *a small fine / a short sentence / life / the death penalty.*

7 He only _____ *half his sentence / eight years of a twelve-year sentence / a year in prison.*

8 She's *launched an / lost her / going to / won her* _____ .

9 It was *his first / a really serious / only a minor / a public order* _____ .

10 She got a *£50 / huge / small / €10,000* _____ .

2 Underline any new collocations for you in Exercise 1. Where possible, notice the grammar they are used with.

3 Use language from Exercise 1 to say what punishments people who commit the crimes in Exercise 2 on page 70 usually get in your country. Do you think these punishments are appropriate? Why? / Why not?

SPEAKING

4 Work in pairs. Discuss the questions.

- Are TV shows about crime and the police popular in your country?

- Which do you think are the most widely watched?

- Do you like any TV shows or films about crime? Which ones? Why?

- Why do you think crime shows are so popular around the world?

- Look at the film poster. Discuss what you think the film might be about and how it might be connected to crime.

LISTENING

5 ▶ 42 Listen to the first part of a radio feature. Take notes on what you learn about the film *Reality* and its star Aniello Arena. Compare your notes with a partner.

6 ▶ 42 Listen again. Are the sentences true (T) or false (F)?

1 Aniello Arena was still in prison when he was making the film *Reality*.

2 He was serving a ten-year sentence.

3 *Reality* is a crime film.

4 Arena still denies any involvement in the crime he was convicted of.

5 The Fortezza Theatre Company stages all their plays in prison.

6 Prisoners choose to get involved with acting to avoid having therapy.

7 Prison authorities elsewhere have shown interest in the project.

7 Work in pairs. Discuss the questions.

- Do you think it's a good idea for prisoners to get involved in drama groups and acting? Why? / Why not?
- Should they be let out on day release to film and allowed to tour?
- Which of the statements below do you agree with? Why?

1 Prisoners ought to be made to do hard manual labour.

2 They need to learn basic literacy skills – how to read and write.

3 They should be forced to meet the victims of their crimes.

4 They should do community service while they are in prison.

5 It's a good idea for them to learn how to use technology.

6 There ought to be some interaction with normal members of society.

7 Encouraging them to keep pets and tend gardens makes sense.

8 ▶ **43** Listen to the second part of the radio feature. Which ideas from Exercise 7 are mentioned? Why?

9 ▶ **43** Work in pairs. Discuss why you think each of the things below was mentioned. Then listen again to check your ideas.

1 public opinion

2 70 to 75%, 30% and 20%

3 death penalty

4 21 years

5 plumbing

6 liberal attitudes

10 Work in groups. Discuss how you feel about prisons like Bastøy and whether the Scandinavian approach to prison would work in your country. Explain why / why not.

GRAMMAR

Nouns and prepositional phrases

We often add prepositional phrases to nouns to help define the noun.

*Public opinion often demands longer sentences and harsher conditions **for those inside**.*

11 Work in pairs. Can you remember which prepositions were used with the nouns in this sentence from the radio feature? What kinds of words follow the prepositions (e.g. adjectives, adverbs, nouns, verbs, etc.)?

The main problem [1]_____ prisons is that we place too much emphasis [2]_____ punishing prisoners and don't pay enough attention [3]_____ rehabilitation.

Ⓖ Check your ideas on page 175 and do Exercise 1

12 Complete the second sentence so that it means the same as the first by adding the nouns in bold, the correct prepositions and any other words necessary.

1 I've always thought the police do an amazing job.

I have tremendous ___respect for___ the police and the work they do. **RESPECT**

2 If they're not careful, the government could easily make this situation worse.

The government are running the _____ things worse if they're not careful. **RISK**

3 If the police think it's necessary to stop and search me then that's OK with me.

I don't have a _____ stopped and searched, if the police think they need to do it. **PROBLEM**

4 If you worry too much about becoming the victim of crime, you'll never do anything!

There's _____ too much about becoming the victim of crime. **POINT**

5 No-one has ever escaped from this prison.

Prisoners have _____ from here. **HOPE**

6 Many police officers have never had to deal with riots.

Many police officers have _____ riots. **EXPERIENCE**

7 The number of people that report hate crimes has gone up.

There's been an _____ of hate crimes. **INCREASE**

8 The government has rejected the call for increased police funding.

The government has rejected the _____ the amount of police funding. **PROPOSAL**

13 In pairs, discuss if you agree or disagree with sentences 1–8. Explain why.

1 There's never any excuse *for committing crime*.

2 The government has no interest *in improving prisons*.

3 There's no point *in trying to rehabilitate some criminals*.

4 There's no need *for more police*.

5 We don't have a problem *with drugs in our country*.

6 We need a return *to the values of the past*.

7 The *quality of life* here is the best in the world.

8 There's a strong focus *on foreign languages in our schools*.

14 Choose four sentences from Exercise 13. Make new sentences by changing the prepositional phrases in italics.

There's never any excuse for dropping litter.

There's no point in politics.

15 Share your ideas in groups. Do people agree with you?

Ⓖ For further practice, see page 175 and do Exercise 2.

RISE AND FALL

READING

1 Work in pairs. Discuss the questions.

1 How would you rate the following in terms of crime and security?

- your country
- your city or town
- the area you live in

2 Do you think crime has increased, decreased or stayed the same over the last few years? Why? Is it the same for all kinds of crime?

2 Read the first two paragraphs of the article (up to *Education*) and discuss these questions.

- Does anything surprise you? Do you believe it? Why? / Why not?
- How would you answer the question at the end of the second paragraph?

3 Discuss what reasons might be given for the trend connected to the following sub-headings. Then read the rest of the article to see if you were right.

- Education
- Distraction
- Demographics and environment
- Technology
- Prison and policing

4 Put the missing sentences (a–h) in the correct place in the article.

a The more confidence the public has in the police, the more likely they are to help with enquiries.

b Increased levels in the blood and brain are associated with violent urges.

c Remove the opportunity to start a life in crime and you reduce the number of criminals.

d Education, in other words, makes us more civilised.

e This resulted in less theft, which had previously been carried out to feed addictions.

f Once identified, large numbers of police would focus on these small areas to arrest criminals and discourage incidents.

g Essentially, if young men are indoors, whatever they're doing, they're not causing trouble outdoors.

h While Latvia fits the pattern, neighbouring Estonia reduced its prison population and still saw a similar fall in murders.

5 Work in pairs. Discuss the questions.

- Which of the suggested causes for the fall in crime are seen in Riga and Latvia?
- Do you believe all the suggested causes? Why? / Why not? Which do you think plays the biggest role?
- Have any of the suggested causes happened in your country? Have they had the same results?
- Are there any other factors that you think affect levels of crime?

VOCABULARY Trends and statistics

6 Replace the words in bold in the sentences with these words and phrases.

account for	drop	played a role	rise
coincided	led to	plunged	soared
correlation	peak	ranks	stems from

1 During the noughties, the number of cars that were stolen **fell** by almost 70%.

2 The prison population hit a **high** of 450,000 in 2006 and has slowly declined by 3% since then.

3 The fall in crime has **run in parallel** with an increase in the numbers entering university.

4 There is quite a well-established **link** between poor reading skills and crime.

5 As mobile phone use has **increased sharply**, it has **resulted in** a similar rise in street crime.

6 It's argued that the **fall** in violent crime **is the result of** harsher prison sentences.

7 Experts believe the economic recession may have **been a factor** in the slight **increase** in the overall crime figures this year.

8 The fact that Russia **comes** second for the number of billionaires may **be the reason for** the huge increase in sales of luxury cars.

7 Think of one example of the things below. Then make a note of possible causes and results of these trends. Use words and phrases from Exercise 6 to share your ideas with a partner.

- something that has **soared** recently / over the last few years
- something that has **plunged** recently / over the last few years
- something your country **ranks highly** in
- a **link** which has recently been established

RIGA-ROUS POLICING BRINGS DOWN CRIME

Jonas Grauza, a police officer from Riga in Latvia, gets out of his car to stretch his legs. While the nightlife in the old town is as lively as ever, for him it's been a quiet night. He's had to break up an argument and take a report of a stolen phone, but that's about it. He smiles when asked if it's a typical night. 'It's generally like this, yes, but 20 years ago it was very different. The only reason you'd come to the old town at night was if you wanted trouble. Police work was a lot more risky.' And the statistics tell the tale. Violent crime has plunged in Latvia over the last two decades, with Riga seeing a 70% fall in murders.

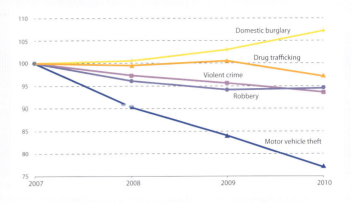

Such changes are not restricted to Latvia. Across Europe, the number of crimes recorded annually has fallen by nearly three million and other countries such as the US and Japan have seen a similar trend, especially in robbery, car theft and violent crime. As this falling trend has become more established, there has been increasing debate about what has caused it and whether it will continue. Are people simply getting nicer?

EDUCATION

Some argue that through raising awareness of issues, people are being turned off crime. Campaigns against drug and alcohol abuse have been successful in that young people are less likely to try illegal drugs than previous generations. [1]_____ . Some have also pointed out that the fall in crime has run in parallel to an increase in the number of people going on to further education. [2]_____

DISTRACTION

However, it is not clear that education in itself drives people away from crime. 18-to-24-year-olds make up the vast majority of criminals and if they are at university, so the argument goes, they don't have the time to commit crimes. This distraction argument has also been put forward as a reason for recent findings that violent video games may account for a percentage of the drop in crime. [3]_____

DEMOGRAPHICS AND ENVIRONMENT

This point that crime is fundamentally a young person's activity has also made researchers speculate that population changes have played a role. It is argued that crime peaked in the 1990s as a result of the children of the 1960s and 70s baby boom reaching their twenties. More controversially, it has been claimed that the banning of lead in petrol in the 70s is a factor as previously the lead particles were released into the atmosphere and breathed in. [4]_____

TECHNOLOGY

While such environmental theories are not widely accepted, there is greater acceptance that technology and prevention have played an important role, at least for certain crimes. For example, with the sophisticated locking systems installed in cars these days, it is far more difficult to steal them. Furthermore, in the past, car crime acted as a gateway crime – an easy first crime to commit, which might lead to further involvement in more serious things. [5]_____ . Having said that, technology is also facilitating new types of crimes such as identity theft, though perhaps these attract a different class of criminal.

PRISON AND POLICING

Others argue that the fall in crime stems from jailing more people for longer and from better policing. They point to the success of programmes in Los Angeles and New York, where police used statistical analysis to identify crime hotspots. [6]_____

THE RIGA EXPERIENCE

Proving causal links when assessing crime is always problematic, not least because correlations are rarely consistent. For example, in several countries, an increase in the prison population has coincided with the fall in crime, but this is not always the case. [7]_____ . In the case of Riga, police targeted key establishments and drove out criminals. Their success allowed legitimate businesses to return as well as wealthier local people to move in. In addition, Latvia has experienced falling birth rates, while university students have almost tripled. Better training of police has also improved relations with the community and a multilingual section has been established to work with the increasing numbers of tourists. [8]_____

Not that everything is perfect: fraud and pickpocketing have increased and the police themselves receive more complaints. However, Jonas Grauza is happy. 'If people complain, it shows the public trust us – and fewer murders means my wife worries about me less.'

VIDEO 4

THE GREENHOUSE EFFECT

1 **Look at these words and phrases. Do you know what they mean? Compare your ideas with a partner.**

a blizzard	a famine	a heatwave
a drought	a flood	a volcanic eruption
an earthquake	forest fires	

2 🎥 **15** **Watch the first part of the video. Find out which of the events in Exercise 1 happened in the following places:**

1 Queensland, Australia
2 Russia
3 Pakistan
4 The United States
5 Chicago

3 🎥 **15** **Work in pairs. Compare your notes. Discuss what you think the root cause of extreme weather is. Then watch the second part of the video and check.**

4 **Work in groups. Compare how well you understood the explanation of the root cause.**

5 **Complete the sentences about the video by adding these nouns.**

core	fuel	potential	source
decades	gallons	record	tracks

1 The state of Queensland was hit by the worst floods in _____ .
2 Russia had one of the hottest summers on _____ , which led to droughts and forest fires.
3 The blizzard hit so hard and so fast that it stopped rush-hour traffic dead in its _____ .

4 At its _____ , the problem is all about water.
5 The ocean is the main _____ of all the water in the atmosphere.
6 The water in the atmosphere provides the _____ for storms.
7 When the sun comes up, millions and millions of _____ of water evaporate from the ocean.
8 The more gases there are in the atmosphere, the greater the _____ for extreme weather events.

6 **Work in pairs.**

• Have any of the events in Exercise 1 happened in your country? When? What happened?
• How many people were affected? In what way?
• How well was the situation dealt with?
• How much do you know about the causes of global warming?
• How worried about global warming are you?

UNDERSTANDING FAST SPEECH

7 **Look at this extract from the video. To help you, groups of words are marked with / and stressed sounds are in CAPITALS. Pauses are marked //. Practise saying the sentence.**

If you're WONdering where all this exTREME RAINfall / COMES from // it starts HERE // at the Ocean's SURface // The Ocean is a SOURCE of WAter in the ATmosphere // and we can SEE it in VArious FORMS // in CLOUDS / in RAIN.

8 🎥 **16** **Listen to how the presenter said this sentence. Now you have a go! Practise saying the extract again fast.**

REVIEW 4

1 Complete the text with the correct option (A, B or C).

We ¹_____ some work done on our house, so we decided to go away for a few days to a little place on the coast. We ²_____ there once years before and had really good memories of it. When we arrived, though, we found that the only hotel in town was full. There ³_____ been a conference or something, because there were people walking round with name tags on. Anyway, someone suggested a place a few miles away. It was a bit of a dump, to be honest, but we didn't have any alternative as it was getting late. We ⁴_____ before we left home. Maybe then we could ⁵_____ somewhere else a bit more decent. Anyway, the following day, we were driving around and we came across a little hotel ⁶_____ the sea. It was quite posh – not the kind of place we ⁷_____ normally stayed in, but we decided that there was no point ⁸_____ back home and so we checked in. We had a fantastic few days, even if we spent a bit more than we'd planned to!

	A		B		C	
1	A	were	B	had	C	were having
2	A	had been	B	were going	C	have been
3	A	must have	B	can't have	C	should have
4	A	should ring	B	would have rung	C	should have rung
5	A	find	B	be finding	C	have found
6	A	overlook	B	overlooking	C	overlooked
7	A	must have	B	should have	C	would have
8	A	go	B	to go	C	in going

2 Complete sentence b using the correct form of the word in brackets, so that it has a similar meaning to a.

1 a I find politics totally boring.
  b I have _____ politics at all. (interest)

2 a I imagine she didn't hear you. She wouldn't ignore you.
  b She _____ you. She wouldn't ignore you. (heard)

3 a It's possible that they're waiting for us outside.
  b They _____ for us outside. (might)

4 a They should ban advertising which targets children.
  b Advertising _____ should be banned. (aimed)

3 Complete the text with the correct form of the verb in brackets.

On Saturday 14 August at around 10pm, I ¹_____ (sit) in my living room watching TV with a couple of friends. It was unbearably hot, so we ²_____ (open) all the windows. Suddenly, we heard some loud bangs outside and I ³_____ (look) out of the window to see what was happening. A nearby car ⁴_____ (be) on fire. I realised

that someone must have thrown fireworks at it and it ⁵_____ (catch) fire. Just down the street I saw a group of youths acting suspiciously. I went out with a friend to see what they ⁶_____ (do), but they ⁷_____ (run off). I ⁸_____ (chase) after them, but I couldn't keep up.

4 Complete the sentences with the correct preposition.

1 There's no excuse _____ not being able to cook.

2 A return _____ old-fashioned values would be no bad thing.

3 We need to place more emphasis _____ staff development.

4 My boyfriend doesn't pay enough attention _____ me!

5 I went on a demonstration _____ corruption.

5 Match the verbs (1–8) with the nouns (a–h).

1 spark	a a fine
2 contest	b fire to a building
3 smash	c a bomb
4 monitor	d a will
5 set	e a lot of damage
6 pay	f emails and phone calls
7 plant	g a window
8 do	h a heated debate

6 Choose the correct option to make phrasal verbs.

1 She *went* / *passed* out suddenly and was unconscious for about five minutes. It was quite scary.

2 We had to *stay* / *put* up with a lot of noise because our room overlooked the main road.

3 There are lots of people begging there. Quite a few people *came* / *approached* up to us and asked us for money.

4 I heard on the news that a bomb has *gone* / *blown* off in the capital.

5 It started *throwing* / *pouring* down, so we had to pull over to the side of the road and wait until it *went* / *eased* off.

7 Complete the text with the correct words. The first letter(s) are given.

Pirates have ¹s_____ another ship off the east coast of Africa. Ten crew members are being held ²ca_____ and the pirates are demanding ten million dollars to ³re_____ the men and return the ship to its owners, JShipping.

A man has been arrested on ⁴su_____ of murder following the ⁵di_____ of a 25-year-old woman. The man is being held in ⁶cu_____ at Bow Street police station, where he is being questioned.

8 ▶ 44 Listen. Write the six sentences you hear.

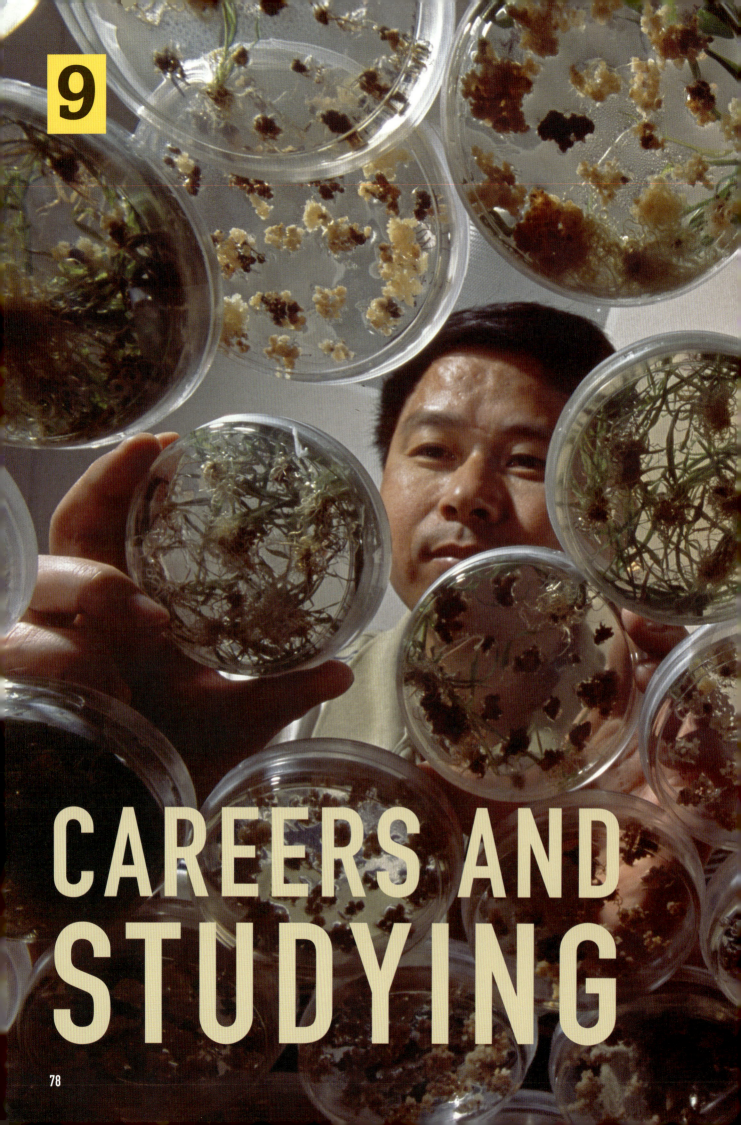

9

CAREERS AND STUDYING

IN THIS UNIT YOU LEARN HOW TO:

- describe good and bad aspects of working life
- explain your feelings about the future
- talk about education and starting work
- give better presentations

SPEAKING

1 **Work in pairs. Discuss the questions.**

- What kind of job do you think the person in the photo has?
- What do you think this job might involve on a day-to-day basis?
- What kind of qualities do you think you'd need to have to do this kind of work?
- Could you do a job like this? Why? / Why not?

2 **Change partners. Discuss the questions.**

- Are you working at the moment? Have you worked before?
- If yes, what do you do and what jobs have you done in the past? What were they like?
- If no, what would you like to do in the future? Why? What will you need to do to get the job you want?

THE WORLD OF WORK

VOCABULARY Working life

1 Work in pairs. Discuss whether the following are usually positive or negative and why. What are the causes and/or results of each thing?

I got promoted is positive. It means you're doing well at work and get moved to a higher position. It usually happens because you're good at your job. One result is you usually get offered more money.

1 I got promoted.

2 I handed in my notice last week.

3 I got a pay rise last month.

4 I'm getting on-the-job training.

5 I actually got made redundant last month.

6 I'm slowly getting the hang of everything.

7 I'm struggling to cope, to be honest.

8 My boss never delegates responsibility to the rest of the team.

9 I'm finding it very rewarding.

10 It's really stimulating. I feel I'm really stretching myself.

11 I'm finding it quite emotionally draining.

12 The work is pretty menial most of the time.

2 Work in pairs. Find out if any of the sentences in Exercise 1 have ever been true for your partner or for any of their friends or family. Tell each other as much as you can about any true sentences.

My older sister actually got promoted quite recently. She works for this big international corporation and they just made her head of her branch. I'm really proud of her.

LISTENING

3 ▶ 45 Listen to the first part of a conversation between two friends, Melissa and Richard. Answer the questions.

1 How is Richard feeling about his job? Why?

2 What does his job mostly seem to involve?

3 What are his plans for the future?

4 What does Melissa say to cheer Richard up?

4 ▶ 46 Listen to the second part of the conversation. What do Richard and Melissa say about the following?

1 training

2 business trip

3 presentation

4 employee

5 clients

6 firm

7 college

8 promotion

5 Work in pairs. Discuss the questions.

• What advice would you give Richard? Why?

• Do you know anyone whose job is going really well at the moment? In what way?

• What do you see yourself doing in five years' time?

• Think of two people you know well. What do you see them doing in five years' time?

GRAMMAR

6 Look at the conditional sentences in the Grammar box below. Then work in pairs to discuss the questions.

Conditionals with present tenses

We often use conditional sentences to talk about real or probable events now or in the future.

a **If I ask** about doing other stuff, **he** just **tells** me to be patient.

b **If it's** that bad, maybe **you should think about** handing in your notice.

c **It might get** better **if I** just **give** it a bit more time.

d **If the worst comes to the worst, I'll end up** knocking on the door of your office.

---

1 What tense is used in the *If* part of the sentences?

2 Which two sentences are talking about the future? Which one is talking about now? Which is talking about something that's usually, generally true?

3 Which result clause is talking about a definite future result? How do you know?

4 Which sentence is giving advice? How do you know?

5 Which result clause is talking about a future possibility? How do you know?

G Check your ideas on page 176 and do Exercise 1.

7 Match each of the sentence beginnings below with two possible endings.

1 If you really want to get into the film industry,

2 If things really are that bad at work,

3 If I get made redundant,

4 If I get good enough grades,

a I might try and set up my own business.

b I'm going to do Law.

c I'll put you in touch with a friend of my dad's who works as a sound engineer.

d you can always request a meeting with management to sort it all out.

e I don't need to sit the entrance exam.

f you have to start at the bottom and work your way up.

g maybe you should start looking for something else.

h at least I'll be able to live on the money I get for a while.

8 Work in pairs. Think of one more possible ending for the sentence beginnings 1–4 in Exercise 7.

9 Write two *if* sentences you could say to someone in each of the situations below. Try to use two different patterns. Then compare your sentences in pairs. Do you agree with each other's ideas?

1 I had a huge row with my boss last week. It was awful.

2 I'm thinking of quitting my job and retraining in another field.

3 We want to try and launch our own website later this year.

4 We might send her overseas to study for her degree.

G For further practice, see page 176 and do Exercise 2.

DEVELOPING CONVERSATIONS

Feelings about the future

When we answer questions about the future, we use a range of different expressions to show how sure we are that something will happen.

You're bound to get lots of offers. (= I'm 95% sure you will.)

I doubt I'll pass the entrance exam. (= I'm 90% sure I won't.)

---

10 Below are five answers to the question *Do you think you'll get the job?* Choose the correct option.

1 *I doubt it. / I'm bound to.* I'm not qualified enough.

2 *Definitely. / I might.* Stranger things have happened!

3 *Probably not / Hopefully not* – but it's worth a try.

4 *Hopefully. / Probably.* I really need the money!

5 *I'm bound to. / I doubt it.* They're desperate for new staff at the moment.

PRONUNCIATION

11 ▶ **47** Listen and check your answers. Notice where the stress is in each of the expressions. Then listen again and repeat.

12 Write four questions about careers and studying to ask other students. Use the pattern *Do you think you will (ever) …?* For example:

Do you think you'll ever do a Master's?

13 Ask other students your questions. Answer using the responses in Exercise 10.

CONVERSATION PRACTICE

14 Work in pairs. Choose a role.

Student A: imagine you are working and your job is going really well. Think of at least three reasons why.

Student B: imagine your job is going badly. Think of at least three reasons why.

15 Roleplay the conversation. Follow the guide below. Continue as long as you can.

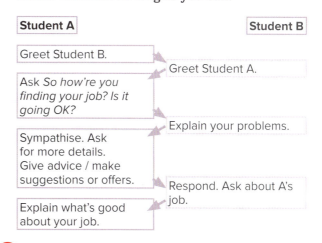

Student A	Student B
Greet Student B.	
	Greet Student A.
Ask *So how're you finding your job? Is it going OK?*	
	Explain your problems.
Sympathise. Ask for more details. Give advice / make suggestions or offers.	
	Respond. Ask about A's job.
Explain what's good about your job.	

🎥 **17** To watch the video and do the activities, see the DVD-ROM.

STARTING OUT

SPEAKING

1 Work in groups. Discuss the questions.

- Do you know if there's a minimum age for a person to have a paid job in your country?
- Are there any part-time jobs that young people in your country typically do when they are at school or at college or university? Would you do them? Why? / Why not?
- What are the advantages and disadvantages of young people working while studying? And of them getting money for everything from their parents?

LISTENING

2 ▶ **48** Listen to a news report about the way a particular job is done. Answer the questions.

1 What job is discussed? Why?
2 What changes are happening to the way the job is being done?
3 What three factors have contributed to the changes?
4 Why does Bud Keynes from the *Milwaukee Herald* newspaper think the changes are bad?

3 Work in pairs. Discuss the questions.

- Can you think of any other jobs where either the people who do them or the way they're done has changed over time?
- What caused the change? Is it a good thing?

READING

4 Read about four first jobs on page 83. Decide who you think had the best first job. Explain and discuss your choices in groups.

5 Answer the questions below. Then compare your ideas with a partner. Discuss which lines helped you make your decisions.

1 Who was recommended for the job?
2 Who never got a break?
3 Whose job is sometimes misunderstood?
4 Who used to get a lift to work?
5 Who started to find their work a bit boring after a while?
6 Who received training?
7 Who now has doubts about 'facts' they hear about?
8 Whose job didn't live up to expectations?
9 Who knew they were being exploited, but didn't mind?
10 Whose manager interfered a lot?
11 Who thinks certain people are better at a job?
12 Who didn't pay any income tax on their earnings?

6 Find the adjectives and/or verbs that go with these nouns from the text.

benefits	foot	labour
laugh	novelty	rank
trays	word	

7 Work in pairs. Discuss how far you agree with these statements.

- I would never do manual work or a low-paid job.
- People should never be forced to retire.
- University students should also work, not just study.
- The army is a good career choice.
- Women are better at some jobs than men.
- Getting a good job is about who you know, not what you know.

GRAMMAR

8 Look at these conditional sentences from the texts. Then work in pairs to discuss the questions below.

Conditionals with past tenses

We use conditional sentences with past tenses to talk about imagined/hypothetical situations.

a *Even **if they doubled** my money, **I wouldn't want to** work near a beach again.*

b ***It would** probably **have been** a different story **if I'd been doing** it on my own!*

c ***If it hadn't been** for her, **I might never even have heard** about the job.*

d ***If I wasn't** in the army, **I would never have gone** somewhere like Haiti.*

1 Which two sentences are talking about imagined/hypothetical situations in the past? What was the reality of each situation?
2 Which sentence is talking about an imagined/hypothetical situation in the future?
3 What tenses are used in the conditional *If* part of each sentence? Which structure is used in the result clause?
4 Which sentence is talking about imagined/hypothetical situations now AND in the past? What's the reality of the situation?
5 Which sentence shows a possible hypothetical result – not a definite one? How do you know?

G Check your ideas on page 176 and do Exercise 1.

EDUARDO, BRAZIL

I got my first job this summer, working in a bar on a beach in Porto Seguro. It sounded ideal – chill out on the beach, get a suntan and earn some money before going back to university. Big mistake! I started work at two in the afternoon, cleaning the place, and then worked solidly through till five in the morning – re-stocking the bar, rushing from one table to the next, taking orders, carrying **trays**, clearing tables – it was non-stop! It didn't help that my boss was a complete control freak. By the time I got home, I was dead, and slept till one. I never actually set **foot** on the beach! Still, by the end of the summer, I'd saved enough to take my girlfriend on holiday. It was great to have money I'd earned myself and to be able to spend it as I wanted, but to be honest, even if they doubled my money, I wouldn't want to work near a beach again. It's far too frustrating seeing what you're missing all the time!

JOCELYN, SCOTLAND

I grew up in a rural community where it was common for kids to help out on the nearby farms. When I was about fifteen or sixteen, I started working Saturdays picking potatoes. We'd be collected at seven in the morning and driven out to the fields, where we'd walk behind these huge machines and bag all the potatoes they'd dig up. It was exhausting, but I enjoyed being outside and we all had a **laugh** together. It would probably have been a different story if I'd been doing it on my own! Of course, as a teenager, I provided cheap **labour**, but that didn't bother me. The £30 I earned every week – cash-in-hand, of course – felt like a fortune back then.

ELA, POLAND

I did Politics at university and I really wanted to go and see more of Europe, so I figured I needed a part-time job. A friend of mine did market research for this local company and she put in a good **word** for me. To be honest, if it hadn't been for her, I might never even have heard about the job. I mostly worked weekends, but once in a while they'd ask me to do the odd evening as well. I basically went door to door asking specific questions – what people drank, who they were planning to vote for, all sorts. It was fun to begin with, meeting so many new people, and the money was quite good too, but the **novelty** soon wore off. It soon got very repetitive. I don't regret it, though. I learned that a smile goes a long way – and as I know that some people were lazy and made up their data, I've learned to be sceptical about statistics too!

CARLA, CHILE

I joined the army after leaving school because I was a restless person and didn't like 'academic' things. Funnily enough, I've actually spent quite a lot of time in a classroom since I joined, as we get training for things like logistics. It's OK, though – you see the practical **benefits** more than at school, so I don't regret joining at all. And if I wasn't in the army, I would never have gone somewhere like Haiti. I went there as part of a UN humanitarian mission. For sure, people associate the army with war, but nowadays it's more about peacekeeping and helping people involved in conflicts. My area – logistics – is really about solving problems and communication and women are often better than men in those roles, so I'm certainly staying in the army and hopefully I'll achieve a high **rank**.

9 **Complete the sentences with the correct form of the verbs in brackets.**

1 To be honest, I _____ this job if I _____ a choice, but I don't really. My parents aren't that well-off, so I basically have to. (not do / have)

2 I hated it, but the boss was a family friend. If my dad _____ me the job, I _____ sooner. As it was, though, I stayed three years before quitting. (not get / leave)

3 If it _____ for my old Geography teacher, I _____ an urban planner. (not be / not become)

4 If it _____ for my high school English teacher, I _____ this presentation to you today. (not be / not give)

5 I love my job. Honestly, even if I suddenly _____ loads of money, I _____ work entirely. (win / not give up)

G For further practice, see Exercise 2 on page 177.

For further practice, see Exercise 2 on page 177.

PRONUNCIATION

10 ▶ **49** Listen to six sentences featuring contracted forms of *would* and *had*. Write what you hear.

11 Work in pairs. Compare what you wrote. Then check your ideas by looking at the audio script on page 203. Then repeat the sentences.

12 Think of four events, situations or people that have had an impact on your life. In groups, explain their importance using conditional sentences with past tenses.

I met my wife Melanie through an old friend of mine, Thorsten. If it hadn't been for him, we'd never have met and we wouldn't be together now, so I owe all that to him. If I'd never met Melanie, we would never have started our own business and we obviously wouldn't be doing as well as we are.

IN SHORT

LISTENING

1 Work in pairs. Discuss the questions.

  1 Who might give a presentation in these places and situations and what might it be about?

- a bank
- a primary school
- a university
- a medical conference
- a company sales conference
- a film production company

  2 Have you ever given a presentation in English or in your own language? Where? What about? How long was it? How did it go?

2 ▶ 50 Listen to the introduction of a presentation given by a Finnish student who is studying Economics in a foreign university. Find out the following:

  1 what the presentation is about

  2 what Kimi will talk about in the rest of the presentation

3 Work in pairs. Discuss the questions.

- Do you know anything about PISA?
- Look at the table. What things might Kimi talk about?
- Why do you think Kimi believes PISA is not very helpful?

Rank	Country	Maths
1	China	613
5	South Korea	554
9	Switzerland	531
12	Finland	519
17	Vietnam	511
22	New Zealand	500
28	Latvia	491
34	Russia	482
40	Croatia	471
48	UAE	434
56	Costa Rica	407
62	Qatar	376

4 ▶ 51 Listen to the presentation and take notes. Then work in pairs to compare your notes. Whose notes are more useful? Why?

5 ▶ **51** Are the sentences true (T), false (F) or not stated (NS)? Listen again to check.

1 There are the same number of students taking the test in all 65 countries.

2 The schools taking part are normally from a variety of places within each country.

3 The results for Finland have plunged since 2000.

4 There's not much difference between the Finnish and Russian results.

5 Kimi doesn't want to get a higher PISA score if it means a long school day.

6 Qatar spends more on education than any other country.

6 Work in pairs. Discuss the questions.

- Do you know how your country ranks in PISA?
- How far do you agree with Kimi's conclusions in the presentation? Explain.
- What do you think education at school is for? What about at university?
- What factors could affect educational performance?

VOCABULARY

Presentations

Presentations usually have an **introduction** where we introduce ourselves, generate interest in the topic, explain the point of the presentation and describe the different sections it will have. In the **main part** the speaker indicates when these sections start and/or end.

We then finish with a **conclusion** where we summarise the points we have made and/or state our final opinion based on the arguments we gave.

7 Decide if the following phrases come from the introduction, main part or conclusion of the presentation. What is the purpose of each phrase?

For those who don't know me already, I'm … and I'm … [introduction]

Purpose: to introduce yourself

1 In short, I think … . Thank you very much.

2 So moving on to the results …

3 I'll go on to conclude that …

4 So those are the problems, what are the solutions?

5 So hands up everyone who … ? OK. Lots of you.

6 If we take a look at this table now, it shows … and as you can see …

7 So to sum up, I hope I have shown that …

8 Today, I'm going to talk to you about …

8 Work in pairs. Discuss the questions.

- What ways can you think of to generate interest in a topic at the start of a talk?
- What might be good or bad about stating your conclusion in the introduction?
- What other advice would you give about giving a good presentation?

9 Complete the sentences with the verbs in the boxes. Then make sentences from parts 1, 2 and 3 and join them together to make the introductions to four different presentations.

1 What I'm going to try and do today is …

summarise	take	talk	tell

a _____ a look at McDonald's recent performance.

b _____ you a bit about the history of the video game industry.

c _____ to you about the way immigration has changed over the last 30 years.

d _____ the main reasons for the war on terror, as I see them.

2 I'd like to begin by …

commenting	giving	outlining	reviewing

e _____ you an overview of the way in which gaming has developed since the 1970s.

f _____ what the literature has to say about the matter.

g _____ on their sales figures for the last five years.

h _____ the main trends in the mass movements of people.

3 I'll then move on to …

consider	focus	make	highlight

i _____ on why these developments occurred.

j _____ why these movements have happened.

k _____ some recommendations about how the company could improve things in the years to come.

l _____ some of the problems with conventional ways of viewing recent military campaigns.

PRONUNCIATION

10 ▶ **52** Listen to the first introduction and read the audio script on page 204. Notice how grouping words together and stressing key words make the speech clearer and more fluent.

11 Write out one of the introductions from Exercise 9. Mark which words you'll group together with a /. Mark a longer pause with //. Underline the key words you'll stress. Practise saying it to a partner.

SPEAKING

12 Choose one of the topics below. Plan a five-minute presentation on the subject. Structure your talk with language and ideas from Exercises 7 and 9.

- the history of your town or city
- the state of the economy in your town/country/region
- the achievements of someone important

13 In small groups, take turns to give presentations.

IN THIS UNIT YOU LEARN HOW TO:

- talk about celebrations and parties you've been to
- suggest different times or places to meet
- talk about awkward situations
- start and end different kinds of conversations

10

SPEAKING

1 **Look at the photo. Discuss the questions.**

- Who are the people?
- Where do you think it is?
- What do you think they've been doing? Why?

2 **Work in pairs. Look at the box and answer the questions.**

- Which of the occasions do you celebrate?
- How do you usually celebrate them?
- What is the biggest celebration of the year where you're from. What happens?

birthday	Eid al-Fitr	Valentine's Day
carnival	Mother's Day	Workers' Day
Christmas	New Year	

SOCIALISING

CELEBRATE GOOD TIMES

VOCABULARY Celebrating

1   Work in pairs. Check you understand the words in bold. Then discuss the questions below.

- I had **a small get-together** at home with some friends.
- I **went clubbing** with a **bunch** of friends.
- I **treated myself** to a day in a spa.
- I had **a weekend break** in Prague.
- I went shopping and **went mad** with my dad's credit card.
- I **wasn't really up for** going out so I just had a quiet night in.
- A bunch of us **rented a karaoke booth** for the night.
- My boyfriend took me out for **a romantic dinner** in this **posh** restaurant.
- I had **a big do** with about 150 people.
- A friend **threw me a surprise party**.

1   Which things have you done to celebrate something?

2   When? What were you celebrating?

3   Which things would you *not* do to celebrate? Why not?

4   Can you think of three other ways of celebrating?

LISTENING

2   ▶ 53 Listen to three friends planning a celebration. Answer the questions.

1   Why are they going out to celebrate this Friday?

2   What do you hear about: Equinox? Rico's? Guanabara?

3   What time do they agree to meet?

3   ▶ 53 Work in pairs. Try to complete the sentences from the conversation. There are two words missing from each. Listen again to check your answers.

1   So _____ go out and celebrate on Friday, then?

2   I'd be _____ that as well. Do you have anywhere _____ ?

3   I thought that Equinox might _____ .

4   I _____ the music down there and besides – it's _____ horrible guys.

5   Well, personally, I'd _____ to get something to eat at some point, if that's _____ with you?

6   Rico's is always a _____ .

7   Yeah, whatever. _____ .

8   I'm working till six and it'd be nice if I could go home first, so could we _____ eight?

GRAMMAR

4 Look at these examples with future forms from the conversation in Exercise 2. Then work in pairs to answer the questions below.

> ### The future perfect
> We occasionally use the future perfect instead of more basic future forms to show the time by which something will be complete.
>
> a *By four o'clock Friday, we'll have finished every single one.*
>
> b *If I revise much more my head's going to explode!*
>
> c *Could we make it eight? I'll have had time to get changed and freshen up a bit by then.*
>
> d *I'll phone and book a table – just to be on the safe side.*

1 Which sentences above contain the future perfect?

2 How is the future perfect formed?

3 Which examples have a reference to time?

4 Does the action happen *before* the time or does it start *at* that time?

G Check your ideas on page 177 and do Exercise 1.

5 Complete the sentences with the future perfect form of the verbs in the box. You may need to use a negative form.

be cook eat find leave lose pass process

1 It's my grandparents' anniversary next Friday. They _____ married for fifty years!

2 I'll order a takeaway for everyone. He said they were going to come straight from work, so they _____ anything.

3 It's a shame you're not coming back till next Tuesday. I _____ for Greece by then, so I'll miss you.

4 I sent my passport to be renewed ages ago, but apparently it _____ in time to go on my end-of-year trip to Disneyland. It's really annoying.

5 I'll have my results by the time you visit and hopefully I _____ , so we'll be able to go out and celebrate.

6 Do you think the lamb _____ properly by 8 or shall I tell people we'll be eating a bit later?

7 Yeah, he looks OK now but imagine him by the time he's forty – he _____ all that lovely hair and he'll probably weigh twenty kilos more.

8 Unfortunately, my grandfather's lost his memory now, but hopefully they _____ a cure for it by the time I'm his age.

6 Spend three minutes thinking about how (a) your life and (b) the world will be different in 30 years' time. In pairs, share your ideas. Use the future perfect.

I imagine I'll have started losing my hair by then.

Hopefully, they'll have found a cure for AIDS by then.

DEVELOPING CONVERSATIONS

> ### Arranging to meet
> We often suggest alternative times/places to meet using *Can/Could we make it ...?* We also explain why.
>
> A: *So what time do you want to meet? Seven?*
>
> B: *I'm working till six and it'd be nice if I could go home first, so could we make it eight?*

7 Complete 1–5 by adding a–e below.

1 A: When do you want to meet? Would about nine tomorrow night be OK?

  B: Can we make it a bit earlier? ...

2 A: When would you like to meet? Would sometime this week suit you?

  B: Could we make it some other time? ...

3 A: What day works for you? Is Friday any good?

  B: Could we make it earlier in the week? ...

4 A: Where shall we meet? How about that new café on the other side of the river?

  B: Can we make it somewhere more central? ...

5 A: Why don't we meet at Janet's place?

  B: Can we make it somewhere nearer mine? ...

a It's quite awkward to get to, that place.

b I've got a lot on at work at the moment.

c She lives miles away from me.

d It's my girlfriend's birthday that day.

e I need to try and get an early night if I can.

8 Work in pairs. Take turns having conversations like the ones in the Developing Conversations box. Use the questions below and suggest your own alternatives. Explain why.

What time do you want to meet? Is ... OK?

Where shall we meet? Would ... suit you?

CONVERSATION PRACTICE

9 Individually, think of what you're going to celebrate. Make notes on the following:

• two ideas for what to do and why

• where exactly you would do them

Then work in groups of three and have a conversation like the one you heard in Exercise 2. Follow this guide.

Student A gives a reason to celebrate.

Student B suggests an idea of how to celebrate.

Student C rejects the idea and explains why.

All three discuss other ideas and come to an agreement.

Arrange where/when to meet and if anyone needs to do anything such as book a table.

 18 To watch the video and do the activities, see the DVD-ROM.

PUTTING YOUR FOOT IN IT

READING

1 Read the dictionary definition of *faux pas*. Then discuss what the faux pas and its consequence might be in each of the situations.

> **faux pas** /ˌfəʊ ˈpɑː/ (n).
>
> If you make or commit a faux pas, you say or do something which unintentionally causes embarrassment in a social situation.

1 Someone says, 'You must be Tim's wife'.

2 Someone complains about their teacher in a cafeteria.

3 A businessperson makes a joke about their company in a speech.

4 Airline attendants share their work experiences on Facebook.

5 An actor kisses an actress during a charity event.

2 Read the article on page 91 and find out what actually happened in each case.

3 Work in pairs. Discuss the questions.

1 Do you agree that no harm was done when the author 'put his foot in it'?

2 Why does the author see Ratner as unfortunate? Do you agree?

3 In what way are the airline attendants and Charlie Sheen similar to Ratner? Do you have any sympathy for them?

4 What has been the impact of 24-hour news? Do you agree with the author?

5 Why does the author think it's good that he's not famous?

VOCABULARY Making mistakes

4 Complete the sentences with these pairs of words. You may need to reverse the order of the words.

burst out – realised	~~pregnant – due~~	live – stupid
turned up – dressed	copying in – send	see – meant
politician – clue	foot – surprise	

1 I asked her when the baby was __*due*__ , but she wasn't actually _*pregnant*_ ! I felt awful afterwards!

2 I asked him how his girlfriend was – and he _____ crying! I hadn't _____ they'd spilt up.

3 I wanted to _____ a private email to a friend, but I ended up _____ everyone in the office by accident.

4 On my first day at work, I _____ in a suit and tie – and found everyone else _____ really casually! I felt so stupid!

5 I pretended I'd lost his passport. It was _____ to be a joke, but he didn't _____ the funny side of it.

6 I nearly put my _____ in it with my brother last week. He's organising a _____ party for my birthday – and I forgot I wasn't supposed to know about it.

7 A top _____ was asked on a live TV show how much bread costs – and he didn't have a _____ !

8 A government minister made a _____ joke about the war – without realising he was _____ on air.

5 Which of the eight mistakes above do you think is the most serious? Explain your ideas to a partner.

SPEAKING

6 Work in pairs. Discuss the questions.

- Do you use social media like Facebook and Twitter? If so, are you careful about what you say? What privacy settings do you use?

- Can you think of any other famous people who have made mistakes in public?

- Have you ever put your foot in it – or done anything embarrassing in public? When? What happened?

- Has anything caused outrage in the media in your country recently?

FROM FAUX PAS TO FRONT PAGE NEWS

Joe Jackson has some sympathy for those whose silly mistakes hit the headlines

We have probably all had moments when we said the wrong thing. I certainly have – like at an office party once, when I introduced myself to a woman a colleague was with by saying, 'Oh, you must be Tim's wife. I've heard so much about you!' The woman then turned to Tim and screamed, 'You're married?' before slapping him in the face. Then there was the time at university when I met a friend in a coffee bar after class and immediately started moaning about our tutor, who was called Dr Gray. I was going on and on about how miserable she was – strict, boring, unfriendly – and my friend wasn't really saying much. After a minute or so, she interrupted me and said, 'Um, I think I should introduce you'. She then turned to this other student who I hadn't really noticed up till then and said, 'This is Tracy. Tracy *Gray*'!

Fortunately, the result of putting my foot in it was only an awkward moment and a stony silence. Maybe my friends thought a little less of me, maybe they thought I was an idiot, but no real harm was done. The same is not true for everyone, particularly if you are famous.

Take Gerald Ratner. He was the multimillionaire owner of a chain of shops that sold cheap jewellery. In what was supposed to be a light-hearted speech to some fellow businessmen, he joked about the quality of some of his products. He said some earrings were 'cheaper than a sandwich, but probably wouldn't last as long'. Other products could be sold at such low prices because they were rubbish. Unsurprisingly, when his customers heard about the jokes they didn't see the funny side and the share price of the company crashed. Ratner had to resign as director and shortly afterwards the company was taken over by a rival.

In some ways, Ratner could be seen as unfortunate in that he was in a semi-private meeting with friends and colleagues he was at ease with, but there happened to be a journalist there. As a result, what was private suddenly became public. And with the rise of social media, there have been plenty of others who have been caught out by the increasingly vague boundaries between our private and public faces. For example, a group of flight attendants made jokes about the engines on their planes failing and moaned about their airline and clients – the kind of thing many people might do privately when they get together with colleagues after work. Unfortunately, they did it publicly on Facebook and it led to thirteen of them being sacked. Similarly, the actor Charlie Sheen managed to send his personal phone number to over five million followers on Twitter when he thought he was sending a private message to his friend Justin Bieber.

What makes things worse for the famous is that these mistakes become even more widely publicised because of 24-hour news channels and websites: there is so much time and space to fill, even a slight faux pas can become big news. For example, the actor Richard Gere caused outrage in the Indian media by kissing the Indian actress Shilpa Shetty on the cheek at an AIDS awareness rally in India. Such public displays of affection are still frowned on in India, but would he have been threatened with arrest or the cause of an international incident without the media storm and the internet? In the end, it came to nothing, but such incidents can actually undermine relationships between countries as well as destroying business deals and careers. All I can say is that it's just as well I'm not famous!

'Oh dear, we forgot to invite the Woods.'

SMALL TALK

SPEAKING

1 Work in groups. Discuss how you would feel in the following situations and what you would say or do.

1 A friend invites you to a party. When you get there, you don't know the host or anyone else apart from your friend, who spends the whole evening with someone else.

2 You get bored during a lecture and sneak out. You then meet someone else coming out of the lecture theatre.

3 You get stuck talking to someone who seems OK to begin with, but turns out to be a complete bore.

4 You go to a friend's house for dinner and are served a special dish – made from something you really don't like.

5 You're in a club or a café and there's a really long queue for the toilet.

6 Someone you don't know interrupts a conversation you're having.

LISTENING

2 ▶ 54 Listen to five conversations. Match each conversation with a situation from Exercise 1. You can match one conversation with two situations.

3 ▶ 54 Work in pairs. Can you remember which conversations you heard the following sentences in? Listen again to check your ideas.

1 The speaker wasn't exactly helping either, was he?

2 They're so versatile.

3 I think I might just go and grab a coffee.

4 It's a real boom town at the moment.

5 I've been meaning to talk to her all evening.

6 My flatmate dragged me here.

7 I love your top.

8 I'm his fiancée.

9 She's always moaning about it.

10 It's attracting a huge amount of inward investment.

4 Work in pairs. Discuss the questions.

• In Conversation 1, the speaker made an excuse and left. Would you have reacted in the same way?

• Have you ever been to a party where you hardly knew anyone? What did you do?

• Have you had any conversations with people you didn't know recently: on public transport? in the street? at a party? in a café or restaurant?

• What did you talk about? How did the conversations start and end?

GRAMMAR

5 Look at these sentences from the conversations in Exercise 2. Then answer the questions below.

> ### Question tags
>
> We often use question tags to ask for agreement or to ask for confirmation of an idea. Question tags are also used in polite requests.
>
> a *They have music later on down there,* ***don't they****?*
> b *You couldn't pass me the salt,* ***could you****?*
> c *The speaker wasn't exactly helping either,* ***was he****?*

1 How are the question tags formed?
2 Which sentence asks for agreement?
3 Which sentence asks for confirmation of an idea?
4 Which sentence is a polite request?

G Check your ideas on page 177 and do Exercise 1.

6 Complete these conversations by adding question tags in the appropriate places.

1 A: Miserable weather.
   B: Yeah, awful. It's been like this for weeks now.
   A: I know. I can't remember when I last saw the sun.

2 A: You don't remember me.
   B: It's Yuka.
   A: No. It's Naomi.

3 A: Excuse me. You haven't got a light.
   B: Yeah. Here you go.
   A: Thanks.
   B: You couldn't lend me a pound.
   A: No, sorry.

4 A: You missed the class on Monday.
   B: There wasn't one. The school was closed for the holiday.
   A: No. Mind you, you didn't miss much. It was quite boring.
   B: Well, to be honest the whole course is a bit disappointing.

5 A: I love that jacket. It's from Zara.
   B: No, I got it from a shop called Monsoon.
   A: Really? You wouldn't happen to have the address.
   B: No. Sorry. I honestly can't remember.

7 ▶ **55** Listen. Check your ideas.

G For further practice, see page 178 and do Exercise 2.

PRONUNCIATION

8 ▶ **55** Listen to the conversations again. Notice how the voice goes up on some tags (to show a genuine question) and down on others (to show a comment). Then practise reading the conversations in pairs.

9 Spend three minutes thinking of questions to ask using the patterns below. Then take turns asking your questions. Your voice should go up when you ask. Answer each question any way you want to.

- *You haven't got … , have you?*
- *You couldn't … , could you?*
- *You wouldn't happen to know … , would you?*

10 Write four comments about the weather, the news, food or sport. Include question tags. Say your comments to a new partner. Your voice should go down. Your partner should make up a suitable reply.

VOCABULARY Talking about parties

11 Match the words in bold with the meanings a–j.

1 This guy kept trying to **chat me up** and in the end I had to tell him to **get lost**. It was really awkward.

2 They set up a **marquee** in the garden and had a band playing in there. They must've spent a **fortune** on it.

3 It got quite wild! The police had to come and **break it up** in the end because it was getting a bit **out of hand**.

4 We threw a surprise party for my mum's 50th. She didn't have a clue! She **burst into tears** when she saw everyone.

5 I felt a bit sorry for her, because hardly anyone **turned up** and she'd prepared loads of food, which all just **went to waste**.

6 I was invited to a wedding reception, but I hardly knew anyone there and no-one really talked to me, so I felt a bit **left out**.

a go away and leave me alone
b a big tent used for events held outside
c ignored and not included
d large amount of money
e was left unused and was thrown away
f uncontrolled
g stop
h talk to me because he wanted a relationship with me
i came
j suddenly started crying

12 Work in groups. Discuss the questions.

- Have you had any of the experiences in Exercise 11? When? Give more details.
- What's your best and/or worst party experience ever?
- Do you usually take a gift when you go to a party?
- Do you usually arrive early, on time or late? Why?
- What would your perfect party involve?

VIDEO 5

THE
REAL INDIANA JONES

1 Read the short introduction about the archaeologist in the video and look at the picture. Then discuss the questions.

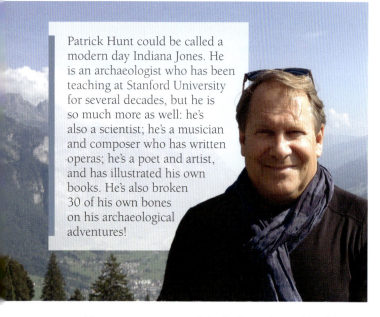

Patrick Hunt could be called a modern day Indiana Jones. He is an archaeologist who has been teaching at Stanford University for several decades, but he is so much more as well: he's also a scientist; he's a musician and composer who has written operas; he's a poet and artist, and has illustrated his own books. He's also broken 30 of his own bones on his archaeological adventures!

- Have you seen any of the Indiana Jones films? What do you think of them?
- What different subjects do you think it helps to study for archaeology? Why?
- What do you think the archaeologists are doing in the picture?
- What dangers and obstacles might archaeologists encounter in their work?

2 📹 19 Watch the video and find out what obstacles Patrick talks about. Make notes under the following headings:
- Politics
- Environment and climate
- Infrastructure
- Preparation

3 📹 19 Work in pairs. Use your notes from Exercise 2 to discuss 1–5. Then watch again to check.

1 Match these words with a heading in Exercise 2.

data set	flames	research	sleet
democratic	geological map	scorpion	slippery
FAA standards	outsider	services	trafficking

2 Why is it so important to collaborate with people where you are working?

3 Why might you need helicopter insurance?

4 Why does he mention the fire on the plane?

5 Why is lack of preparation one of the most important obstacles?

4 Work in pairs. Discuss the questions.

- Do Patrick Hunt and his experiences have any similarities with the film character Indiana Jones? Why? / Why not?
- What other jobs might experience the obstacles Patrick talks about?
- Have you experienced any of the kinds of problems Patrick talks about? When? Where? What happened?
- Would you like to be an archaeologist? Why? / Why not?

UNDERSTANDING FAST SPEECH

5 Look at this extract from the video. To help you, groups of words are marked with / and stressed sounds are in CAPITALS. Pauses are marked //. Practise saying the sentence.

YOU know / you may be in a reMOTE loCAtion / where there's / THERE'S no AMbulance that can come GET you // you MIGHT have to have HELicopter inSURance inSTEAD.

6 📹 20 Listen to how Patrick said this sentence. Now you have a go! Practise saying the extract again fast.

REVIEW 5

GRAMMAR

1 Choose the correct word or form.

1 If I get made redundant, *I am going to set up / I set up* my own business.

2 I can't believe that in September I *will work / will have worked* here for ten years already!

3 It was a fantastic party, *was / wasn't* it?

4 I hope some more people turn up or this food *is going to go / will have gone* to waste.

5 Sorry, I'm so late. I *would've called / would call* you, if the battery on my phone hadn't died.

6 You wouldn't happen to know if they're recruiting people, *would / do* you?

7 I would have told him to get lost too if he *spoke / had spoken* to me like that.

8 If the worst *comes / will come* to the worst, *I'll go back / I go back* and live with my parents.

2 Complete the second sentence so that it has a similar meaning to the first sentence, using the word given. Do not change the word given. You must use between two and four words, including the word given.

1 It was a shame more people didn't come to the party.

The party would have been better if more people _____ . **TURNED**

2 Would it be possible to give me a lift home?

You _____ home, could you? **DRIVE**

3 All staff are going to get training before we start using the new system with clients.

By the time the new system goes live, all staff _____ how to use it. **TRAINED**

4 The situation became quite chaotic because the police didn't intervene soon enough.

If the police had intervened sooner the situation _____ of hand. **GOT**

5 I want to do a Masters, but it depends on the cost.

I'm going to do a Masters, if _____ too much. **COST**

6 It's pretty menial work, right?

The work _____ is it? **STIMULATING**

3 Complete the email with one word in each space.

Dear Simon,

I'm writing to say I don't think I [1] _____ make it to your leaving do. As you know, the new store's opening in two weeks and I [2] _____ finding things hard, to be honest. If my boss [3] _____ actually taken on a couple more people as I asked him to, perhaps things wouldn't [4] _____ so bad, but he just won't listen and, as he hardly sets foot in the office, he doesn't really know how much pressure we're under. If everything [5] _____ to plan, I might [6] _____

done everything I need to do before your party, but to be honest I [7] _____ it. You know how it is – something unexpected is [8] _____ to delay things.

So anyway, if I don't see you next week, let's get together soon, [9] _____ we? We could even rent a karaoke booth again, if you're [10] _____ for it!

4 ▶ 56 Listen. Write the six sentences you hear.

VOCABULARY

5 Match the verbs (1–10) with the collocates (a–j).

1 the police broke up	a crying / laughing
2 he just burst out	b in a good word / my foot in it
3 I treated myself to	c the main reasons / the key stages
4 it was meant to be	d quite casually / very smartly
5 he was dressed	e the demonstration / the party
6 she didn't see	f a joke / a surprise
7 she achieved	g a beauty treatment / a new outfit
8 I actually put	h a high rank / her main aim
9 she's handed in	i the funny side / the practical benefits
10 she summarised	j her notice / her assignment

6 Complete the presentation introduction with one word in each space. The first letters are given.

Hello. [1] W_____ everyone. For those who don't know me already, I'm Steffi from Switzerland and I'm here studying Economics as part of the student exchange programme. Today I'm going to talk about Glencore Xstrata. So [2] h_____ up everyone who has heard of Glencore Xstrata? Well it might [3] s_____ you to learn that in fact it's currently the 12th largest company in the world with a market value of $90 billion. So what I'm going to do today is take a [4] c_____ look at this company and where it stands. I'll begin by [5] ou_____ its main businesses and providing a brief [6] ov_____ of the company's history. I'll then [7] m_____ on to [8] re_____ its recent performance before [9] h_____ some of the current threats to growth and future opportunities. Finally, I'll [10] c_____ that on the whole the future remains quite bright for this company.

7 Complete the sentences. Use the word in brackets to form a word that fits in the space.

1 The company currently has 300 _____ . (employ)

2 Working with prisoners can be very rewarding, but it can also be _____ draining. (emotion)

3 It's very _____ working with children. (reward)

4 Working in market research was fun to begin with but the _____ soon wore off. (novel)

5 The minister made a stupid joke without _____ he was on air. (realise)

6 We'd often work _____ for twelve hours. (solid)

7 It's ridiculous. She was made redundant only three months after they gave her a _____ . (promote)

11

TRANSPORT AND TRAVEL

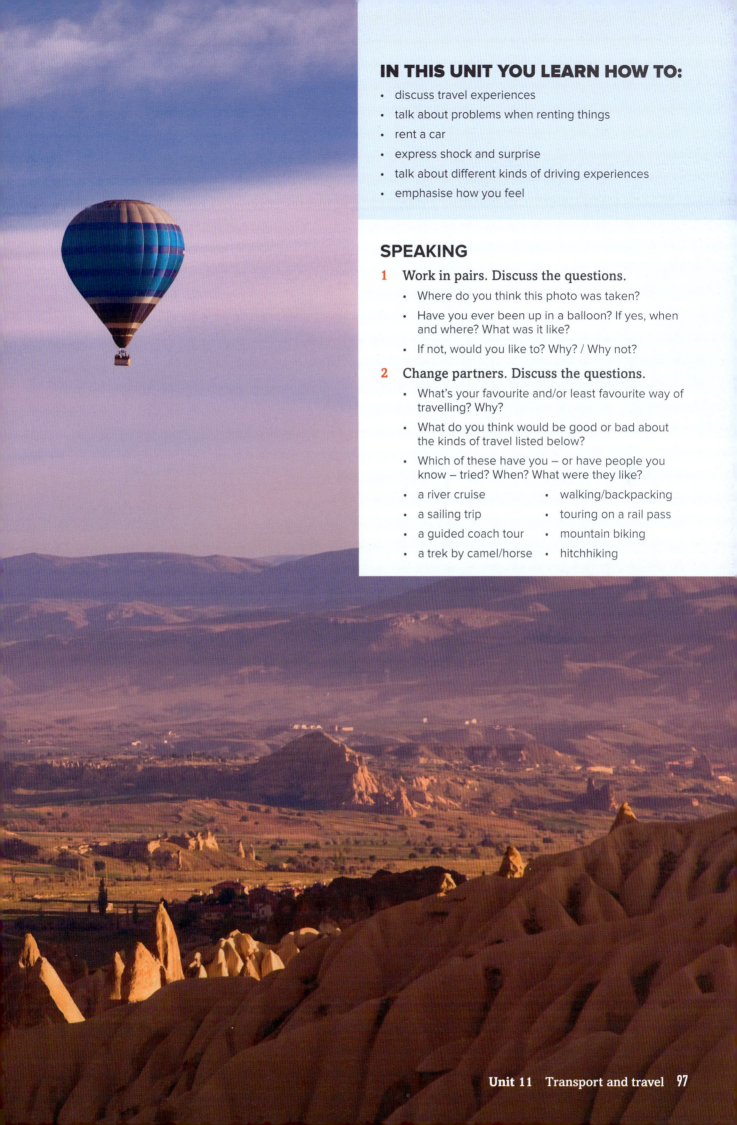

IN THIS UNIT YOU LEARN HOW TO:

- discuss travel experiences
- talk about problems when renting things
- rent a car
- express shock and surprise
- talk about different kinds of driving experiences
- emphasise how you feel

SPEAKING

1 Work in pairs. Discuss the questions.

- Where do you think this photo was taken?
- Have you ever been up in a balloon? If yes, when and where? What was it like?
- If not, would you like to? Why? / Why not?

2 Change partners. Discuss the questions.

- What's your favourite and/or least favourite way of travelling? Why?
- What do you think would be good or bad about the kinds of travel listed below?
- Which of these have you – or have people you know – tried? When? What were they like?

a river cruise	walking/backpacking
a sailing trip	touring on a rail pass
a guided coach tour	mountain biking
a trek by camel/horse	hitchhiking

ON THE ROAD

VOCABULARY Problems when renting

1 Complete the sentences with these nouns.

brakes	deposit	insurance	safety
chain	engine	leak	small print
dent	gears	rental	tyre

1 It cost €50 a day to rent a board, but we had to pay a returnable _____ of €200 on top of that.

2 They tried to sell us _____ to cover any damage to the windscreen or tyres.

3 It was difficult to change _____ . They were very stiff and I couldn't get into fifth at all.

4 We couldn't get the _____ started on the way back and we were just floating there for about two hours before they came to rescue us.

5 There was obviously a _____ in the tank because you could smell petrol.

6 They didn't provide any _____ equipment like life jackets or helmets.

7 When I put the _____ on, they weren't very effective, so going downhill was a bit scary.

8 They wouldn't give our deposit back because there was a _____ and some scratches in the side.

9 We got a flat _____ so we had to call the rental place to come and pick us up.

10 I hadn't read the _____ and I found out there was a $500 excess which wasn't covered by the insurance.

11 They weren't very well maintained. The _____ kept coming off my one and the handlebars were loose on my friend's one.

12 We were a little late getting back as there wasn't much wind and so they charged us an extra half-day's _____ .

2 With a partner, discuss what you think was rented in each of the sentences in Exercise 1.

3 Work in pairs. Discuss the questions.

- What things have you rented?
- Have you ever had any of the problems in Exercise 1?
- Give six examples from your own life, each using a noun from the box in Exercise 1.

LISTENING

4 Work in small groups. Imagine you/your family wanted to rent a car. Discuss which of the features below would be: (1) really important (2) quite important, but not essential (3) not very important.

- It's automatic.
- It has GPS.
- It's fuel-efficient.
- It's diesel.
- The insurance covers everything.
- It has a great sound system.
- You get unlimited mileage.
- There's plenty of room in the boot.

5 ▶ 57 Listen to a conversation in a car rental office. Answer the questions.

1 What's the special offer for the week?

2 Does the customer take it? Why? / Why not?

3 What else has the customer ordered?

4 Does he take the extra insurance?

5 What else do you hear about the car he's renting?

8 Write responses to each of the sentences below. Repeat surprising information as a question and then add another question or comment.

1 A: The taxi fare to your hotel will be €100.

   B: _____ .

2 A: The cheapest ticket we have left is $875.

   B: _____ .

3 A: Our flight leaves at five in the morning.

   B: _____ .

4 A: It's a bit old, but it's a nice car! I could let you have it for 1500.

   B: _____ .

5 A: If you just wait at the station, I should be able to get there within an hour or two.

   B: _____ .

6 A: I'm afraid the contract does state that there's a €50 penalty if you return the car more than an hour late.

   B: _____ .

PRONUNCIATION

9 ▶ **59** Listen to the conversations from Exercise 8. Notice the way the questions have strong stress and high intonation. Then read the conversations with a partner, using your own extra questions and comments. Continue each conversation for as long as you can.

CONVERSATION PRACTICE

10 Work in pairs.

Student A: read File 19 on page 191.

Student B: read File 9 on page 186.

Plan some of the things you will say. Then read the audio script for track 58 on page 205 and underline any expressions you want to use.

11 Roleplay the conversation.

12 Then, Student A: you are going to phone the company and report a problem. Decide if you are happy with B's response.

Student B: A is going to phone and report a problem. Deal with it however you want to.

Roleplay the telephone conversation. Use some of the language from the box below.

> I wonder if you can help me.
>
> I'm calling because we have a problem with the car we're renting from you.
>
> I'm so sorry to hear that.
>
> I'm not sure we'll be able to help you, I'm afraid.
>
> I'm sorry, but that's just not good enough.
>
> That's the best we can do, I'm afraid.

🎥 **21** To watch the video and do the activities, see the DVD-ROM.

---

6 ▶ **57** Work in pairs. Can you remember the verbs you heard in each of these sentences from the conversation in Exercise 5? Listen again to check your ideas.

1 Hi. I _____ a car online.

2 We have your car ready, but we're _____ a special offer this week.

3 You can _____ to the next range for just two euros a day.

4 You _____ GPS, yes?

5 What are the chances of anything _____ wrong?

6 So should I _____ the tank full?

7 So could you just _____ where I've marked with a cross?

8 You may want to _____ the car as well before you leave.

7 ▶ **58** Listen to a man calling a car rental office. Answer the questions.

1 What's the problem with the car John Farnham rents?

2 How does he feel about the proposed solution?

DEVELOPING CONVERSATIONS

Expressing surprise or shock

When we are surprised, shocked or annoyed by what we are told, we often repeat the information as a question and then add another question or comment.

A: *We guarantee they'll be with you within four hours.*

B: ***Four hours?*** *Is that really the best you can do?*

A: *I'll be able to come and look at your car next Wednesday.*

B: ***Next Wednesday?*** *That's almost a week away!*

THE TRIP OF A LIFETIME

SPEAKING

1 Look at the three journeys below. Then work in pairs to discuss the questions.

Journey 1: a 6000-kilometre train journey from Moscow to Beijing

Journey 2: a 4500-kilometre drive across the United States

Journey 3: an 800-kilometre walk from the south of France to northern Spain

- What do you think the good things about each journey might be?
- Would it be better to travel on your own or in a group? Why?
- What kind of problems might happen on each one?
- Which of the three journeys most appeals to you? Why?
- Have you ever heard of anybody making any similar journeys?

READING

2 Read about the three journeys on page 101. Answer the questions.

1 Why did each person decide to make their journey?

2 What was good or bad about each one?

3 Was there anything in the three stories that surprised you?

4 Have you changed your mind about which journey most appeals to you?

3 Without reading the stories again, try to complete the sentences. Then check your ideas by looking at the expressions in bold in the texts.

1 It was an incredible experience being so close to a _____ of elephants like that in the wild.

2 I know you're upset, but you need to _____ things into perspective. I mean, it's not the end of the world!

3 We drove right across the desert – through some incredibly desolate _____ .

4 It's a remote area – and still very traditional. It's almost _____ by the modern world.

5 I've seen that movie so many times that I know most of it by _____ .

6 We're all from quite different backgrounds but we share a common _____ in our love of music.

7 A quick _____ of advice for you: make sure you take out travel insurance before you set off.

8 The main station must've been incredible once, but over the years it's slowly _____ into disrepair.

9 Everyone was so kind and generous to me. The whole trip really reaffirmed my _____ in humanity.

4 Work in groups. Discuss the questions.

- What other pilgrimages do people make?
- What other famous journeys have you heard of?
- What's the best journey you've ever made? What kind of scenery did you go through?
- Are there any journeys you'd love to make one day?
- Can you think of any famous road movies?

GRAMMAR

5 Read the Grammar box. Then choose the correct option in the sentences below.

> ### Uncountable nouns
>
> Uncountable nouns have no plural forms and are never used with *a/an*. We use no article or *the* or *some*. We also use *much* – not *many* – before them.
>
> a *I don't have **much** money.*
>
> b *I've spent **all the** money you gave me.*
>
> c *Money is the root of **all** evil.*

1 Roisin and her friend bought all the *equipments / equipment* they needed for their walk in France.

2 Felix got *a / some* useful *information* from local guides about spots tourist don't normally see.

3 Artur and Attila didn't do *many researches / much research* before setting off for Chicago.

G Check your ideas on page 178 and do Exercise 1.

6 Complete the sentences with one word.

1 I've just had _____ really good news.

2 You travel light! You've got hardly _____ luggage with you!

3 I'm really looking forward to this break. I've had so _____ time to myself lately!

4 I don't think I'll get the job. I don't have _____ experience.

5 I'm not making _____ progress at all with my German. If anything, I think I'm getting worse!

6 I couldn't find very _____ information about the place on the internet.

7 Come and sit with us. There's _____ of room.

8 I spent a great _____ of time trying to avoid the people in the tent next to ours!

7 Work in pairs. Discuss the questions.

- Who do you usually talk to when you need advice?
- Do you do much research before going on holiday?
- How much luggage do you usually take when you go on holiday?
- How much time do you usually spend packing?
- Have you had any good or bad news recently?

G For further practice, see Exercise 2 on page 178.

ARTUR: ROUTE 66

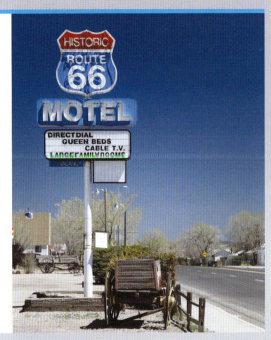

Growing up in Hungary in the 70s, Route 66 was like a mythical highway. The Rolling Stones' version of the song was very popular back then and I **knew** the lyrics **by heart**. Route 66 represented a dream vision of America: colour, freedom, speed, the romance of the open road. Ever since then, I've wanted to drive it – and last year my dream finally came true.

To celebrate our 50th birthdays, I flew to Chicago with an old friend, Attila. We then hired a Cadillac and set off for LA – more than 2000 miles away! We hadn't done much research before we left – and soon discovered that the road is no longer really in use! Its peak years were the 1930s through to the 60s and since then it's **fallen into disrepair**. As a result, much of the journey was quite bumpy; we went through some really out-of-the-way places – and got lost quite a bit as well! We drove through some really **desolate scenery** – mile after mile of farmland – and, of course, we had the occasional row. Spending all that time together meant they were bound to happen! Having said that, though, we ended up better friends than ever.

Strangely, one of the movies they showed on the plane home was the Pixar animated film, *Cars*, much of which is set along the road!

FELIX: THE TRANS-SIBERIAN RAILWAY

I'm studying Chinese at university and last year I went to Beijing. I've always loved trains, so I decided to go via Russia on the Trans-Siberian express. I had wanted to travel alone as my image of group tours is middle-aged people following a guide around like a **herd of sheep**. However, other people advised against travelling independently and the *Vodkatrain* group tour turned out to be quite different from the usual tour. There were only eight of us – all in our twenties. I guess being stuck on a train for hours day after day you either end up bonding or wanting to kill each other and luckily we **formed a strong bond**.

The guides in the cities we stopped off at were local students who gave us useful information about spots most tourists don't get to see. Their friends even came along sometimes, so we not only passed through some amazing countryside, but we also met some remarkable people. There were many highlights, but Lake Baikal was the best. It's this vast expanse of incredibly pure water and the whole area is almost **untouched by the modern world**. Mind you, I wouldn't advise anyone to swim in it. I almost froze to death.

ROISIN: THE CAMINO DE SANTIAGO

The Camino de Santiago is a pilgrimage route to the cathedral of Santiago de Compostela in northern Spain, where – according to legend – the remains of St James are buried. Pilgrims have been walking this path for centuries, and a few years ago one of my best friends decided to embark on the journey, so I thought I'd go along and keep her company.

We started in Saint-Jean-Pied-de-Port, in France, where we bought all the equipment we'd need, and set off. The walk took over a month and for my friend, who's far more religious than I am, I think it really **reaffirmed her faith**. Even for me, though, it was a strangely spiritual journey. As we walked through the countryside, I slowly came to accept all the things that had happened to me over recent years. I just found that the peace and quiet along with the slow pace of the journey through this incredible scenery really helped me to **put things into perspective**, and I came home feeling incredibly refreshed.

A **word of advice**, though, if you're thinking of doing the walk yourself: learn some Spanish first. It'll make life easier! Oh, and buy good walking boots. I ended up with holes in mine – and got terrible blisters as well!

WHAT DRIVES ME MAD

VOCABULARY Driving

1 Match the verbs 1–10 with the groups of words a–j.

1	drive	a	a red light
2	flash	b	by a car coming off the motorway
3	overtake	c	really close behind you
4	get cut up	d	your lights
5	go through	e	the car in front
6	run over	f	20mph over the speed limit
7	swear	g	a guy crossing the road
8	get	h	to avoid it
9	do	i	a fine and three points on your licence
10	swerve	j	at the other driver

2 Work in pairs. Discuss what might be the reasons for and/or results of the ten actions in Exercise 1.

LISTENING

3 ▶ 60 Listen to two friends talking about driving experiences. Lily is from Britain and Sanjar was born in Iran. Answer the questions.

1 What laws did Lily break?
2 What's her punishment?
3 How did she feel about driving in Paris, and why?
4 What's driving in Tehran like?

4 ▶ 60 Listen again. Are the sentences true (T) or false (F)?

1 Lily went over the time she'd paid for on the machine.
2 Lily argued with a police officer about it.
3 Lily's not going to appeal against the fine.
4 She was stopped by the police for speeding.
5 Sanjar doesn't think speeding is a problem in Britain.
6 Some other drivers didn't like Lily's driving when she was in France.
7 Sanjar was surprised that pedestrians in Britain weren't more careful.
8 They both agree that drivers are more polite in Britain.

5 Work in pairs. Discuss the questions.

• Who's the worst and/or best driver you know? What makes them bad or good?
• Do you think driving is getting better or worse in your country? Why?
• Are some cities worse to drive in than others?
• Do you think speed cameras are a good thing? Why? / Why not?
• Is there anything you need to be careful (not) to do in your town or city?

GRAMMAR

6 Read the sentences in the Grammar box. Work in pairs and discuss the questions below.

Emphatic structures

In English, we sometimes change the order of words in a sentence to emphasise how we feel.

1a *It happened when I'd actually gone to look for change for the machine, which **is** really irritating.*

1b *What's really irritating **is** (the fact) that it happened when I'd actually gone to look for change for the machine.*

1c *The thing that's really irritating **is** (the fact) that it happened when I'd actually gone to look for change for the machine.*

1 Which two sentences emphasise how you feel?
2 In your language, can these sentences be constructed in the same way?

G Check your ideas on page 178 and do Exercise 1.

7 Complete the sentences with the pairs of words.

annoys + the number	find + sitting	's + parking
concerns + the amount	gets + when	scares + the way
drives + the whole	hate + the fact	

1 What _____ bad is people _____ on the pavement so you can't get past.
2 The thing that _____ me is _____ some people swerve in and out of the lanes.
3 What I _____ most boring is _____ in traffic jams all morning.
4 The thing that _____ me most is _____ of pollution there is in the city centre.
5 What _____ on my nerves is _____ men go on about how women can't drive.
6 What _____ me is _____ of speed cameras there are.
7 What _____ me mad is _____ one way system and the lack of signposting.
8 What I really _____ is _____ that so much money is spent on cars.

8 Write a response to each of the complaints in Exercise 7. Use one of the patterns below. Work in pairs. Take turns saying the complaints and replying.

I know. It's really …

I know. They should …

Really? That doesn't bother me. What (annoys me more) is …

Really? I don't mind that. I think …

G For further practice, see page 179 and do Exercise 2.

SPEAKING

9 Read through the transport questionnaire below and choose one answer for each question. Think of the reasons you will give.

10 Work in groups of three. Find out more about your partners by discussing your choices and explaining your reasons. When you disagree, use some of the language and patterns you learnt in Exercises 6, 7 and 8.

11 Write one more possible answer to each of the questions in the questionnaire, but use a pattern from Exercises 6, 7 and 8. Then share your ideas.

A: *Another thing that stops people using public transport is the fact that the metro stops running at night.*

B: *Maybe, but what I think stops them is sheer laziness!*

A QUESTION OF TRANSPORT

1 What stops people using public transport most?
a The cost.
b That it doesn't run frequently enough.
c The amount of crime you get on the buses and trains.
d The fact that it's filthy and run-down.
e The fact that it's so crowded.

2 Which of these do you think is a real problem with transport?
a The shortage of parking spaces in the city centre.
b The lack of investment in cycle lanes and facilities.
c The fact that public transport is badly co-ordinated.
d The speed limits that are imposed on drivers.
e The sheer number of cars on the roads

3 Which single thing would most improve your town or city?
a Introducing a charge for vehicles to enter the centre of town.
b The introduction of stricter speed limits.
c Reducing the number of bus stops.
d Creating a new underground line.
e Getting rid of all parking restrictions.

4 Which of these is the scariest?
a Being in a car when the driver texts while they're driving.
b Being in a car when the driver overtakes on a corner.
c Being on a very bumpy flight.
d Cycling in the city on a busy main road.
e Being stuck in a tunnel on a train.

5 What bad driving habit do you find most annoying?
a When people stick to the middle lane on the motorway.
b When people drive too slowly.
c People not indicating before they pull out or turn.
d Drivers not giving enough space to cyclists.
e Drivers not stopping to let pedestrians cross the road when they're waiting at a crossing.

6 What do you like best about train travel?
a That you can work during the journey.
b The fact you can relax and sleep.
c The amount of space you have.
d The fact that you get to meet new people.
e That I hardly ever have to do it.

7 Which behaviour do you find most strange?
a Standing in the queue to board a plane an hour before it starts boarding.
b Leaping up to get off the plane as soon as it lands.
c People wearing masks when cycling or walking to work.
d Parents taking their kids to school by car.
e People taking cabs when there's perfectly good public transport available.

8 Which concerns you most?
a The amount of pollution caused by traffic.
b The number of accidents on the roads.
c The high rate of bicycle thefts.
d Oil running out sometime in the not-too-distant future.
e The ever-increasing number of aeroplanes in the skies.

12

IN THIS UNIT YOU LEARN HOW TO:

- describe health problems in more detail
- pass on sympathetic messages
- talk about operations
- discuss issues connected to health systems
- talk about research and surveys
- tell jokes better

SPEAKING

1 **Work in pairs. Discuss the questions.**

- Where do you think this photo was taken?
- What do you think is going on in the picture?
- Why do you think people still use traditional medicines?
- Would you try – or have you ever tried – herbal medicine at all? Why? / Why not?

2 **Change partners. Discuss the questions.**

- When was the last time you were ill?
- What symptoms did you have?
- What did you do to get better?

HEALTH AND MEDICINE

I FEEL AWFUL

VOCABULARY Health problems

1 Match the health problems 1–9 with the groups of symptoms a–i.

1 I've got the flu.
2 I've got an allergy.
3 I broke my leg.
4 I'm suffering from stress.
5 I suffer from asthma.
6 I suffer from eczema.
7 I've got an upset stomach.
8 I've got a cold.
9 I was in an accident.

a I can't stop sneezing.
  My throat swells up.
  I get a terrible rash.

b I've got a temperature.
  I feel stiff all over.
  I keep feeling hot and then cold.

c I had it in plaster for six weeks.
  I had to use crutches.
  I was off work for a while.

d I suffered cuts and bruises.
  I had to have twelve stitches.
  I got a big bump on my head.

e I get really short of breath.
  I have to use an inhaler.
  It's made worse by smoke and fumes.

f My skin cracks and gets really itchy.
  I can't stop scratching it.
  It's stress related.

g I've got a runny nose.
  I've got a bit of a sore throat.
  I've got a bit of a cough.

h I've got diarrhoea.
  I feel really rough.
  I threw up three times last night.

i I've been having trouble sleeping.
  I fainted.
  I get panic attacks.

2 Work in pairs. Discuss the questions.

1 Do you know anyone who:
  - has an allergy? What to? What reaction do they have?
  - has a chronic condition like asthma or eczema? How bad is it?
  - has had stress-related health problems? Why? What happened?
  - has ever broken a bone? When? What happened?

2 What do you usually do if you have:
  a cold? / the flu? / an upset stomach?

3 Have you ever missed something important or nice because of illness or an accident? What happened?

LISTENING

3 ▶ 61 Listen to two telephone conversations. Answer the questions.

1 Why are the people phoning?
2 What health problems have the speakers' partners had?

4 ▶ 61 Listen again. Are the sentences true (T) or false (F)?

Conversation 1

1 Joop's girlfriend, Kaatje, fainted earlier.
2 She's been suffering from insomnia.
3 Kaatje has an appointment to see someone in a few days.
4 Michelle gives Joop some advice.

Conversation 2

5 They're still not completely sure what caused Lachlan's problem.
6 They had to call an ambulance.
7 He'll be in hospital for two nights.
8 Nina is annoyed they'll miss the concert.

5 Work in pairs. Discuss the questions.

- Which problem sounds worse to you – Kaatje's or Lachlan's? Why?
- What advice would you give each of them?

GRAMMAR

6 Look at these sentences from the conversations in Exercise 3. Then work in pairs to discuss the questions below.

Supposed to be -ing and *should* for talking about the future

We often use *supposed to be -ing* and *should(n't)* + infinitive (without *to*) to talk about the future.

a *We**'re supposed to be going** away for a few days next week.*

b *I know we**'re supposed to be coming** to the concert tonight.*

c *It **shouldn't be** too late.*

d *We **should get to** yours by lunchtime.*

1 Which two sentences talk about something that has already been organised, but which the speakers may not be able to do?

2 Which two sentences contain the meaning *I (don't) think + will*? Are they being positive about the future or negative?

G Check your ideas on page 179 and do Exercise 1.

7 Complete the sentences with *should, shouldn't* or *be supposed to be -ing* and the verb in brackets.

1 The medicine the doctor gave me is working really well, so I _____ back at work soon. (be)

2 I _____ a friend later, but I think I'm just going to go home to bed. I feel really rough. (meet)

3 You'll probably feel something when the needle goes in, but it _____ too much. (hurt)

4 He _____ the operation next week, but he may have to go away for work, in which case he'll need to delay it. (have)

5 Apparently, it's not a bad break so it _____ long to heal. Hopefully, she'll only be on crutches for a few weeks. (take)

6 I _____ to a concert tonight, but I've got so much work to do. You don't want to buy my ticket, do you? It _____ really good! They're a great band. (go, be)

PRONUNCIATION

8 ▶ 62 Listen to five sentences that feature the normal contracted form of *supposed to be* – /səˈpəʊztəbi/. Write what you hear.

9 Work in pairs. Practise saying the sentences. One of you should say the sentence you heard. Your partner should add a second part starting with *but*.

A: *I'm supposed to be revising for my exams tonight*

B: *but I might have to work in the shop instead.*

10 Change partners. Tell each other about the following:

- something you're supposed to be doing sometime soon, but might cancel
- something that's supposed to be happening sometime soon, but might not
- something happening soon that you think should be good
- something you're doing soon that shouldn't be too hard / shouldn't take too long

DEVELOPING CONVERSATIONS

Passing on messages

In the first conversation, Michelle showed sympathy for Joop's girlfriend, Kaatje, like this:

***Tell her** there's no need to apologise and I understand.*

***Send her** my love and **tell her** I'm thinking of her.*

Using imperatives to ask people to pass on messages like this is polite.

11 Put the words in the correct order to make messages.

1 best / them / regards / give / my

2 me / her / a / hug / give / from

3 coming / them / not / apologies / give / for / my

4 thinking / tell / say / I'm / hi / and / of / them / them

5 tell / not / love / her / send / worry / my / and / to / her

6 to / tell / soon / him / better / it / take / and / get / easy

7 himself / need / there's / tell / him / apologise / to / look / and / after / no / to

8 give / tell / the / baby / my / them / wait / and / them / can't / congratulations / I / to / see

12 Are there any messages in Exercise 11 that you don't like or would feel uncomfortable saying? Why?

CONVERSATION PRACTICE

13 Work in pairs. Have similar telephone conversations to the ones in Exercise 3. Use the guide below to help you plan what to say or ask and use some language from these pages.

14 Roleplay the conversation. Follow the guide. Continue as long as you can. Then swap roles.

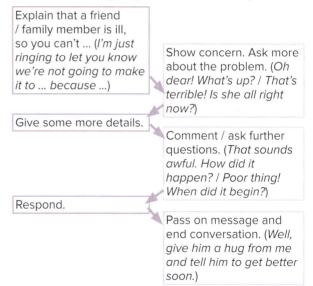

Explain that a friend / family member is ill, so you can't … (*I'm just ringing to let you know we're not going to make it to … because …*)

Show concern. Ask more about the problem. (*Oh dear! What's up? / That's terrible! Is she all right now?*)

Give some more details.

Comment / ask further questions. (*That sounds awful. How did it happen? / Poor thing! When did it begin?*)

Respond.

Pass on message and end conversation. (*Well, give him a hug from me and tell him to get better soon.*)

🎥 **22** To watch the video and do the activities, see the DVD-ROM.

FOREIGN BODIES

VOCABULARY Parts of the body and operations

1 Label the picture with these words.

ankle	brain	chest	elbow	finger	hip	kidney	knee
liver	lung	rib	skull	spine	toe	wrist	

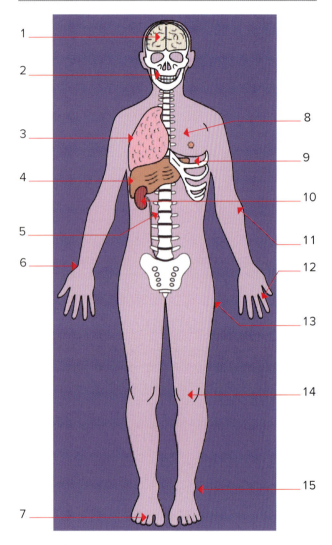

2 Discuss which of the parts of the body in Exercise 1 the following sentences could be about.

1 It was badly broken and she had to have an operation to put a pin in it.

2 In the end the only option was to have a transplant.

3 It was causing him a lot of pain so he had an operation to replace it.

4 She had an operation to remove the tumour.

5 He tore a ligament and he had to have an operation to sort it out.

6 It was a minor operation. She was only in hospital for the day.

3 Tell a partner about people you know who have had an operation on any of these parts of the body.

LISTENING

4 Read the Fact File below. Work in groups. Do you find each fact interesting, surprising, shocking, unsurprising or dubious? Explain why.

5 ▶ **63** Listen to the introduction to a programme about medical tourism. Complete these notes.

> Ways globalisation already affects healthcare:
> Medical staff moving from country to country
> Hospitals outsource record keeping and the reading
> of ¹ _____ to cut costs
> ² _____ Americans have medical and dental
> treatment abroad at knock-down ³ _____ .
> Mexico, Jordan, ⁴ _____ ,
> ⁵ _____ and Thailand could benefit from trade.
> Expected to be worth more than
> ⁶ _____ dollars a year.

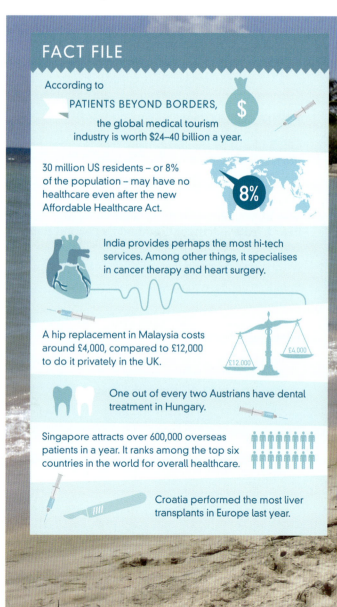

FACT FILE

According to **PATIENTS BEYOND BORDERS,** the global medical tourism industry is worth $24–40 billion a year.

30 million US residents – or 8% of the population – may have no healthcare even after the new Affordable Healthcare Act.

India provides perhaps the most hi-tech services. Among other things, it specialises in cancer therapy and heart surgery.

A hip replacement in Malaysia costs around £4,000, compared to £12,000 to do it privately in the UK.

One out of every two Austrians have dental treatment in Hungary.

Singapore attracts over 600,000 overseas patients in a year. It ranks among the top six countries in the world for overall healthcare.

Croatia performed the most liver transplants in Europe last year.

6 Work in groups. Think of three negative and three positive aspects of medical tourism.

7 ▶ **64** Listen to the rest of the programme. Take notes on any good and/or bad things about medical tourism they mention.

8 ▶ **64** Decide if 1–6 apply to Damian (*D*), Cindy (*C*) or Charlotte (*CH*). Some may apply to more than one person. Listen again and check.

1 They have had some kind of treatment.

2 They are trying to address the lack of care for those at the bottom of society.

3 They believe that some doctors are more interested in money than in their patients.

4 They are concerned about the rising number of scams.

5 They became frustrated with the health system.

6 They mention cutting edge medical techniques.

9 Work in groups. Discuss the questions.

• Would you ever go abroad for treatment? Why? / Why not? Do you know anyone who has been? How did it go?

• Have you heard any stories about operations going wrong? What happened?

• Have you heard of any scams? How do they work?

GRAMMAR

10 Work in pairs. Discuss if you agree or disagree with the quotations below.

'Hospitals are **no** places to be sick!'

'**Many** people spend their health gaining wealth – and then **most** of them have to spend their wealth regaining their health!'

'**The** best medicine in the world is to love **your** job and to know who **all** of **your** enemies are!'

'**Most** people spend so **much** time watching their health that they don't have time to enjoy it!'

'**Any** doctor will tell you that the most dangerous patients are **the** ones with a **little** knowledge!'

'**A** healthy attitude is contagious but don't wait to catch it from **other** people.'

'**Every** rich man should remember that a **few** difficulties in life are good for your health.'

Determiners

All the words in **bold** in Exercise 10 are determiners. They go before nouns to show which or how many things we mean, and if we are talking about something in general or a specific thing/person. Some determiners (*the*, *no*, *any* or *my*, *your*, etc.) can go before any kind of noun, but others can only be used with singular nouns, plurals or uncountable nouns.

11 Look at the words in bold in Exercise 10 and discuss the questions.

1 Find two determiners that go with:

a a singular noun   c an uncountable noun

b a plural noun

2 When do you use *of* after a determiner?

3 Which determiner shows a negative?

G Check your ideas on page 179 and do Exercise 1.

12 Choose the correct option.

1 *Every* / *All* hospital provides similar care.

2 *Every* / *All* dental care is private. You have to pay for *any* / *no* dental work you need done.

3 *Many* / *Much* trainee nurses never actually complete their training and many *other* / *others* nurses leave the profession soon after qualifying.

4 *Most* / *Most of* people get free healthcare.

5 *Both* / *Both of* nurses and doctors are underpaid.

6 Far too *many* / *much* doctors end up only working in private healthcare.

7 They're investing *less and less* / *fewer and fewer* money in healthcare.

8 A *few* / *several of* incidents of negligence in hospitals have resulted in legal action.

9 In most *case* / *cases*, patients have *none* / *no* choice about how or where they are treated.

10 More and more people are looking for *another* / *other* treatments outside the normal health service.

13 Tick the sentences in Exercise 12 that you think are true for your country. Discuss your ideas in groups.

A DOSE OF HUMOUR

READING

1 Work in pairs. Look at the photo and discuss the questions.

- What is happening? Why?
- Have you heard of or seen anything similar?
- What effects might laughter or a sense of humour have on health? Why?

2 Read the article about humour and healthcare. Answer the questions.

1 Is the author writing the article to criticise or support clowns in hospitals?

2 Which of the following does research show, according to the article?

a Children don't want to be visited by clowns in hospital.

b People who hadn't watched a comedy movie needed more painkillers after their operation.

c People with a sense of humour had a longer life expectancy.

d People don't get a positive effect from humour if they don't actually laugh.

e Doctors tell jokes to each other in stressful situations.

f Doctors don't talk to their patients enough.

g You can inherit a sense of humour.

h Doctors make patients laugh more after they have done a course.

3 Work in pairs. Discuss the questions.

- Why do you think people have a fear of clowns? Do you have any fears?
- Why do you think it's important that patients choose their comedy movie for it to help with pain relief? What would you choose?
- Why might the kind of jokes doctors may tell each other not be appropriate with their patients? Do you speak differently to different groups of people? How?
- Why might it be important for doctors and nurses to use humour? What health professionals have you talked to? What were they like?
- Do you think all humour is healthy? Why? / Why not?
- How do you think you can learn to be funnier? Do you make people laugh much? How?

4 Complete the sentences with some of the words in bold connected to research from the article.

1 Over 25% of those who were _____ stated they had suffered stress-related conditions.

2 The study showed that financial literacy is essential if the financial system is to be run effectively. This, in _____ , would have a positive effect on the economy as a whole.

3 The study provided _____ that laughing has a positive _____ on productivity at work.

4 The study _____ _____ how nurses interacted with patients on hospital wards.

5 The research _____ that much back pain was in fact the result of an infection in the spine.

6 The survey was _____ over the phone with people from 26 countries.

7 The new study appears to _____ what researchers have long suspected: ape and human laughter share a common origin.

8 The study stresses _____ _____ of green space on feelings of well-being.

5 Work in pairs. Tell a partner about any research you have heard reported in the news recently.

PRONUNCIATION

6 Read the joke to yourself. Follow the stresses and pauses that are marked. Guess how the joke might end.

A <u>man</u> goes to a <u>doctor</u> // and <u>says</u> // 'Doc. // I <u>think</u> there's something <u>wrong</u> with me // Every time I <u>poke</u> myself // it <u>hurts</u>. // <u>Look</u>!' // And he starts <u>poking</u> himself. // He <u>pokes</u> himself in the <u>leg</u>. // 'Ouch!' // He <u>pokes</u> himself // in the <u>ribs</u> // 'Aagh!' // He <u>pokes</u> himself // in the <u>head</u> // and he literally <u>screams</u> in <u>agony</u>. // 'Aaaaagh! // You <u>see</u> what I <u>mean</u>, Doc? // You <u>see</u> how <u>bad</u> it is? // What's <u>happening</u> to me?'// And the <u>doctor</u> <u>replies</u> // 'Yes ...

7 Tell a partner the joke with your ending.

8 ▶ 65 Listen. Find out the actual ending.

SPEAKING

9 Work in groups of three. Read the jokes and choose your favourite.

Student A: look at File 15 on page 191.

Student B: look at File 3 on page 186.

Student C: look at File 8 on page 189.

10 Prepare your favourite joke. Mark the words that are grouped together and that are stressed. Practise saying the joke quietly to yourself.

11 Take turns telling your jokes. Use actions if you think they will help.

'Laughter is the best medicine, but it's not covered in your health plan.'

JUST CLOWNING AROUND

Gene Clark discovers hospital entertainers still have a role to play.

A survey **conducted among** 250 children **has revealed that** all of them would prefer not to see hospital walls decorated with clowns' faces. Many hospitals, in an attempt to provide a more positive environment, have painted children's wards with pictures of cartoon figures. While the children liked the bright colours, even some of the teenagers **who were questioned** found the clowns' faces 'scary'. Fear of clowns is, in fact, quite a common phenomenon and can provoke sweating, shortness of breath and panic attacks – hardly the reaction the hospitals were after!

Some might argue that **these findings** also **question the value of** real-life clowns working in hospitals, which is an increasingly common practice all over the world. However, as Pau Pujol, a hospital clown from Barcelona, says 'Most clowns in hospitals don't use the traditional heavy make-up because we're aware it can scare kids. We're only about magic and joy and contributing to the recovery of patients'.

There is certainly **some evidence that** humour can have a **positive impact** on health. One study has found that patients with a good sense of humour had better outcomes in cases of kidney failure. Another found that patients who had watched a comedy film of their choice following an operation required substantially less pain medication afterwards than a **control group**.

Exactly why that is is not entirely clear. The act of laughter is known to release chemicals in the brain, which reduce stress as well as exercise the lungs and muscles. However, a Norwegian study, which showed how a sense of humour reduces mortality up to retirement age, **stresses that** laughter is not always necessary for humour to work. The **lead researcher**, Sven Svebak, says 'Commonly, people with the same sense of humour tend to enjoy themselves together and

can communicate humour without huge gestures. A twinkle in the eye can be more than enough.' He argues that humour builds stronger communities (and vice versa), **which in turn** leads to less insecurity and stress.

In hospitals, **research shows how** humour is often used by doctors and nurses to reinforce working relationships in a similar way and enables them to cope with the stress of being surrounded by illness and death. Obviously, the kind of jokes doctors may tell each other might not be appropriate with their patients, and they feel they should maintain a professional front. Some argue that this **contributes to** a wider problem in modern health services. With new technology and drugs, the focus can be too much on technical solutions and the importance of individual attention and warm, human contact in the healing process is sometimes lost. While clowns and comedy can obviously help to fill that gap, it is argued that the nurses and doctors themselves should use more humour in their daily interactions with patients.

But what if they are not 'naturally' funny? Is it something we can learn or are we born that way? A study that **looked at how** twins reacted to Gary Larson cartoons **showed that** a sense of humour wasn't genetic, but **was due to** environmental factors such as family and friends. Svebak's research seems to **confirm** this and he believes humour is learnable.

In fact, there are now a number of courses available for health professionals to improve their humour skills. Courses look at how to tell jokes and funny stories better, as well as noticing opportunities for humour in everyday conversation as well as when it is to be avoided. As Pau Pujol says 'clowning is a skill which you have to work on and scaring people is really a sign of inadequate training rather than a problem with the idea of clowns in hospitals'.

VIDEO 6

WILD HEALTH

1 Look at the photo. Work in pairs. List the ways in which you think people and animals can sometimes be similar.

2 [▶ 23] Watch the first part of the video. Which similarity does it describe?

3 Work in pairs. Discuss what you understand by the idea of self-medication. How might it apply to animals? Can you think of other ways in which humans self-medicate?

4 [▶ 23] Watch the rest of the video. Complete these notes.

> Zoopharmascognosy is the study of how animals
> [1]_____ .
>
> Common misconception that animals just use
> [2]_____ . Reality is more complex.
>
> Early medicine based on observing
> [3]_____ .
>
> Chimps have shown us [4]_____ important new compounds.
>
> <u>Three main areas of animal self-medication</u>
>
> 1 Curative measures: help to cure illnesses they contract.
>
> 2 [5]_____ measures: taking positive action against illness.
>
> 3 [6]_____ measures: developing knowledge of what to eat – and what not to!

> Cows prefer grass grown in [7]_____ because it's easier to digest.
>
> Wildebeest migrate to areas rich in
> [8]_____ , as it contains minerals needed for lactation (milk production).
>
> A snow leopard in a zoo was put on
> [9]_____ because she had some kind of
> [10]_____ .
>
> She started eating [11]_____ because she was feeling sick.
>
> Buffalos sometimes eat mud to [12]_____ .
>
> Primates use plants to deal with [13]_____ .

5 Work in pairs. What do you think are the main implications of the research Cindy Engels has done?

UNDERSTANDING FAST SPEECH

6 Look at this extract from the video. To help you, groups of words are marked with / and stressed sounds are in CAPITALS. Pauses are marked //. Practise saying the sentence.

ALL the WHILE SHE // was SUffering from NAUsea / she was EAting GRASS / conTINuously // and WHEN the COURSE of antibiOtics STOpped / SO did the GRASS EAting.

7 [▶ 24] Listen to how the narrator said this sentence. Now you have a go! Practise saying the extract again fast.

REVIEW 6

GRAMMAR

1 Complete the second sentence so that it has a similar meaning to the first sentence, using the word given. Do not change the word given. You must use between two and five words, including the word given.

1 I honestly can't believe how much some sports stars are paid. It's crazy!

What _____ that some sports stars are paid such unbelievable amounts of money! **AMAZE**

2 It really scares me, the way people still trust him and are happy to vote for him.

The thing that I _____ people will still vote for him, after everything he's done. **SCARY**

3 I've arranged to meet some friends later, but I guess I could cancel.

I'm _____ some friends later, but I guess I could always cancel. **SUPPOSED**

4 I don't expect you'll have any problems.

_____ problems. **SHOULDN'T**

5 Every one of my friends is still single.

_____ married yet. **NONE**

6 They said they didn't have any idea what had caused the explosion.

They said _____ what had caused the explosion. **NO**

2 Choose the correct word or form.

1 The news last night *was / were* so depressing.

2 They've been lucky to have had such *a long and happy marriage / long and happy marriage*.

3 *It / What* really annoys me that you can't leave negative feedback on their website.

4 I've been doing some *researches / research* on food marketing to children.

5 I ordered it yesterday, but the postal service is so slow! *I bet it'll / It should* take ages to arrive.

6 *Most / Most of* the English people I've met have been very friendly and fun to be around.

7 *Is / It's / I find* really boring always having to explain how to spell my name.

8 They said they had *any / no / none* intention of signing a new contract with us.

3 Complete the text with one word in each space. The first letters are given.

Operating in these kinds of conditions is a logistical nightmare. A great ¹d_____ of our equipment needs to be flown in to the area, which is very problematic when fighting is continuing on the ground. They're ²s_____ to be holding peace talks sometime in the next week or so, so there ³s_____ be some progress made, but everything is taking longer than we were ⁴e_____ . Luckily, we have plenty of ⁵e_____ of dealing with these kinds of situations. The thing that most ⁶w_____ us at the moment

is the ⁷n_____ of people living without access to clean drinking water. There have been outbreaks of disease in one camp and we're hoping it doesn't spread to ⁸o_____ . If it does, we may well have a huge crisis on our hands.

4 ▶ 66 Listen. Write the six sentences you hear.

VOCABULARY

5 Match the verbs (1–8) with the collocates (a–h).

1	read	a	cuts and bruises
2	boost	b	a special offer
3	conduct	c	the car in front
4	suffer	d	tourism in the area
5	run	e	the small print
6	overtake	f	the value of the treatment
7	question	g	gears
8	change	h	a survey

6 Decide if the language in the box is connected to transport and travel or to health and medicine, and in what way.

automatic	an inhaler	swell up	a temperature
a dent	a leak	swerve	a transplant
get cut up	in plaster		

7 Complete the story with one word in each space. The first letters are given.

It was supposed to be the trip of a lifetime, but it all ¹w_____ horribly wrong. We didn't have enough money for the bus, so we ²hi_____ up into the mountains. The first guy who stopped and gave us a lift seemed nice enough, but he turned out to be a crazy driver! He went ³t_____ three sets of red lights, nearly ⁴r_____ over a cyclist, kept ⁵sw_____ at other drivers and at one point told us he didn't even have any ⁶in_____ , so we were lucky we didn't have an accident! Once we got up the mountains and started ⁷tr_____ , I thought it was all going to be OK, but on the second day, my friend slipped and tore a ⁸li_____ in his knee. He couldn't walk anymore. He was in terrible ⁹p_____ . I had to get him to a hospital and in the end he had to have an ¹⁰o_____ on it. Afterwards, he couldn't walk properly for ages!

8 Complete the sentences. Use the word in brackets to form a word that fits in the space.

1 70% of those _____ said they would like to see child-free zones on aeroplanes. (question)

2 The _____ clearly show that leading a full life is strongly associated with taking part in activities. (find)

3 All of our vehicles come with _____ mileage as standard at no extra cost. (limit)

4 Please give them my _____ for not being there in person. (apologise)

5 You'll need to pay a _____ deposit of €100. (return)

6 It's an amazing area. It's managed to remain almost _____ by the modern world. (touch)

13

LIFE-CHANGING EVENTS

IN THIS UNIT YOU LEARN HOW TO:

- describe major life events in more detail
- report information you are not 100% sure of
- discuss gossip and news about people
- complain about annoying habits
- discuss ceremonies
- talk about values and concepts

SPEAKING

1 Work in pairs. Discuss the questions.

- Which major event in life do you think this photo shows?
- How do you think the people in the photo are feeling? Why?
- What do you remember about this moment in your own life?

2 Change partners. Make a list of ten life-changing events. Then discuss which you have already experienced and what you remember about each one. Which do you think changed you the most? Why?

GOING THROUGH CHANGES

VOCABULARY Life-changing events

1 Work in pairs. Which life-changing events do you think are described in 1–10 below?

1 He was convicted of corruption. Apparently, he'd been taking bribes for years.
For example: *Number 1 must be about being found guilty of a crime and then getting sent to prison – or going to prison.*

2 He'd been struggling for a while and he just decided he'd had enough. Then he got offered a job, so he decided not to bother graduating.

3 It wasn't as straightforward as they'd been hoping. The baby was two weeks overdue and weighed five kilos! I was told she was in labour for ages.

4 They'd been saving up for it since they first moved in together, which helped. Then they had their offer accepted on the second place they saw, luckily, and managed to take out a mortgage.

5 I heard her husband had treatment for cancer for over a year, but unfortunately it just continued to spread. It's all been really tough for her.

6 He'd been thinking about it for a while, as he was fed up with all the travelling, so he retrained as a counsellor.

7 I think their marriage had been through a rough patch before and they had got through it, but this time they decided to call it a day.

8 Apparently, he'd fancied her for ages, but she was seeing someone else, so when they split up, he asked her out on a date and they've been together ever since.

9 His team had been on a terrible run. They'd only won one game in ten. Then they got knocked out of the cup, and the board just decided it was time for him to go.

10 The ceremony was just for close friends and family, but then we invited about 500 people to the big reception in the evening.

2 Complete the collocations below with nouns from Exercise 1.

1 take ...	6 retrain as a ...
2 get offered a ...	7 call it a ...
3 be in ...	8 ask her out on a ...
4 take out a ...	9 get knocked out of the ...
5 ... spread	10 invite people to the ...

3 Think of your own examples for five of the events described in Exercise 1. The examples could be things you have heard about or involve people you know. Tell a partner as much as you can about each one. Use language from Exercises 1 and 2.

GRAMMAR

4 Look at these sentences from Exercise 1. Then work in pairs to answer the questions.

The past perfect simple and continuous

Past perfect forms emphasise something that happened before another past event that has already been mentioned.

A: *So why did he drop out of the course?*

B: ***He'd been struggling*** *for a while and he just decided* ***he'd had*** *enough.*

---

1 Which of the structures in **bold** is the past perfect simple? Which is the past perfect continuous?

2 What is the form of each structure?

3 Which structure describes something that happened just once? And which describes something that happened over a period of time?

4 Which time expression shows the period of time?

G Check your ideas on page 180 and do Exercise 1.

5 Complete the sentences using the past perfect simple or continuous form of the verbs in brackets.

1 When I found out I _____ , I was speechless. I just couldn't believe it.
(win)

2 Apparently, they discovered she _____ money from them for months.
(steal)

3 I suddenly realised I _____ the fire on, and by the time I got back to the house, the whole place was in flames.
(leave)

4 She _____ from the illness for some time, but she _____ anyone about it.
(suffer, not tell)

5 We finally realised we _____ the turning and we _____ in the wrong direction for half an hour!
(miss, go)

G For further practice, see Exercise 2 on page 180.

PRONUNCIATION

6 ▶ **67** Listen and check your answers. Then listen again and repeat what you hear.

7 Think of a response to each of these sentences using the past perfect simple or continuous. Then work in pairs. Take turns asking the questions and giving responses.

1 So why did your father decide to take up running?

2 But how come she didn't have any money?

3 What made them decide to move to Brazil?

4 How come he gave up playing basketball?

5 So how come you sold your flat?

LISTENING

8 ▶ **68** Listen to two conversations where the speakers gossip about other people. Answer the questions for each conversation.

1 Why do they start talking about the other people?

2 What pieces of news surprise one of the speakers?

9 Work in groups. Discuss the questions.

• What are the most popular gossip magazines in your country? Do you ever read them? Why? / Why not?

• Would you ever consider adopting children?

• Have you ever completely changed your opinion of someone? Why?

• Do you know anyone who has ever been in a long-distance relationship? How did it work?

• Would you consider moving to a different country for love? If not, why not?

DEVELOPING CONVERSATIONS

Showing uncertainty

We use lots of different expressions to show we are reporting information that we're not sure is true.

As I understand it, she'd already had a son with Scott Blake.

Apparently, she's got a really good job there.

10 Complete the phrases in the conversation with one word in each space.

A: Did you hear about Gavin getting married?

B: Yeah. It was a bit sudden, wasn't it?

A As [1]f_____ as I know, they'd only been going out for five weeks!

B: Really? [2]A_____ I understand it, they'd actually been at school together.

A: Right. Well, [3]f_____ what I've heard, she's a really nice woman and, [4]a_____ , she's from an incredibly rich family.

B: Really? I was [5]t_____ they didn't invite many people to the wedding because they couldn't afford it.

A: Well, [6]a_____ to my friend Justin, she had a falling-out with her father because he didn't really approve.

11 You are going to have a conversation like the one in Exercise 10 about an imaginary man called Bill. Invent 'facts' about where he has moved to, why, what it's like and who he is living with. In pairs, have the conversation using your ideas and the expressions from Exercise 10.

A: *Did you hear about Bill moving?*

B: *Yeah. From what I've heard, he's gone to Greece.*

CONVERSATION PRACTICE

12 Think of some news you've heard recently about someone you know or a celebrity. Then work in pairs and have similar conversations to the ones you heard in Exercise 8. Use the guide below to help you get started. Then swap roles.

Ask if your partner knew / has heard about …

Say no. Ask for more details.

Give more details about the news. Include some information you're not sure is true.

Ask more questions and/ or add comments.

Answer any questions. Continue to give more details and extra information.

25 To watch the video and do the activities, see the DVD-ROM.

WORKING IT OUT

SPEAKING

1 Work in groups. Discuss the questions.

- Do you argue a lot or do you tend to avoid confrontation?
- When you argue, who do you usually argue with? What about?
- Is there anything you'd like your friends and people in your family to stop or start doing?

GRAMMAR

2 Look at these sentences. Then work in pairs to answer the questions below.

> ### be always/constantly -ing, wish and would
>
> We can use the present continuous and *I wish + would* to show our feelings about habits.
>
> a *She's constantly arguing with people.*
>
> b *He's very charming. He's always complimenting you.*
>
> c *I wish he would listen more carefully.*
>
> d *I wish she wouldn't smoke inside the house.*

1 Which structure emphasises habits that could be positive or negative?
2 Which two adverbs are used with the present continuous here?
3 Which structure shows you'd like someone to behave differently (but don't expect them to)?

G Check your ideas on page 180 and do Exercise 1.

3 Add a second sentence to these comments using *be always/constantly + -ing* or *wish + would* and the follow-up idea in brackets.

She's so affectionate. (give me hugs and kisses)

She's always/constantly giving me hugs and kisses.

1 He's not a very good listener. (shut up and let others speak sometimes)
2 He's such a bore. (talk about something else apart from his job)
3 Honestly, he's so romantic. (buy me roses and say he loves me)
4 She's so intense about everything. (lighten up a bit and have a laugh a bit more)
5 Don't be so defensive! (take everything I say as a personal attack)
6 My sister's so bad-tempered and spoilt. (my dad let her get her own way)

4 Write comments similar to those in Exercise 3 describing people with these characteristics.

ambitious	generous	polite	stubborn
competitive	mean	selfish	vain

5 Work in pairs. Talk about the following:

- Five people you know who should change their habits. Use the structure:

  I (sometimes) wish ... would(n't) ...

- Five people you know with the characteristics in Exercises 3 or 4. Use the structures:

  ... is so / such a ... (S)he's always ... / (S)he never ...

G For further practice, see page 181 and do Exercise 2.

READING

6 Read the introduction to a Wiki page on how to manage conflict. In groups, answer the questions.

1 Can you imagine yourself in any of the four situations? Why? / Why not?
2 Which is the most difficult situation to be in?
3 Do you think any of these conflicts could have been avoided? How?
4 How would you try to end each situation if you were involved or were watching?

HOW TO
MANAGE CONFLICTS

Imagine these situations:

> A three-year-old has a tantrum while her parents are shopping. She throws herself on the floor, kicking and screaming.

> A parent shouts at a teenager 'This place is a mess. I'm constantly clearing up after you and I'm sick of it. I wish you'd put your stuff away and stop being so untidy.'

> Two lads start fighting after one of them bumps into the other and spills a drink he was carrying.

> Two colleagues – a woman, who is relatively new to the company, and a man – have stopped talking to each other after clashing several times. The woman complains that her colleague is stubborn and never accepts any of her ideas. The man says that she is constantly making comments which undermine his authority in the office.

Conflicts are bound to happen on occasion. However, many can be avoided and when they do happen, we can learn to handle them better so things don't get out of control. Furthermore, the techniques apply to all conflicts, whether with babies and toddlers or between adult colleagues.

7 Read the Wiki below. Match the headings a–i with paragraphs 1–8. There is one extra heading you won't need. In pairs, check your answers and explain your choices.

a Mind your language
b Not getting angry doesn't mean giving in
c Give choices
d Stay calm
e Don't wait to repair the damage
f You need to pay attention to body language
g Remember there are two sides to every story
h Know the flashpoints
i Be flexible

8 Read these sentences. Underline a sentence – or part of a sentence – from each paragraph in the Wiki that has the same meaning.

1 If you end up insulting people, the situation won't improve.
2 When you speak to each other again, don't talk about what you said or did before.
3 Another person's body language may show us that we are annoying that person unintentionally.
4 We shouldn't continue to argue just because we want to avoid seeming weak.
5 It's OK to provide rules and defend your beliefs.
6 Don't start shouting.
7 Attempt to delay awkward discussions until less stressful times.
8 When you think about it, different backgrounds can make you think in different and reasonable ways.

9 Work in pairs. Discuss the questions.

- Do you agree with all the techniques mentioned?
- Do you think they would work in the four conflicts described in the introduction?
- Do you think you could learn from any of the pieces of advice? In what way?

[1]

You may be in the right. The child might be screaming because you won't buy him chocolate, a colleague might be genuinely setting out to block your ideas. Setting children boundaries or standing up for yourself is sometimes necessary. What's important is to successfully steer a path through these confrontations in a calm manner – not to avoid them altogether or to simply let others get their own way all the time.

[2]

Don't raise your voice. If you do, your 'opponent' will also inevitably increase their volume and the discussion will just turn into a shouting match.

[3]

Saying *always* or *never* is likely to immediately make people defensive, while *wishing* someone would do something suggests the idea is an impossibility already! Resorting to personal abuse will then only make matters worse. Instead, try using *sometimes*, or describe your feelings without directly referring to the other person: 'I don't like it when people scream, "I want", or 'Seeing an untidy room upsets me.'

[4]

Sometimes it's best to postpone an argument. We all have buttons that certain people know how to push and which are guaranteed to annoy us. It is best to acknowledge this and attempt to step back when you see things coming. In the same way, if you're not a morning person, for example, try to put off sensitive topics of conversation until later on in the day, when you will be naturally less tense.

[5]

Listen to others. When it comes down to it, differences in gender, generation, character or nationality may produce a different perspective to yours, and one that is equally valid. Is the child asking for chocolate really saying he's tired? Is your colleague in a vulnerable position within the company? Is the underlying message he's giving actually 'I'm worried about redundancy'?

[6]

Don't get stuck defending an unreasonable position just for the sake of not losing face. Be prepared to accept that you may have been wrong or that there might be some middle ground where you could compromise.

[7]

Never tackle sensitive or controversial matters over the phone or by email. Remember that gestures and facial expressions can provide warning signs that you're rubbing someone up the wrong way, which may lead you to change your approach to the subject. The way you stand can also send messages.

[8]

Despite your best efforts, you may occasionally fall out with people. The key then is to try and get in touch as quickly as possible rather than letting things drift and making an upsetting incident worse. When you get in touch, don't go over old ground again. Say 'I'm sorry we argued' or 'Can we agree to disagree?' And in return, accept any such offers you receive with good grace and move on.

FROM THE CRADLE TO THE GRAVE

SPEAKING

1 Work in pairs. Discuss the questions.

- Do you know anyone who's had a baby recently? Do you know any rites or ceremonies around pregnancy and birth?
- When do people come of age in your country? What might people do to mark the event? Are there any other special ages which people celebrate?
- Have you been to any weddings? What were they like?
- Do people usually celebrate wedding anniversaries in your country? How? Are there any special anniversaries?
- Are funerals big events in your country?
- Is it better to be buried or cremated? Why?

LISTENING

2 Work in pairs. Look at the groups of words and, without using a dictionary, discuss the following:

- Which words do you already know the meaning of?
- What kind of ceremony or rite do you think links the words in each group? How?

1 reception / a toast / groom / vows

2 turn 20 / traditional outfits / mayor / gather

3 preserve / coffin / respects / grave

4 lips / a blessing / labour / an astrological chart

3 ▶ 69 Listen and find out what ceremony or rites each person talks about and how the words in Exercise 2 are used.

4 ▶ 69 Decide if the statements 1–8 are true (T) or false (F). Then listen again and check.

Speaker 1

1 The speaker is a good singer.

2 The person who says 'I do' loudest will be the decision maker in the relationship.

Speaker 2

3 The girls spend thousands of pounds on their outfits.

4 They receive a present at the ceremony.

Speaker 3

5 The body is always displayed in a coffin before the funeral.

6 Taking photos of the dead is a sign of respect.

Speaker 4

7 The speaker is very positive about the Hindu rites carried out at birth.

8 The rites connected with new babies happen ten days after birth.

6 Complete the quotations below with these nouns.

ambition	courage	integrity	love
compromise	honesty	justice	responsibility

1 ❝ Money can't buy you _____ , but it sometimes helps to find a wife! ❞

2 ❝ Children should be given _____ from an early age or they will never become adults. ❞

3 ❝ _____ is always the best policy in life. Lies will always get you into trouble. ❞

4 ❝ You need _____ and greed to get ahead in life. ❞

5 ❝ The key to a successful marriage is friendship and _____ . Love fades and you can never have everything you want. ❞

6 ❝ Freedom and _____ for all is something worth dying for. ❞

7 ❝ It's better to have _____ and experience failure, than to lose your principles and have success. ❞

8 ❝ _____ is not only what it takes to stand up and speak, it's also what it takes to sit down and listen. ❞ (Winston Churchill)

7 Work in groups. Think of six more values or concepts.

8 Work in pairs. Discuss the questions.

- Do you agree or disagree with the quotations in Exercise 6? Why?
- What examples or symbols can you think of for the nouns in the box in Exercise 6?
- What core values do you think guide you?
- What do you think are the core values that might guide the following?
  - a doctor
  - a soldier
  - a school
  - a business

9 Choose three of the ideas or concepts below and one of the values and concepts you thought of in Exercise 7 and write your own 'quotation'.

Curiosity
Dignity
Faith
Friendship
Hatred
Liberty
Loyalty
Success

5 Work in groups. Discuss the questions.

- What aspects of the four experiences you heard about are different in your culture? What happens in your culture?
- Do you like the sound of any of the traditions the speakers talk about? Which ones? Why?
- Are there any traditions around birth, coming of age, weddings and funerals that are changing? Why? Is it a good thing?
- Are there any traditions you'd like to change? Why? / Why not?

VOCABULARY

Values and concepts

When we talk about values (e.g. *honour*, *courage*, etc.) and when we talk about a concept in general or an abstract concept, we don't use an article (*a* / *the*).

People here find **death** an awkward subject.

Family is core to the Hindu faith.

14

BANKS AND MONEY

IN THIS UNIT YOU LEARN HOW TO:

- describe problems connected to personal finances and banking
- deal with banks
- apologise and explain problems in formal settings
- use descriptive literary language
- express regrets
- use financial metaphors

SPEAKING

1 **Work in pairs. Discuss the questions.**

- What do you think is happening in the photo?
- Where do you think it was taken?
- Do you like the idea of giving money as a present? Why? / Why not?
- Have you ever given or received money as a present? If so, when?

2 **Change partners. Discuss the questions.**

- How good with money are you? In what way?
- Do you know anyone who has invested money in anything? What?
- Do you know anyone who has won any money? How?
- Do you earn money? Are you happy with what you make?
- How do you feel about getting into debt? Why?

MONEY TROUBLES

VOCABULARY Money problems

1 Complete the sentences with the pairs of words.

account + insurance	currency + inflation
budget + debt	limit + charges
cash flow + credit	market + bailout
credit card + loan	savings + pension

1 I had a £250 overdraft _____ , but I went over it and ended up having to pay something like £80 in _____ . It was so annoying!

2 During the crisis, the _____ basically collapsed and then _____ rocketed. Prices went up by something like 500% in just a few months!

3 The company had awful _____ problems and the bank wouldn't extend them any _____ , so in the end, they went bankrupt.

4 The economy there basically collapsed and it wiped out all of her grandparents' _____ , so now they just have to live on the state _____ , which is tiny!

5 He's never really learned how to manage a _____ and so he's always getting himself into _____ .

6 Someone somehow hacked into my _____ and took a load of money, but luckily I was able to claim it all back on the _____ .

7 The bank had to write off billions in bad loans when the housing _____ collapsed. In the end, they were saved from collapse by a government _____ .

8 She ran up huge debts on her _____ , which affected her ability to borrow money. She couldn't even take out a _____ to buy a new laptop.

2 Write the verb + noun collocations in each sentence in Exercise 1.

have a £250 overdraft limit / go over my overdraft limit

3 Work in pairs. Discuss the questions.

• Which of the problems in Exercise 1 have happened to people, banks, private companies or countries you know? When? What happened?

• What other money problems often affect (a) individuals? (b) banks or private companies? (c) national economies?

• What are the worst problems that can affect each of these (a–c)? Why?

LISTENING

4 ▶ **70** Listen to two conversations involving problems with banks and money. Answer the questions for each conversation.

1 What does the customer want?

2 What problems does the customer encounter?

3 What happens in the end?

5 ▶ **70** Listen again. Are the sentences true (T) or false (F)? How do you know?

Conversation 1

1 The customer can prove where he's currently living.

2 He pays a regular monthly sum of money towards the bills.

3 He wants to pay some cheques into an account.

4 There's a trial period for a current account without fees.

Conversation 2

5 The customer wants around £500 worth of foreign currency.

6 They usually hold some Venezuelan currency, but don't have any left.

7 The customer is pleasantly surprised by the exchange rate.

8 They charge 3% commission when they change money.

6 Work in pairs. Discuss the questions.

• Have you ever opened a bank account? What kind? Who with? Was it easy to do?

• How are banks generally seen in your country? Why?

• Who do you think are the best or worst banks to be with? Why?

• Have you ever had any problems changing money or using cashpoints abroad? If yes, what happened?

GRAMMAR

7 Look at these sentences. Then answer the questions below.

Passives

a *The £30 **will be refunded**.*

b *It looks as if it's **all been bought**.*

c *They're **often accepted** instead of the local currency.*

d *I've **been caught out** before thinking that.*

1 Why is the passive used in each sentence a–d?

2 How is the passive formed in each case?

3 Do you know how to use the passive in any other tense?

G Check your ideas on page 181 and do Exercise 1.

8 Complete the sentences with the correct active or passive form of the verbs in brackets.

1 I only realised that my card ¹_____ last Saturday when I was doing my shopping in my local supermarket and the machine wouldn't ²_____ the transaction. I ³_____ my bank and they said my card ⁴_____ because of suspicious activity over the previous few days. (copy, process, call, block)

2 His business had serious cash flow problems last year and he ¹_____ huge debts trying to keep things going. In the end, he ²_____ bankrupt. All his employees ³_____ redundant, the bank ⁴_____ his house and he ⁵_____ without a penny to his name. (run up, go, make, repossess, leave)

3 A politician has been accused of ¹_____ in a financial scandal. Michael Hurley, 46, allegedly ²_____ over £1.3 million from a local council account to a secret account in Belize. He ³_____ last week after a lengthy police investigation. If found guilty, he could ⁴_____ to up to ten years in jail. Mr Hurley ⁵_____ all charges against him. (involve, transfer, arrest, sentence, deny)

DEVELOPING CONVERSATIONS

Apologising and offering explanations

In formal settings, we can use these expressions to apologise:

***I'm really / terribly / awfully sorry**.*

***I do apologise**.*

When dealing with problems in business situations, it is common for people to apologise and then offer a polite explanation or solution.

***I'm awfully sorry**, sir, **but I'm afraid** we're actually completely out of bolivars.*

***I'm terribly sorry** this is taking so long, madam. The computers aren't usually this slow!*

9 Put the words in the correct order to make explanations often given after apologies.

1 the / look / at / once / I'll / into / matter

2 are / the / very / being / today / computers / slow

3 have / some / of / there / been / kind / must / mix-up

4 down / at / the / I'm / our / moment / is / afraid / system

5 can / we / absolutely / afraid / nothing / there's / I'm / do

6 afraid / to / make / decision / I'm / not / authorised / I'm / that

7 word / can / see / manager / do / and / I'll / a / with / my / what / I / have

PRONUNCIATION

10 ▶ **71** Listen and check your answers to Exercise 9. Notice where the main stresses in each sentence are and the weak forms that are used. Then practise saying the sentences.

11 Work in pairs. Take turns saying and responding to the sentences below. When responding, apologise and offer an explanation or solution.

1 Why is it taking so long?

2 Why don't you have any record of my deposit?

3 My driving licence should be sufficient identification, shouldn't it?

4 The cashpoint outside has eaten my card.

5 I keep forgetting my PIN number. Can I change it?

6 I've just had my bank statement. Why am I being charged every time I withdraw money from my local cashpoint?

CONVERSATION PRACTICE

12 Work in pairs.

Student A: read File 4 on page 184.

Student B: read File 13 on page 189.

Spend a few minutes preparing what to say. Decide which language from these pages you want to use.

13 Roleplay the conversations. Take turns being the customer and the bank clerk. Sort out the problems that arise.

▶ 26 To watch the video and do the activities, see the DVD-ROM.

MADE OF MONEY

SPEAKING

1 Read the traditional Chinese sayings connected to money. Decide what you think each one means and how far you agree.

1 'Be careful what you wish for.'

2 'A long march starts with the very first step.'

3 'An ambitious horse will never return to its old stable.'

4 'When you have only two pennies left in the world, buy a loaf of bread with one, and a flower with the other.'

5 'Without rice, even the cleverest housewife cannot cook.'

6 'A single tree makes no forest; one string makes no music.'

7 'Giving your child a skill is better than giving them a thousand pieces of gold.'

8 'A bird can only sit on one branch; a mouse can't drink more water than flows in a river.'

9 'An inch of time is worth an inch of gold, but it is hard to buy one inch of time with one inch of gold.'

2 Work in pairs. Discuss your ideas. Do you know any similar sayings to those in Exercise 1?

READING

3 Read the first part of a Chinese folk tale about attitudes to work and wealth. Then answer the questions in pairs.

1 Why do you think the bundles of wood were taken up to the heavens?

2 Why do you think the old man refused to let the woodcutter take the moneybag he wanted?

3 What problems and/or opportunities did the magic moneybag bring?

4 Work in pairs. Look at the words in italics in the sentences below. Can you remember some of the more literary words that were used in the story in their place? Read again and check.

1 The bundle in the courtyard had *completely disappeared* again.

2 The poor man decided to *hide* inside the big bundle of wood.

3 At midnight, a huge rope *came down* from the sky.

4 It eventually *stopped* on a cloud and he *carefully looked* through the sticks.

5 The old man *laughed*.

6 The young man was *shown* into a magnificent palace, its golden walls *shining* in the sunlight.

7 The first bag was *full of* precious things.

8 *Holding tightly* onto the enormous rope, the woodcutter was lowered to the ground.

5 ▶ 72 Discuss how you think the story will end. Then listen to the end of the story and see if you were right.

6 Work in groups. Discuss the questions.

· Which of these topics does the story deal with?

death	fame and fortune	greed	justice
dignity	fear	honesty	poverty

· Do you agree with the values of the story?

· Do you know any similar stories – or any other folk tales – connected to money?

GRAMMAR

7 Look at these sentences from the folk tale. Then complete the rule with the names of the correct tenses.

wish

I wish we didn't have to, but we are penniless.

How I wish I'd never opened that bag.

After *wish*, we use [1]_____ to refer to current situations that can't be changed and [2]_____ to talk about regrets about past situations.

G Check your ideas on page 181 and do Exercise 1.

8 Choose the correct form.

1 I wish I *hadn't taken out / didn't take out* the loan, but at the time I really needed the cash.

2 I really wish I *hadn't had to / didn't have to* do this, but I've got no choice.

3 I wish *I'd stuck / I stuck* with my old job.

4 I miss travelling. I wish *I'd been better / I was better* with money so I could save up enough to go away again.

5 I wish I *could've paid / could pay* you, but I'm still waiting for people to pay me back what they owe me.

6 I wish *you'd said / you said* something. I might not have made such a fool of myself!

7 I wish there *had been / was something* I could say to make you feel better, but I know there isn't.

8 I sometimes wish *I'd never started / I never started*. It's turning out to be a bit of a nightmare.

9 Discuss what actually happened or what the situation is now in Exercise 8.

10 Write five wishes on a piece of paper.

I wish I was a millionaire ...

11 Work in pairs. Play a game of 'Be careful what you wish for'. Exchange your paper with a partner. Your partner should think how the wishes will go or have gone wrong. Then say and respond to the wishes.

A: *I wish I was a millionaire.*

B: *Your wish is granted, but now you'll get married to someone who's only interested in your money. They'll divorce you and leave you penniless.*

THE MAGIC MONEYBAG

There once was a poor young couple who lived in a tiny hut. To survive they had to chop extra wood to sell. They kept one small bundle for themselves to make a fire and cook and keep themselves warm and they left a big bundle in their courtyard, to take to market the next day. One morning when they woke up, they found that the bundle they had left in the courtyard the previous night had mysteriously disappeared. There was nothing to do but sell the one they'd been keeping for themselves.

That same day, they chopped more firewood, left a large bundle in the courtyard again and kept a small amount of wood for themselves. The following morning, the bundle in the courtyard had vanished again. The same thing happened on the third and fourth days as well and by the fifth day the poor man was so desperate, he decided to conceal himself inside the big bundle in the courtyard in order to find out where his wood had been vanishing to. At midnight, an enormous rope descended from the sky, attached itself to the bundle and lifted it up to the heavens, with the poor woodcutter still inside it.

It eventually came to a halt on a cloud and he peered through the sticks and saw an old man with long, grey hair approaching. As the old man was untying the bundle, he found the woodcutter inside and asked, 'Other people only cut one bundle of firewood a day. Why do you cut two?'

The poor man replied, 'I wish we didn't have to, but we're penniless. We keep a little for our own use but we have to cut the rest to sell so we can buy rice.'

The old man chuckled. 'I know you are struggling to provide food for you and your wife,' he said. 'I'll give you a present. Take it with you and it'll provide you with a proper living.'

The young man was then ushered into a magnificent palace, its golden walls sparkling in the sunlight. He was taken to a room full of moneybags and told to choose whichever he wanted.

The woodcutter grabbed the largest moneybag, which was crammed with precious things. At that moment, the old man became very serious. 'No! I'm sorry. Not that one. Take this one. It is empty now but will provide you with money for your whole life – but only as long as you take just one piece of silver from it each day and never more than that.' The poor man reluctantly agreed. He took the empty bag and, clinging onto the enormous rope, was lowered to the ground.

Once home, he told his wife the story and she was full of joy. From then on, they'd open the moneybag every morning and a lump of silver would roll out. They started saving up.

Time passed slowly. One day, the husband suggested buying an ox, but his wife disagreed. Later, he suggested buying some land, but his wife didn't agree to that either. More time went by, and the wife proposed building a proper cottage with a good roof. The husband was desperate to spend the money and said, 'As we've got so much, why don't we build a big mansion?' The wife couldn't dissuade her husband and reluctantly went along with the idea.

THE LUCK OF THE DRAW

SPEAKING

1 Work in pairs. Discuss the questions.

- Are there lotteries in your country?
- What do you know about them?
- Which of the facts about lotteries below do you find interesting, surprising or unsurprising? Explain why.

- The first lottery occurred in China about 200BC. The Great Wall of China may have been partly funded by it.

- Winners of Dutch lotteries in the 17th century received paintings.

- The word lottery comes from the Dutch word *loterij*.

- Lotteries were banned in the United States between 1890 and the mid-1960s.

- The hardest lottery to win is the Italian *SuperEnalotto* – with odds for the top prize of over 622 million to one.

- The biggest jackpot win for a single person is currently $370,900,000.

- 28% of the money spent on the lottery in the UK goes to 'good causes'. These include charities, preserving British heritage, funding Olympic athletes, and subsidising theatre and the arts.

PRONUNCIATION

2 ▶ 73 Listen to an alternative way to express three of the statistics in the Fact File in Exercise 1 and find the numbers they match with.

3 ▶ 74 Think of two different ways to express each of these figures. Then listen and repeat the numbers you hear.

1 3,700,000
2 1,500
3 0.02
4 2/3
5 40%
6 -10°

4 ▶ 75 Listen and write down the numbers you hear in the six statistics. Then compare your answers in pairs. Can you remember the complete statistics?

5 Work in pairs. Discuss the questions.

- How do you think these statistics are worked out?
- Do you think the statistics are true, probably true or a bit dubious?
- Have you heard any interesting or dubious statistics recently? What about?

UNDERSTANDING VOCABULARY

Metaphor

Many words and expressions, such as those connected to money, are used metaphorically. Often this metaphorical usage is more common than the literal usage.

The **odds** of winning the SuperEnalotto are 622 million to one. (literal)

A: *What are the **odds** he'll be late?* (metaphorical)

B: *Oh, he's bound to be!*

6 Complete each pair of sentences with one of these words. You may need to change the form.

bet	gamble	lottery	stake
earn	jackpot	odds	waste

1 a He doesn't _____ much. He's still a junior in the firm.

   b After all that hard work, I think we've _____ a break.

2 a I wish we hadn't bought it. It was a _____ of money!

   b I wouldn't _____ your breath. You'll never persuade him to change his mind.

3 a He _____ £50 on a horse to win, but it came second.

   b I _____ it was nice to have a break after all that work.

4 a I don't _____ , especially at casinos. I'm not lucky.

   b A recent report has warned that people are _____ with their lives by buying cheap medication online.

5 a He's the clear favourite to win at _____ of 2 to 1.

   b She recovered from the illness against all _____ .

6 a I won £10 on the _____ . I got three numbers out of six.

   b Finding a decent restaurant there is a bit of a _____ .

7 a There's a rollover on the lottery because no-one won last week. The _____ is something like $30 million now.

   b He hit the _____ when he got that job. It's great.

8 a We sometimes play poker for money, but only for a very small _____ each – one cent – and you can only raise it to ten!

   b It's important voters understand the issues because there's a lot at _____ – people's jobs and their future security!

7 Work in pairs. Choose one of the questions to talk about.

- What aspects of life do you think are a lottery in your country? Explain why.
- What is at stake in the next election in your country? Explain why.
- Can you think of someone you know or have heard about who survived against great odds? Explain what happened.

LISTENING

8 Work in groups. List reasons someone might give for banning a lottery.

9 ▶ 76 Listen to the first speaker (Zak) in a debate about banning lotteries and note what reason he gives in favour of banning them.

10 Explain the points Zak was making when he mentioned the following:

1 promising to give people $2.6 million in the next quarter of a million years

2 the focus of the marketing of lotteries

3 subsidising opera and Olympic sportsmen

4 only having to choose six numbers to get rich

5 dreaming of a mansion and a Ferrari

6 the story of John from Sydney

11 ▶ 76 Listen again and check your ideas. Then discuss the questions.

1 What mark out of ten would you give Zak's speech?

2 Do you agree with his points? Why? / Why not?

3 What counter arguments could someone make?

12 ▶ 77 Listen to the opposing speaker, Stacy, in the debate. Take notes on Stacy's reply to Zak.

13 Compare your notes in pairs and then in groups. Finally, compare what you understood with the audio script of Stacy's arguments on page 209.

14 Work in groups. Discuss the questions.

- What mark would you give Stacy?
- Who do you think won the debate? Why?
- Do you think any of the points they made were irrelevant, clever, stupid or confusing?

SPEAKING

15 Work in small groups to prepare a debate similar to the one you heard between Zak and Stacy. Decide which of the topics below you want to debate, or propose your own topic.

- 'Money is the root of all evil.' Discuss.
- 'The best things in life are free.' Discuss.
- 'The world would be a better place without banks.' Discuss.
- 'Everyone should have to vote.' Discuss.
- 'Debating should be part of everyone's schooling.' Discuss.

16 Divide your group into two teams. One team should defend the statement for the topic you have chosen; the other team should counter it. Prepare your arguments. Look back at the debate you heard to find techniques and expressions you want to use.

17 Each team should nominate a speaker. Then have your debate in front of another group. The other group will give each team marks out of ten and decide the winner. Your group will then do the same for them.

NUBIAN WEDDING

1 You are going to watch a video about a ceremony which the girls in the photo take part in. Before you watch, discuss:

- what country you think they are from
- what they're doing

2 🎥 27 Watch the video and take notes about the people and their celebration. Then complete each of the following in ways that are true for you.

> I didn't quite understand …   The … is similar to …
>
> I was surprised that …   I'd like to know …
>
> I found … interesting.

3 Work in pairs. Compare your notes and discuss what you thought of the film using the ideas from Exercise 2.

4 Complete the sentences with a singular or plural form of the words in the box.

blood	exchange	mean	mud	paper
dam	land	mine	noon	ritual

1 The _____ is celebrated by the entire village for seven days and nights.

2 The couple met once and were reunited when an official came to sign the legal _____ .

3 The perfumes and incense are supposed to get the groom's _____ moving and give him energy.

4 The people were removed from their ancient _____ when they were flooded to build a _____ .

5 The old village had _____ houses and lacked _____ of transport, but the old man preferred it.

6 The dancing continues from early evening till _____ the next day.

7 Nubia derives from an old word for gold and refers to gold _____ that used to be in the area.

8 After the _____ of rings, the bride's mother kisses the couple.

5 Work in groups. Discuss the questions connected to the video.

- In what ways are Nubian weddings similar or different to weddings in your country?
- What other people have had to move from their homelands? What happened? Why?
- What's the longest party / celebration you have been to? How long did it last? What did you do?
- Have you ever had to sign legal papers? What for?
- Are there any mines in your country? What kind? Have you ever visited one?

UNDERSTANDING FAST SPEECH

6 Look at this extract from the video. To help you, groups of words are marked with / and stressed sounds are in CAPITALS. Pauses are marked //. Practise saying the sentence.

even THOUGH / there in the old VILLage / there was no electRIcity / or MEANS of transporTAtion like we have here NOW // STILL // LIFE there was BEtter // THERE we USED to KEEP our NUbian traDItions / and NUbian LANguage // NUbian LANguage could be in DANger here toDAY.

7 🎥 28 Listen to how the narrator said this sentence. Now you have a go! Practise saying the extract again fast.

REVIEW 7

GRAMMAR

1 Complete the text with one word in each space.

After we had ¹ _____ married for a few years, my husband and I decided to close our separate bank accounts and put all our money into one joint account. He ² _____ been telling me what a good idea it was for ages and in the end, I just gave in. Looking back on it, though, I wish I ³ _____ . The problems started a few weeks ago. My joint card ⁴ _____ rejected a couple of times and when I phoned the bank about it, they said our overdraft limit ⁵ _____ been repeatedly exceeded over the preceding weeks. At first I thought perhaps our account had ⁶ _____ hacked into, but when I spoke to my husband about it, he admitted he'd been spending too much. We're so badly in debt now that we're going to have to sell our car. I wish we ⁷ _____ have to, but what can we do? Still, at least everything should ⁸ _____ paid back by the end of this year!

2 Complete the second sentence so that it has a similar meaning to the first sentence, using the word given. Do not change the word given. You must use between two and four words, including the word given.

1 He never really helps me with the housework.

I _____ me with the housework from time to time. **WISH**

2 I wish he wouldn't take things from my room without asking me first.

He _____ things from my room without asking me. **ALWAYS**

3 He's a terrible listener. He's always talking over the top of everyone else.

He's a terrible listener. He _____ to anything anyone else says! **NEVER**

4 I hate being this height. I'm about ten centimetres shorter than all the rest of my friends.

I hate being this height. I really _____ taller. **WISH**

5 I can't give you a lift today, I'm afraid. My car is in the garage.

I can't give you a lift today, I'm afraid. My car _____ at the moment. **FIXED**

6 I can't accept this cheque, I'm afraid. There's no signature on it.

I'm afraid I can't accept this cheque. It _____ . **SIGNED**

3 Choose the correct word or form.

1 When I came out of my house this morning, I saw that our car *was / had been* broken into.

2 I'd *been looking / looked* forward to it for so long but in the end, it was a bit disappointing, really.

3 Have you seen the news? Something terrible *has been / has* happened in Cairo.

4 Of course they all denied *be / to be / being* involved in the scandal.

5 I wish *I'd / I hadn't / I wouldn't have* never met you.

6 I wish I *hadn't to / didn't have to / hadn't had to* do military service. They were the worst two years of my life.

7 I wish he *wouldn't be / hadn't been / wasn't* so selfish. He only ever thinks of himself.

8 I feel so useless. I wish there *was / is / could've been* something I could do to help.

4 ▶ **78** Listen. Write the six sentences you hear.

VOCABULARY

5 Match the verbs (1–8) with the collocates (a–h).

1	run up	a	a loan / a mortgage
2	take out	b	a rocky patch / a tough time
3	live on	c	face / your temper
4	stand up	d	an offer / you may be wrong
5	go through	e	huge debts / a big bill
6	accept	f	your voice / taxes
7	lose	g	for yourself / against racism
8	raise	h	ten pounds a day / very little

6 Complete the sentences. Use the word in brackets to form a word that fits in the space.

1 I'm in charge of 35 people, so the job carries quite a lot of _____ . (responsible)

2 We've known each other since we were kids. It's maybe the most important _____ of my life. (friend)

3 On the whole, I try to avoid _____ whenever I can. (confront)

4 The national bank collapsed, and that totally wiped out all our _____ . (save)

5 The bank just said they wouldn't _____ any more credit to a new business. (extension)

6 He was a controversial figure who inspired _____ and affection in equal measures. (hate)

7 Decide if these words are connected to life-changing events, banks or gambling and in what way.

a bailout	currency	in labour	an overdraft	stakes
charges	the jackpot	odds	retrain	vows

8 Complete the story with one word in each space. The first letters are given.

From what I've ¹h_____ , the board basically decided that it was ²t_____ to let him go quite a while ago. ³Ap_____ , he didn't get on with some of the other directors – ⁴r_____ them up the wrong way, you know. Then when the company started suffering during the crisis and having serious cash-⁵f_____ problems, he got the blame. He was accused of mismanaging the ⁶bu_____ and getting the firm into serious ⁷d_____ so, as I understand it, despite the official statement saying how he's always acted with absolute ⁸in_____ and everything, he's really getting sacked!

15

FOOD

IN THIS UNIT YOU LEARN HOW TO:

- explain how to cook things
- give approximate meanings
- get better at linking ideas together
- talk about food programmes and memories of food
- discuss food-related stories in the news

SPEAKING

1   **Work in pairs. Discuss the questions.**

- What do you think the relationship between the people in the photo is?
- What do you think they're cooking? Why?
- How do you think they might cook the food they're preparing?
- Have you ever done any cooking like this?

2   **Change partners. Discuss the questions.**

- Can you cook? What's your best dish?
- How did you learn to cook the dishes you can make?
- Is there any food you typically prepare together with your family or friends? When?
- Do the men or women in your family do the bulk of the cooking? Or does it depend?

WHAT'S COOKING?

VOCABULARY Food and cooking

1 Look at the pictures in File 16 on page 190. In pairs, discuss the questions.

- Are there any foods you've never tried?
- Are there any you didn't know in English?
- Are any of them difficult to buy where you live?
- Which five of these foods do you like the most?
- Are there any you can't stand? Why not?
- Are there any foods you love that aren't pictured?

2 Work in groups. How many of the foods from page 190 can you remember? Put them into the categories below.

fruits / nuts:	
fish / seafood:	
vegetables / salads:	
pulses / beans:	
herbs / spices:	

3 Complete the sentences with these words.

almonds	chocolate	courgette	mixture	peaches
chickpeas	coconut	grapefruit	parsley	trout

1 **Peel** the _____ and **remove** the stones.
2 **Steam** the _____ . When it's ready, the flesh should come away from the bones easily.
3 **Soak** the _____ overnight in water and then **boil** them for two hours.
4 **Melt** the _____ and mix in the raisins.
5 **Squeeze** some _____ juice over the salad.
6 **Slice** the _____ and **fry** the slices till they are slightly brown on each side.
7 **Crush** the _____ and sprinkle on top of the cake.
8 **Chop** some _____ and **sprinkle** it onto the soup.
9 Add the _____ milk. Bring it to the boil and then leave for about 30 minutes, but stir it occasionally.
10 **Blend** the whole _____ until it's smooth.

4 Work in pairs. Look at the verbs in bold in Exercise 3. Tell each other which you have done in the last month. Then think of two more things you can do each verb to.

You can peel bananas and potatoes.

LISTENING

5 ▶ **79** Listen to a conversation where a woman comments on a dish and asks how it's made. Note down the ingredients.

6 ▶ **79** Discuss with a partner what you remember about how the dish was made. Then listen again and take notes. Finally, compare your notes in groups.

7 Work in pairs. Discuss the questions.

- Do you like the sound of the recipe? Why? / Why not?
- Do you know anyone who has a special diet or who avoids certain things like salt? What do they have to eat or avoid? Why?
- Who's the best cook you know? What are their best dishes?

DEVELOPING CONVERSATIONS

Vague language

We can show something is not exact by adding *-ish* to adjectives or *-y* to nouns. We can also add *kind of* or *sort of* before adjectives and verbs and *like* before nouns.

It's a grey**ish** white stick. It gives a **kind of** citrus**y** flavour.

It looks **sort of like** a spring onion.

You know, **like** a big orange squash.

With quantities, we use words such as *roughly / about / or so*.

Use **roughly** a cupful.

Leave it to boil for fifteen minutes **or so**.

8
Make the sentences less exact by adding the forms in brackets in the correct place. You might have to change the spelling.

1 You bake it in the oven for twenty minutes.
(roughly)

2 I generally sprinkle some herbs on top and two teaspoons of crushed pistachios.
(about)

3 If you add a squeeze of orange, it gives it a sweet finish, which is really nice.
(kind of)

4 The colour put me off at first. It was green blue, but it tasted great.
(kind of / -ish)

5 It has an odd oil texture and a weird egg smell.
(-y / -y)

6 You need a large pan, because you add two litres of fish stock.
(-ish / or so)

7 If it's a small chicken and isn't stuffed, then it should only take 40 minutes to roast.
(-ish / or so)

8 It's a potato, but it's rounder and it's got purple skin and the flesh is orange.
(like / -ish / kind of)

9
Work in pairs. Using vague language, describe different foods for your partner to guess.

A: *It's biggish with a yellowish skin, very juicy flesh and a kind of lemony flavour. It's quite bitter.*

B: *Is it a grapefruit?*

GRAMMAR

Linking words

You have learnt a number of words in this book that make the relationship between two ideas in a sentence or between two sentences clear. For example, **order and time** (*and, when, after, once, then, afterwards, while, during,* etc.), **result and reason / purpose** (*as, so, to*), **contrast** (*although, however*) and **condition** (*if, in case, provided*).

10
Read the Grammar box. Then choose the correct options to complete the recipe below.

First you chop some onions ¹*and / after* put them in some oil. Fry them for a few minutes. Actually, you should heat the oil a bit beforehand and ²*when / then* you put the onion in, it should sizzle. ³*Then / After* you need to turn the heat down, ⁴*as / so* you want the onion to cook slowly ⁵*then / so* it becomes nice and sweet. I also like to add some garlic, ⁶*although / however* I know most people don't. Anyway, ⁷*while / during* the onion is cooking, peel about four big potatoes and cut them into little pieces – quite small, ⁸*otherwise / unless* they'll take ages to cook.

⁹*Once / Afterwards* the onion has started to turn brown, add the potatoes and continue to cook everything ¹⁰*until / when* the potato is soft. The onion won't burn ¹¹*provided / unless* you mix it in with the potato and stir the mixture now and then.

Break about eight eggs into a bowl and whisk them with a touch of milk. Spoon the cooked mixture into the whisked eggs – without any of the oil ¹²*if / in case* you can avoid it – and mix it all together.

You then pour away the oil in the pan – apart from about a spoonful – and heat it up again so it's very hot. ¹³*When / Then* pour the egg and potato into the pan and after about a minute, turn it down low and let it cook ¹⁴*for / during* about ten minutes. You then need to get a big plate or flat lid to put on top of the omelette ¹⁵*for / to* turn it over and cook the other side.

G For further practice, see page 182 and do Exercise 1.

CONVERSATION PRACTICE

11
Work in pairs. Discuss how many of the different kinds of dishes below you could cook. For each dish, decide what ingredients you'd need and how you'd cook the dish.

- a stir fry
- a tart or a cake
- a pasta dish
- a rice-based dish
- a stew
- a curry
- a vegetarian dish
- a salad

12
Choose whichever one of the dishes above you think you would cook best. Change partners. Have conversations similar to the one in Exercise 5. Follow this guide. Then swap roles.

Start by saying: *Mmm! This is delicious! What's in it?*

Explain what's in the dish.

Ask questions about the taste and about how to make the dish.

Answer the questions as best you can.

Check details when you're not sure about ingredients or what to do.

29 To watch the video and do the activities, see the DVD-ROM.

THIS TAKES ME BACK

SPEAKING

1 Work in groups. Discuss the questions.

- What cookery programmes have you heard of? Do you watch any? Why? / Why not?
- What films do you know where food plays an important part? What are they about? Do you like them?
- Do you ever read blogs about food? Do you read any other blogs? What are they about?

READING

2 Read the blog post and decide which of the following opinions the writer gives. Underline any examples or evidence given in the text.

1 *Ratatouille* is more worth watching than *MasterChef*.

2 People should spend more time preparing food.

3 It's a waste of money buying expensive wine.

4 How good we think something tastes is influenced by language and price.

5 We should question the way food is wasted when a lot of people are living in poverty.

6 Cooking is about caring for others, sharing food and creating memories.

3 Work in pairs. Discuss your ideas for Exercise 2 and decide which is the main argument.

4 Work in pairs. Look at the words in bold and think about what they might mean from the context. Then answer the questions.

1 What do you use to **flick through the channels**? What else might you flick through?

2 If you **come across** a film or some research, were you deliberately looking for it?

3 Is a **subtle** difference, change or shift of direction easy to detect?

4 What's the difference between an expert and a **so-called** expert?

5 Can you predict a **random** event or a random choice?

6 What do you think would be examples of a **fancy** car?

7 What word could replace **chuck**?

8 Why might you stop reading an online review if there's a **spoiler alert**?

9 Who else (apart from a critic) might **pass judgement** and on whom?

5 Write a comment about the blog post. Choose two of these ideas to write about. Then share your comments with other students in the class.

- Give an example of a food or smell that reminds you of someone or some time.
- Give an example of a special meal you remember having.

- Give an example of a smell or food you can't stand because of a past experience.
- Explain the opinions you agree with in the post and give a further example.
- Explain what you disagree with in the post and why.
- Explain what's good about *MasterChef* or similar programmes.
- Recommend another film connected to food and say why.
- Explain some other research connected to taste and smell.

UNDERSTANDING VOCABULARY

Prefixes

In the article, the author mentioned ***non-existent differences*** and a ***semi-cooked*** dish.

We make lots of words by using prefixes like *non-* and *semi-* before a root word. They modify the meanings of the words they are added to. For instance, *non-existent* differences are ones that don't exist, while a *semi-cooked* dish is not completely cooked.

6 Complete the definitions with these prefixes.

dis	mis	non	over	pro	semi
ex	multi	out	pre	re	super

1 many – as in _____-cultural or _____-lingual

2 no longer – as in _____-soldier or _____-president

3 wrongly – as in _____manage a situation or _____inform the public

4 more or better than – as in _____perform a competitor or _____grow your clothes

5 too much – as in _____stay your welcome or _____do it

6 not – as in _____-stick pan or _____-existent

7 opposite – as in _____obey an order or _____qualified

8 before – as in _____-war or _____-heat the oven

9 again – as in _____play a game or _____read a book

10 partly – as in _____-professional or _____-conscious

11 in favour of – as in _____-GM food or _____-democracy campaigner

12 extremely – as in _____-fit or a _____-posh hotel

7 Work in pairs. Challenge each other to think of another example for each prefix. Your partner should put their word into a sentence.

A: *pre-*

B: *I buy a lot of pre-cooked meals.*

FOOD, FRIENDS, FAMILY

PREVIOUS POSTS

granny's apple pie; first picnic of the year; other names for the children's menu; simple stews

Flicking through the channels last night trying to find something that wasn't *MasterChef* (apparently there are versions in 40 countries now!), I **came across** the animated film, *Ratatouille*. I've seen it before, but I'd say it's the best ever film about food, so I watched it again and realised it sums up what this blog's about.

If you haven't seen it, the film's a rags-to-riches tale of how a rat becomes a chef in a top Parisian restaurant – silly I know, but bear with me.

The rat has to defeat two rivals. On the one hand, there's the head chef who has plans to use the name of the restaurant to brand frozen fast food. He represents the food industry – processed, cheap, inauthentic. On the other hand, we have the painfully thin food critic writing his reviews with a view to finding fault and roasting reputations. He essentially represents what I call the Masterchefisation of cooking, where drama is created out of **subtle**, not to say non-existent, differences.

The thing is, when it comes to taste, subtleties are actually lost on the vast majority of us. You'll remember my amusement in a previous post at research which showed most people in double-blind tests thought cheap wine tasted better than ridiculously expensive ones. I also came across this research that showed even prizes judged by **so-called** experts turn out to be completely **random**. The same judges assess the same wines differently every time. But of course, if you say something's a prize winner or it costs a lot, people do believe it tastes better (see here for some research) and that's what *MasterChef* is all about: it suggests taste is all about expense and **fancy** technique, so if you don't cook your potato three different ways, using £1000 worth of kitchen equipment, it's essentially inedible.

Honestly, the other day I saw a chef reject one of the competitor's dishes, not because it was semi-cooked, but because the tiny spots of sauce around the edge of the plate were unevenly spaced apart. 'I can't possibly serve that to my customers – start again!' and he **chucked** it in the bin. And this in a country where the number of food banks providing free food for the poor has doubled in the last two years!

Which brings me back to *Ratatouille* and the key scene, which, in contrast to *MasterChef*, always fills me with joy. (**Spoiler alert** for those who haven't seen it.) The miserable food critic has come to the restaurant to **pass judgement** on the new chef (the rat!). How on earth will they impress him? The little chef prepares a dish of ratatouille, shocking the other cooks, who are convinced the critic will destroy them because ratatouille is such an unsophisticated dish – essentially vegetable stew. But on tasting the first mouthful, the critic is transported back to his childhood. He remembers coming home upset because he'd fallen over. His mother sits him down and places a plate of ratatouille before him. It's fresh, it's tasty, but more than anything, it's the taste of comfort and of a mother's love. The critic smiles.

The memories we collect connected with food and meals are so much more valuable and real than technique and expense. They say, 'you are what you eat', but I'd say we're the *memories* of the food we eat. Anyway, let me know what you think. Do you agree? Have you got any memories connected with food?

COMMENTS 6

Come on! He could be a top chef!

I'm sorry, but it'll still taste like a pumpkin!

FOOD FOR THOUGHT

VOCABULARY Food in the news

1 Work in pairs. Look at the newspaper headlines below. Discuss what you think each story will involve. Explain which you'd be most interested in reading.

a FARMERS' PROTEST ENDS IN RIOT

b SHOPPERS URGED TO CHANGE HABITS TO CUT FOOD WASTE

c Call for ban on fast food advertising

d POOR FOOD HYGIENE ACCUSATIONS PROVE TO BE A DIRTY LIE

e BIG DATA ANALYSIS TO SOLVE GLOBAL FOOD SHORTAGES

f GOVERNMENT PROMISE TO ACT IN BID TO END FOOD FRAUD

2 Match the collocations with the headlines in Exercise 1. There are two for each headline.

1 tackle rising rates of obesity
2 cut farming subsidies
3 prevent widespread hunger
4 clash with police
5 exclusive restaurants
6 appalling wastefulness
7 the damage that negative publicity does
8 organised criminal gangs
9 abandon weekly supermarket visits
10 prohibit commercial sponsorship
11 develop more efficient farming techniques
12 uncover illegal activity

3 Work in pairs. Compare your ideas. Then think of one more collocation you would expect to find in each story.

LISTENING

4 ▶ 80 Listen to four news stories about food. Match each one with a headline from Exercise 1.

5 Compare your ideas in pairs. Which eight collocations from Exercise 2 did you hear? Can you remember what was said about each of them?

6 ▶ 80 Listen again and answer the questions about the four stories.

1 a What kind of food fraud has been going on?
  b What effect has the scandal had on shopping habits?
2 a What is Mr Gunning accused of doing?
  b What do you learn about his trial?
3 a What disturbing predictions are made?
  b What's the function of the e-pills and how will they work?
4 a How much food is being wasted in the UK?
  b In what way does wasted food 'cost consumers three times over'?

7 Work in pairs. Discuss the questions.

- One of the four stories you heard is an urban myth. Which do you think this is? Why?
- Have you heard any other urban myths?
- Do you know any news stories similar to the other three you heard? What do they involve?
- What other problems do you think will arise as the global population increases?
- How much do you know about big data – and the issues around the way it's analysed?
- How do you think food waste could best be tackled? Why?
- Do you think you or your family waste much food? What kind? Why?

GRAMMAR

Patterns after reporting verbs

When we report what people said, we often just summarise their main ideas. We use lots of different verbs to do this (*promise, accuse, recommend*, etc.).

The patterns that follow these verbs vary and depend on the first verb used. With some verbs, only one subsequent pattern is possible, while with others different patterns are possible.

8 ▶ **81** Read the Grammar box. Try to complete the four sentences from the news stories in Exercise 4 by using the correct patterns for the verbs in brackets. You may also need to add extra words. Then listen to check.

1 The government is promising _____ a full investigation. (carry out)

2 Gunning is accused _____ habitually _____ a cockroach into his food as he neared the end of his meals. (introduce)

3 Many experts recommend _____ technology and data analysis to help improve the situation. (use)

4 A new report urges shoppers _____ weekly supermarket visits. (abandon)

9 Match each of the sentences in Exercise 8 with one of the four patterns a–d. Then match the verbs in the box below to the patterns.

a verb often followed by infinitive (with *to*)

b verb often followed by *-ing*

c verb often followed by person + (not) + infinitive (with *to*)

d verb often followed by a preposition + *-ing*

advise	consider	intend	suggest
agree	deny	insist	threaten
apologise	encourage	refuse	warn
confess	imagine	remind	worry

G Check your ideas on page 182 and do Exercise 1.

10 Complete the second sentence so it has a similar meaning to the first. Use between two and five words, including the correct form of the word in bold.

1 We strongly recommend that the government rethinks its policy.

We would _____ its policy on this matter. **URGE**

2 The government have accepted an offer for the farmland from a private company.

The government _____ the farmland to a private company. **AGREE**

3 My son is three now and he never wants to eat anything healthy.

My son just totally _____ anything healthy at all. **REFUSE**

4 My grandmother always makes her special apple pie every time we go and visit her.

My grandmother always _____ her special apple pie every time we go and visit her. **INSIST**

5 A friend of mine said we should try this new Vietnamese place near here.

A friend of mine _____ this new Vietnamese place near here. **SUGGEST**

6 Given the cod shortages, fish and chip restaurants are suggesting that customers try alternatives.

Given the cod shortages, fish and chip restaurants are _____ alternatives. **ENCOURAGE**

7 The company has expressed regret after it was caught selling contaminated meat.

The company _____ contaminated meat. **APOLOGISE**

8 The firm rejected all accusations of involvement in the scandal.

The firm categorically _____ involved in the scandal. **DENY**

11 Work in groups. Tell a partner some examples of things that:

• people are currently being urged to do – or not do.

• someone famous has been accused of doing recently.

• you've promised to do recently.

• you've had to apologise for doing recently.

• someone famous has been criticised for recently.

• you have refused to do.

SPEAKING

12 Imagine you are going to make a podcast. With a partner, think of a food-related news story. This could be one of the two stories from Exercise 1 that weren't included in the news stories you listened to – or it could be a different story that you have heard.

13 Prepare a short podcast about your story. Use as much language from these pages as possible.

14 Present your podcast to another pair. Who told the most interesting story?

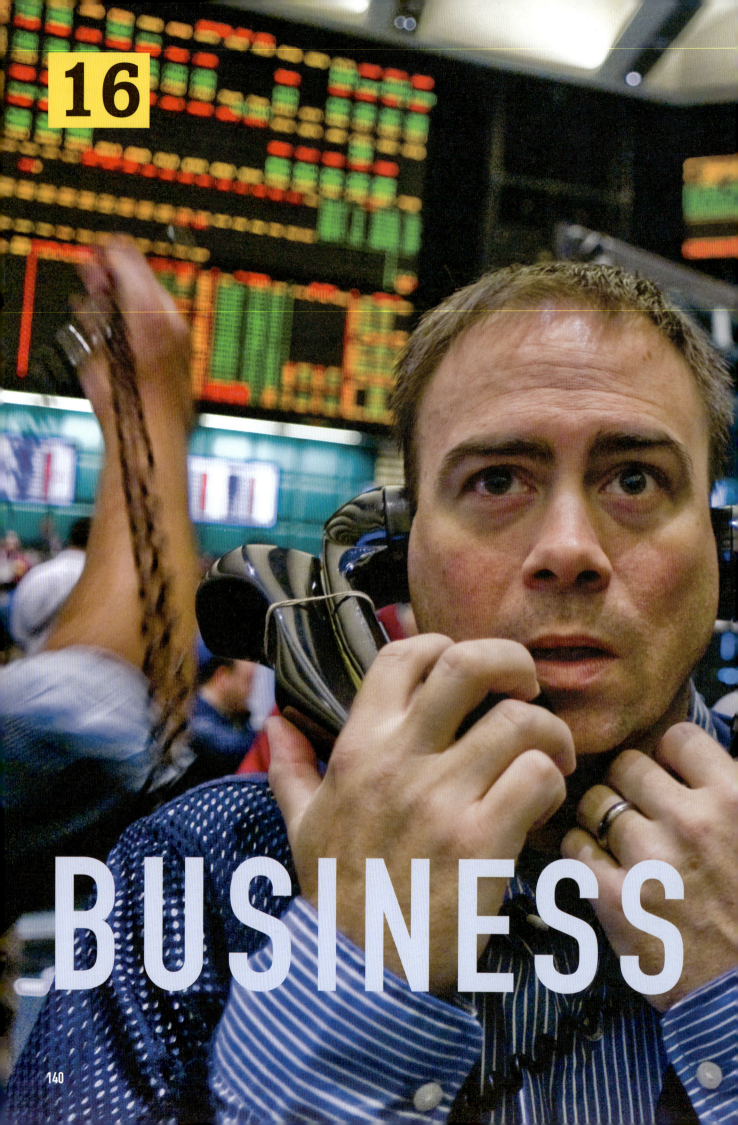

16

BUSINESS

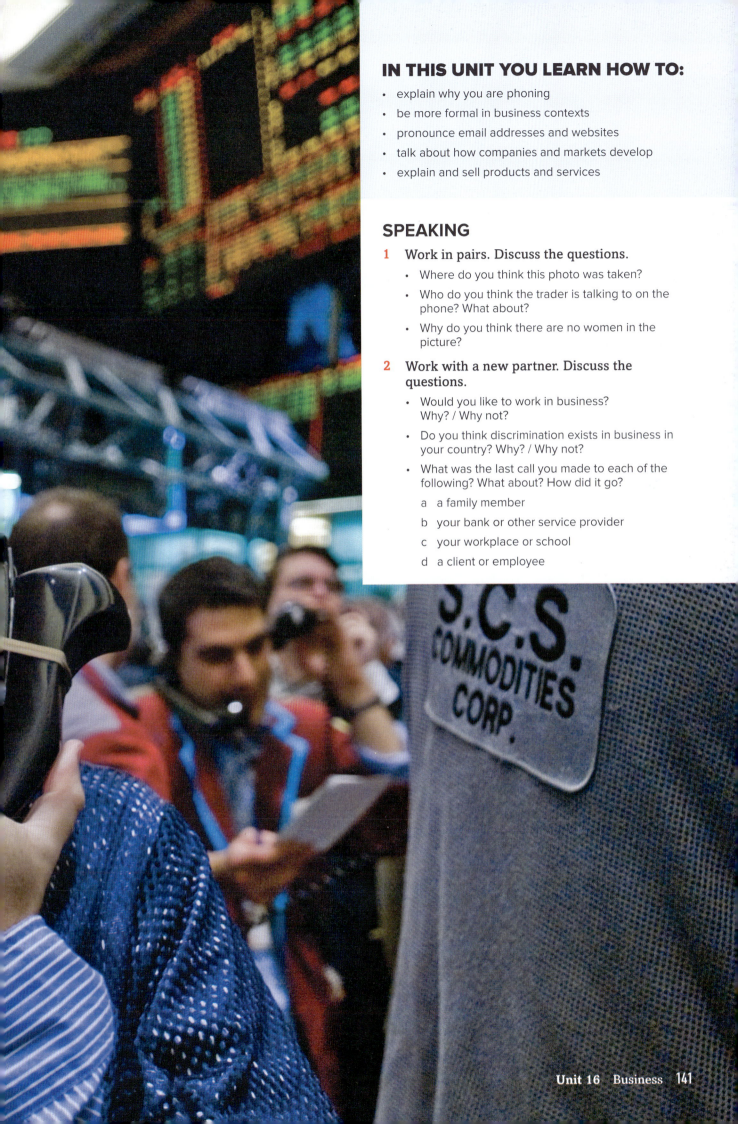

IN THIS UNIT YOU LEARN HOW TO:

- explain why you are phoning
- be more formal in business contexts
- pronounce email addresses and websites
- talk about how companies and markets develop
- explain and sell products and services

SPEAKING

1 Work in pairs. Discuss the questions.

- Where do you think this photo was taken?
- Who do you think the trader is talking to on the phone? What about?
- Why do you think there are no women in the picture?

2 Work with a new partner. Discuss the questions.

- Would you like to work in business? Why? / Why not?
- Do you think discrimination exists in business in your country? Why? / Why not?
- What was the last call you made to each of the following? What about? How did it go?

  a a family member

  b your bank or other service provider

  c your workplace or school

  d a client or employee

I'LL CHASE IT UP

VOCABULARY Reasons for phoning

1 **Match the two parts of the sentences.**

1 I'm just phoning to chase up
2 I'm just phoning to remind you
3 I'm just phoning to try to arrange
4 I'm just phoning to pass on
5 I'm just phoning to check

a an overdue payment on your account with us.
b stock levels in the warehouse.
c that you have an appointment with Mr Tanaka at 3.
d my thanks to you and your team.
e a suitable time and place for the next meeting.

6 I'm just calling to let you know
7 I'm just calling to enquire
8 I'm just calling to confirm
9 I'm just calling to apologise for
10 I'm just calling to see

f the mix-up earlier.
g I won't be able to make the meeting tomorrow.
h whether you're taking on any staff at the moment.
i about the vegetarian options on your menu.
j a booking for three nights next week.

2 **Work in pairs. Think of one other possible ending for each of the sentence beginnings in Exercise 1.**

*I'm just phoning to chase up **an order I placed last month**.*

LISTENING

3 ▶ **82** **Listen to a conversation between two colleagues. Answer the questions.**

1 Why is Ian calling Claudia?
2 What does he suggest?
3 How does Claudia respond?
4 What arrangements do they end up making?

4 ▶ **83** **Now listen to a second conversation between a client and a customer services operator. Complete the note below as you do so.**

Order no.:

Date placed:

Client's name:

Email address:

Action:

5 **Work in pairs to compare your notes.**

DEVELOPING CONVERSATIONS

Using *would* to show formality

One way we can make sentences sound more polite and less direct is to use *would*. It is often used in more formal contexts. We also use other more formal words with *would*. ***I was wondering if** you'd like to join us* sounds more formal than *Do you want to come with us?*

11 ▶ 85 Now listen and write down the email and website addresses you hear. Compare your ideas with a partner.

12 Work in groups. Swap your email address with the other students. Then recommend five websites each. Give the addresses and explain why you like them.

GRAMMAR

13 Look at these sentences from the conversations in Exercises 3 and 4. Then work in pairs to answer the questions below.

> ### The future continuous
>
> We occasionally use a future continuous form when making arrangements and plans.
>
> a **I'll be visiting** Barcelona for a trade fair so **I'll be able to fit** in a day with you then.
>
> b **It'll be going out** today by special delivery so **it'll be** with you first thing tomorrow.

1 Which of the forms in bold is the future continuous?

2 Which shows a previous arrangement or plan?

3 Which shows a more recently made plan or promise?

G Check your ideas on page 183 and do Exercise 1.

14 Complete the sentences by putting the verbs in brackets with *will / won't* and a simple or continuous form.

1 _____ the head office when you're in Japan? We could have a meeting then. (visit)

2 I'm sorry we've got nothing available now, but it's worth contacting us again in the run-up to Christmas as we _____ new staff then. (take on)

3 I _____ to the Cairo office later on today, so I _____ and chase up the projected sales figures. (go / try)

4 We _____ a new flagship store in Tokyo soon, so that _____ our profile quite a bit. (open / boost)

5 Thanks for the offer, but I _____ late tonight, so I _____ able to make the dinner. (arrive / not be)

CONVERSATION PRACTICE

15 Work in pairs. You are going to roleplay four business-related conversations. Together, choose four of the situations from Exercise 1 to roleplay. You should begin each conversation with one of these sentences.

16 Choose your roles for each of the four conversations. Then roleplay the conversations. Use as much language from these pages as possible.

🎥 30 To watch the video and do the activities, see the DVD-ROM.

---

6 Look at audio scripts 82 and 83 on page 211. Find two examples in each conversation where *would* is used to be polite.

7 Rewrite the sentences using *would* and the words in brackets so that they sound softer and more polite.

1 Is Friday good for you? (at all)

2 Can you make the 29th? (able / at all)

3 Do you have the address there? (happen)

4 Can you just spell the street name? (mind)

5 Do you want to come with us? (wondering / like)

6 Can you email me over the details? (possible)

7 Any day next week is good for me. (suit)

8 If it's OK with you, I don't want to. (mind / rather)

8 Work in small groups. Arrange a time and place for a meeting. Each student should reject at least two suggestions. Use polite expressions including *would*.

PRONUNCIATION Emails and websites

9 Work in pairs. How do you say the symbols in the box in an email or website address?

> 1 @ 2 / 3 _ 4 . 5 -

10 ▶ 84 Listen and check your ideas.

STIFF COMPETITION

SPEAKING

1 Work in groups. Discuss the questions.

- Do you know anyone who runs their own business? What kind of business is it? How long has it been going? Do you know how it's doing?
- Would you like to run your own business? If so, what kind of thing and why? If not, why not?

VOCABULARY Building up a business

2 Complete the story with these words.

broke even	expanded	merge	set up	turnover
competition	loss	raised	taken over	venture

Ten years ago, my brother and I decided we'd had enough of working for other people and that it was time to ¹_____ our own company. We had some savings and, with the help of the bank, we ²_____ the rest of the capital we needed. The business took a while to take off. For the first year, we ran at a ³_____ but before too long we ⁴_____ and eventually we started making a healthy profit . We ploughed all the money back into the business and ⁵_____ quite quickly. Next, we went into a joint venture with another company, which was very successful and eventually we decided to ⁶_____ and float the new company on the stock exchange. Our annual ⁷_____ rose to around $80 million and at that point we were ⁸_____ by a rival company. We sold our share of the company for around $50 million. We were happy to sell because we could see we were going to start facing stiff ⁹_____ from a lot of new companies entering the market, and now I've actually got an idea for a new ¹⁰_____ .

3 Work in pairs. Discuss the questions.

- What ways might you raise capital for a business? What's good or bad about each way?
- Do you know any companies that are expanding quickly at the moment? How? Are they making a healthy profit?
- Think of two examples of companies that merged or were taken over. How successful was it?
- What companies are facing stiff competition at the moment? From where? Do you think they'll survive? Why? / Why not?

READING

4 Work in pairs. Look at the ten characteristics of successful people as described on a business website. Give yourselves each a mark from 1–3 (1 = this doesn't sound like me, 3 = this is me!) and explain why. Which of you is likely to be most successful?

5 Compare your scores with another pair. Explain your decisions and discuss the questions.

- What do you think is meant by 'successful' here? Do you agree with this definition? Why? / Why not?
- What evidence is given for the characteristics? How reliable do you think the list is? Does it matter?
- Are there any other characteristics or habits that you think successful people have or do?

TOP TEN — CHARACTERISTICS OF SUCCESSFUL PEOPLE

1. They work incredibly hard, set high standards and put in the hours needed to meet them.
2. They were high achievers at school and are always keen to learn more through reading widely.
3. They're social animals. They have a wide circle of friends and acquaintances and are always networking.
4. They're perfectionists and always focused on improving their company's performance.
5. They display a healthy degree of impatience and tend not to perform well in bureaucracies.
6. They're creative and they're innovative.
7. They don't waste time moaning or looking for people to blame. They accept responsibility for their actions, learn and move on.
8. They're keen observers and often take notes, so they tend to notice changes and opportunities quicker than others.
9. They tend to maintain their cool and their sense of humour under pressure.
10. They have what's called a tolerance of ambiguity. They don't have to have complete knowledge or certainty before making a decision or seizing an opportunity.

6 Now read the profile of Jamila Abass, one of Africa's top new entrepreneurs. Answer the questions.

1. What is her business?
2. Which of the ten characteristics of successful people do you see evidence of in Jamila's story? In what ways?
3. Why do you think the author describes her as being 'remarkable'?

7 Complete the sentences with ONE word from some of the collocations in bold in the text.

1. I showed a _____ from an early age.
2. I don't have enough confidence to _____ on my own business venture.
3. Our country needs to _____ more investment from abroad.
4. We need to _____ the role of disabled people in the workforce.
5. The government has _____ widespread support for its current policies.
6. Local food stores often _____ the resources to compete with supermarkets.
7. I'm quite _____ about the claims businesses make about their products.
8. Promoting academic _____ is not the most important thing about a school.

8 Work in pairs. Discuss if you think each sentence above is true or not. Explain your ideas.

144

NEW AFRICAN ENTREPRENEURS

JAMILA ABASS, CEO OF M-FARM

Jamila Abass, the remarkable CEO of M-Farm, grew up in north-east Kenya, one of 19 children, before her **academic excellence** took her first to a top school near Nairobi and then a scholarship to study at a university in Morocco. She initially planned to become a doctor, but, having started school late, she was judged to be too old to study medicine and her place was given to a man. Instead, at 22 and having never touched a computer, she **embarked on a degree** in software engineering.

On graduation, she returned to Nairobi, where she initially worked as a systems developer and became involved in hacker and business forums, including *Akirachix*, a group to **promote women in** the technology **industry**.

Although Jamila's family is from a nomadic background, her parents had small businesses and she **showed a talent for** business from an early age. With her siblings, she put on puppet shows in English for her neighbours and sold refreshments. She also grew and sold coriander in the harsh desert land, something which also **gave her insight into** the struggles of farmers.

She says she had always believed that by working hard you get what you deserve. However, a few years ago, she came across a story about a farmer who was considering quitting because he was making a loss on the crops he produced. Investigating further, she found that this was a widespread problem: farmers who worked hard to **secure a good harvest** were often unaware of the prices available in different markets around Kenya and **lacked the resources** to find out. As a result, distributors and traders who came directly to the farms to buy the crops were able to lie about the current market rate and **force prices down**.

Shocked at the injustice of the situation, but also seeing an opportunity for a business start-up, Jamila and two friends came up with a mobile phone solution. A bit like eBay, the service uses SMS or a smart phone app to provide pricing information to farmers about prices in a variety of markets around east Kenya, which allows the farmers to **enter into a proper negotiation with** distributors. The M-Farm service also enables farmers to collaborate so they can accept larger and more profitable orders and M-Farm **charges a small commission** on all trades.

The three women put together their proposal as part of a competition, winning a £10,000 grant to **develop the venture**. They subsequently **attracted further investment** of £100,000 from *Techfortrade*, a UK charity. The business took time to get off the ground as farmers were **sceptical about the benefits**. However, through marketing and training, the company slowly took off and those using the service have seen their income double. The company is already reaching a limit in east Kenya in terms of the number of buyers that exist and they are now looking to expand throughout Kenya and other countries in East Africa as well as potentially working with supermarket chains in Europe.

SPEAKING

9 **Work in groups. Discuss the questions.**

- Do you think M-Farm is a good business? Why? / Why not?
- Have you heard of any other groups that are exploited like the farmers are? How?

- Who are the most famous entrepreneurs in your country? How did they achieve their success?
- Have you heard of any business people who have been involved in scandals? What happened?
- Have you heard of any business people who have used their wealth positively? How?

THE MOTHER OF INVENTION

SPEAKING

1 Read the short text below. Then discuss the questions.

Dragon's Den is a popular reality TV programme in the UK. Each week, prospective entrepreneurs who want to set up their own businesses present their plans to a panel of five successful business people. The aim is to persuade members of the panel to invest a certain amount of their own money in exchange for a stake in any new company the entrepreneurs are then able to start. After the entrepreneurs have pitched their ideas, they are then subjected to questioning from the panel, as a result of which each of the business people either offers to give the money the entrepreneur has asked for or declares that they are not interested. There is no negotiation on the amount that is invested, but the entrepreneurs and business people can negotiate what percentage of the new company the business people will end up owning.

1 Does a programme like *Dragon's Den* exist in your country? Is it a programme you would watch? Why? / Why not?

2 What qualities do you think the panel of successful business people are looking for when ideas are pitched to them?

3 Do you know of any other reality TV shows in the areas below? What do they involve? Do you like any of them? Why? / Why not?

- business
- living with a group of other people
- survival or dealing with difficult situations
- music or dance
- romance or meeting people

LISTENING

2 You are going to hear a radio report about a reality TV programme in Afghanistan. First, work in groups. Discuss what you know about Afghanistan.

3 ▶ 86 Listen and answer the questions.

1 What is the programme?

2 Why is it important there?

3 What is different about the programme compared to its British equivalent?

4 ▶ 86 Listen again. Decide if the statements are true (T) or false (F). Then compare your answers with a partner.

1 The show was originally devised in Britain.

2 The Afghan economy has not been sustaining itself.

3 Most people in Afghanistan work for the state.

4 More people need to learn more about how businesses work.

5 Faizulhaq Moshkani's main business is selling electricity.

6 His company is unique in Afghanistan.

7 There are two reality TV shows on Afghan TV.

8 In the past, women in Afghanistan weren't allowed to have paid jobs.

5 Work in groups. Discuss the questions.

- Did anything surprise you about the report? What?
- Do you agree that reality TV is 'overwhelmingly positive'? Why? / Why not?
- Which programmes on TV in your country are educational? Do you watch them? Why? / Why not?

6 ▶ **87** Work in pairs. Try to complete each collocation in bold from the broadcast in Exercise 3 with ONE word. Then listen to check your ideas.

1 *Dragon's Den* is soon to enter a new series, with prospective entrepreneurs trying to _____ **money**

2 millionaires who provide capital and business expertise **in** _____ **for** a stake in their companies

3 Afghanistan still _____ **depends on** foreign aid

4 **Small and medium-sized** _____ are easily the biggest employers

5 The problem at the moment is **a** _____ **of skills** such as financial planning

6 plans for expansion **come under** _____ from local experts

7 high _____ **costs** ultimately forced him to close down

8 the _____ **popular** singing contest *Afghan Star*

GRAMMAR

7 Read the Grammar box. Then look at the mistakes crossed out in the sentences below. Work in pairs. Discuss how you think each sentence should be corrected and why.

Expressing necessity and ability

Must doesn't have an infinitive or *-ing* form and is only used in the present tense. For other tenses, we use forms of *have to* to express necessity. We also use *force somebody to do something* and *make somebody do something* when something or someone creates an obligation.

Can doesn't have an infinitive or *-ing* form and is only used in the present tense. For other tenses, we use forms of *be able to* to express ability. We also use *enable somebody to do something, allow somebody to do something* and *let somebody do something* when something or someone makes another thing possible.

1 The device allows you to share files without you ~~must~~ rely on a computer.

2 If the loan is approved, it will ~~able us~~ buy more stock and take advantage of the interest we've generated.

3 The negative feedback that we got ~~made~~ us to look at the design again.

4 This deal means I'll finally ~~can~~ give up my day job and focus entirely on the business.

5 Over the last few years, we ~~can~~ keep ahead of our competitors by developing new products.

6 We were forced to cut costs ~~for to able us~~ compete.

7 Thanks to all the effort everyone put in, in the end we ~~can~~ fulfil all our orders before Christmas. Well done!

8 If we'd done more market research before launching the first model, we would not have ~~must~~ redesign it so soon. It would've ~~forced~~ us think about our product a bit more.

9 It's a risk more investors are going to ~~must~~ take.

10 We'll soon ~~can~~ generate all our own electricity, which will ~~can~~ us cut costs massively.

G Check your ideas on page 183 and do Exercise 1.

8 Work in pairs. Tell each other about things:

- you haven't been able to do recently.
- you're glad you won't have to do in the future.
- you used to be able to do, but can't anymore.
- everyone should have to do.
- you'd like to not have to do.
- you'd love to be able to do.
- a little more money would enable you to do
- a lot more money would allow you to do.
- getting a particular qualification would enable you to do.
- which you have to force yourself to do.

VOCABULARY Business collocations

9 Decide which of these words completes each group of collocations.

area	company	order	sales
business	market	product	stock

1 the target ~ / exploit a gap in the ~ / break into the American ~ / it's a niche ~ / do a lot of ~ research

2 be in ~ / be out of ~ / check ~ levels / buy new ~ / sell off old ~ cheap

3 fulfil ~s / be flooded with ~s / keep up with new ~s / chase up an ~ / receive a big ~

4 boost ~ / ~ have shot up / ~ have plunged / add to our ~ team / improve ~ and marketing

5 develop a ~ line / launch the ~ / a revolutionary new ~ / the ~ is aimed at teenagers / market the ~

6 branch out into other ~s / it's a specialist ~ / it's a growth ~ / it's an ~ of concern / the ~ manager

7 expand the ~ / build up the ~ / plough money back into the ~ / put them out of ~ / it's a risky ~

8 set up the ~ / head of the ~ / take over the ~ / float the ~ on the stock exchange / have a controlling stake in the ~

10 Underline any collocations in Exercise 9 that are new for you. Then compare what you have underlined with a partner and discuss what you think the collocations mean.

SPEAKING

11 Work in groups of four. Form two pairs: Pair A and Pair B.

Pair A: look at the list of products and services in File 6 on page 185.

Pair B: look at the list of products and services in File 12 on page 189.

12 You are going to try and persuade the other pair to invest in your products. With your partner, spend five minutes discussing what you are going to say and what language from these pages you could use.

13 Take turns for each pair to pitch one of their products or services to the other pair. See how many deals you can make.

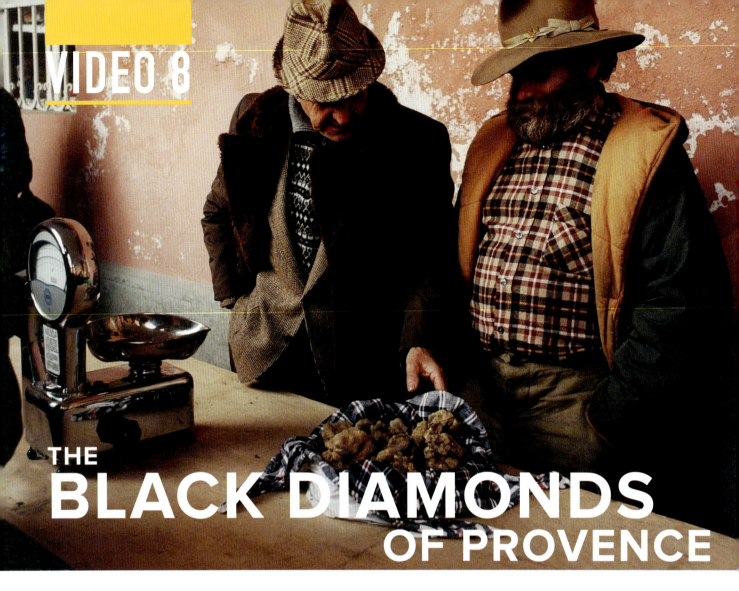

VIDEO 8

THE BLACK DIAMONDS OF PROVENCE

1 Work in pairs. Discuss what you think is happening in the photo.

2 📹 **31** Watch the first half of the video. Complete the sentences.

1 Each year the church has a service to give thanks and pray for a good _____ .

2 Truffles are sometimes called _____ .

3 The truffle market in Richerenche trades _____ worth of truffles a day.

4 When most people think of Provence, they imagine summer holidays, lazy afternoons and _____ .

5 Farmers often work as truffle _____ .

6 Brokers generally trade discreetly. Doing cash deals helps them to avoid paying _____ .

7 Gourmet food companies mainly export truffles to the US and _____ .

8 A century ago, brokers were selling about _____ tonnes a year. The supply has decreased a lot since then.

3 Work in pairs. Discuss the questions. Then watch the next part of the video.

1 Where do you think the truffles come from?

2 How do you think the hunters get them?

3 Why do you think the supply is declining?

4 📹 **31** Watch. Find the answers to Exercise 3.

5 Work in pairs. Discuss the questions.

- Have you ever tried truffles? Do you like them or are they overrated?

- What are the most expensive foods in your country or region? Why are they expensive? What do you think of them?

- What are the most important markets in your country? Where are they based? Who controls them?

- What do you think of black market trading and tax avoidance?

- Have you ever hunted or gathered your own food? What happened?

UNDERSTANDING FAST SPEECH

6 Look at this extract from the video. To help you, groups of words are marked with / and stressed sounds are in CAPITALS. Pauses are marked //. Practise saying the sentence.

HALF of FRAnce's / BLACK TRUffles / are tranSPORted / through the TOWN'S MARket // up to ONE HUNdred ANd EIGHty THOUsand USDOllars' WORTH / a DAY // they're ALL / LOOking for TRUffles // and not just ANY ONE will DO / EIther.

7 📹 **32** Listen to how the narrator said this sentence. Now you have a go! Practise saying the extract again fast.

REVIEW 8

GRAMMAR

1 Complete the text with one word in each space.

The show has sometimes been accused [1] _____ showing off and suggesting dishes that take too long to prepare, and if that's ever been the case, then it's obviously something we'd be keen to apologise [2] _____ . [3] _____ , the recipe we [4] _____ be showing you today is one of the easiest things you'll ever cook. It's a stir-fry and to be honest, the most important thing is the equipment. Make sure you have a good wok – a good Chinese frying pan. Personally, I can't imagine ever [5] _____ anything but a Fissler. They're not cheap, but they're the kind of thing that can [6] _____ even a beginner look good. They [7] _____ you cook a huge range of Chinese food and are super-easy to clean and store – [8] _____ , as I said, they can be rather expensive.

2 Complete the second sentence so that it has a similar meaning to the first sentence. Use the word given. Do not change the word given. You must use between two and five words, including the word given.

1 To ensure the beans are soft enough to cook with, soak them overnight.

Make sure you soak the beans overnight, _____ too hard. **OTHERWISE**

2 There was widespread opposition, but they still went ahead and built the factory.

The factory was built _____ . **DESPITE**

3 To avoid further strikes, we would urge the management to increase its offer.

_____ its offer, there will be further strikes. **UNLESS**

4 The company has been accused of putting profit above people.

The company has been _____ putting people first. **CRITICISED**

5 Don't call between nine and ten, OK? My favourite TV show is on then.

Don't call between nine and ten as _____ my favourite TV show then. **BE**

6 They made me do it even though I'd made it clear I didn't want to.

I _____ it even though I'd made it clear I didn't want to. **FORCED**

7 The terrible weather has prevented us from visiting you over recent weeks.

We _____ you recently because of the awful weather. **ABLE**

3 Choose the correct word or form.

1 I'm happy to lend it to you, *in case / provided / once* you can pay me back this week.

2 Leave to cook *during / once / for* an hour or so.

3 We'll be sending it out today so it *must / can / should* be with you tomorrow.

4 We'll soon *can / be able to / let / enabled to* attract further foreign investment.

5 He strongly denies *doing / to do / about doing* anything wrong.

6 In the end, he confessed *to steal / stealing / to stealing* the money.

4 ▶ 88 Listen. Write the six sentences you hear.

VOCABULARY

5 Match the verbs (1–8) with the collocates (a–h).

1	pass on	a	at a loss
2	chase up	b	judgement
3	pass	c	my thanks to your colleagues
4	raise	d	capital
5	run	e	an overdue payment
6	cut	f	with the police
7	clash	g	them in water overnight
8	soak	h	farming subsidies

6 Complete the sentences. Use the word in brackets to form a word that fits in the space.

1 He was _____ from driving for two years after being caught drink-driving. (qualify)

2 The whole situation has been _____ by the government. It was a disaster. (manage)

3 The school has a reputation for academic _____ . (excellent)

4 I should issue a quick _____ alert in case you've not seen the final episode: it all ends in tears! (spoil)

5 The UK is now an incredibly _____ society. People from all over the world live there. (culture)

6 Within two years, the company had _____ its original premises. (grow)

7 Decide if these words are connected to cooking or business – and in what way.

a commission	a float	a mix-up	plunge	squeeze
crush	hygiene	a niche	sprinkle	subtle

8 Complete the story with one word in each space. The first letters are given.

I run a small firm that designs and markets apps [1]a_____ at helping normal people cook like professionals. To begin with it was really hard trying to raise enough capital to get a new [2]ve_____ off the ground. It took a couple of years before I finally managed to [3]b_____ even, and even after I started making a profit, I still tried to [4]p_____ everything back into the business. The app market is a hard one to succeed in, and the firm lacks the [5]re_____ to compete with the biggest players. Despite that, though, we're doing far better than many so-[6]c_____ experts predicted we ever would. Basically, we've managed to [7]ex_____ a gap in the market and our annual [8]t_____ is now high enough for me to not just live on, but also to employ five other people.

1 WRITING Giving advice

SPEAKING

1 Work in groups. Discuss the questions.

- What do you think of your country's capital city?
- What would you recommend seeing there? Why?
- Are there any things you'd tell people to avoid? Why?
- Have you visited any other capital cities? When? Why? What were they like?

GRAMMAR

Advice and recommendations

There are lots of ways to give advice. Look at the different ways of answering the question: *What would you recommend seeing there?*

I'd go to Montmartre *(if I were you)*.

You should take *a boat trip down the river.*

You're best staying *in an area called Vosstaniya.*

You could take *a tour round the mountains (if you wanted).*

You're better off taking *the train. (= it's preferable)*

We often use the structures above with an *if*-clause + present tense – or another expression that refers to a general topic.

If you want to relax, you should take *a boat trip down the river.*

In terms of accommodation, you're best staying *in an area called Vosstaniya.*

2 Complete these sentences with advice for someone who is going to visit the area you are in now. Use a variety of structures.

1 If you've never been here before, _____ .

2 If you're into art or history, _____ .

3 If you like shopping, _____ .

4 If you want to go swimming, _____ .

5 If you want to escape the tourists, _____ .

6 As far as nightlife is concerned, _____ .

7 When it comes to getting round the city, _____ .

8 In terms of places to stay, _____ .

3 Compare your sentences with a partner. Do you agree with each other's advice?

WRITING

4 A friend of a friend has written to Harriet for advice about where to stay and what to do in London. Read Harriet's reply below and decide which of the pieces of advice you'd follow and which you'd ignore. Explain your decisions to a partner.

To	cceline@shotmail.fr
Subject	Re: London

Hi Celine,

Anna mentioned you might write. I'll actually be away, so you could use my flat, if you wanted. You'd be doing me a favour, as you could feed my cats. It IS in the suburbs, though – quite a long way from the city centre. As far as places to see are concerned, the Tower of London is well worth visiting, although it is a bit pricey. All the museums are free, though. If you want to escape the crowds, I'd recommend Hampstead Heath. It's a beautiful park and you get stunning views across London on a clear day. You could even swim in the ponds if you're brave enough. While you're here, the Thames Festival will be on. It's mainly held on the South Bank. There are workshops, live music, firework displays, parades – all sorts of things. Check out the Thames festival website. Apart from the festival, there's a huge choice of entertainment. When it comes to nightlife, I'd buy *Time Off* magazine, if I were you. Otherwise, you'll miss out on all London has to offer. Generally, I'd steer clear of the clubs in Leicester Square as they can be a bit of a tourist trap. You're better off going to Old Street – I think it's a bit trendier. In terms of eating out, Brick Lane's good for curry. If you want some traditional fish and chips, try here: http://www.timeoff.com/london/restaurants/reviews/9382.html. It's a bit in the middle of nowhere, but it's great. Other than that, lots of pubs do decent food. Anyway, if there's anything else you need, let me know.

Harriet

The email is written as one long text. When we write, it helps the reader if we divide the text into paragraphs that deal with different subjects. In letters and emails, a paragraph may sometimes be only one sentence. We mark a separate paragraph by leaving a line space.

5 Work in pairs. Divide the email into six paragraphs. Mark the beginning and end of each paragraph with /. Underline expressions that start the paragraphs and/or show a new subject is being introduced.

VOCABULARY Describing places

6 **Work in pairs. Discuss what problems or what good things there might be in the following:**

- a tourist trap
- a rough area
- a posh area
- a lively area
- the suburbs
- a high-rise building
- a street market
- an up-and-coming area

KEY WORDS FOR WRITING

otherwise, other than, apart from

We use *otherwise* to show that something bad will occur if you don't do the thing you just mentioned.

I'd buy Time Off magazine if I were you. **Otherwise**, *you'll miss out on some of the best things London has to offer.*

You can also use *otherwise* or *other than* / *apart from that* to mean 'in addition (to that)', not including things you just mentioned.

... it's great. **Other than that** / **Apart from that** / **Otherwise**, *lots of pubs do decent food.*

You can use *apart from* and *other than* to join two parts of a sentence, but you can't use *otherwise*.

Apart from / **Other than** / **~~Otherwise~~** *the festival, there's a huge choice in entertainment.*

7 **Decide if one or both options are correct. Cross out the incorrect ones.**

1 There's quite a lot of street crime, so don't leave anything valuable on café tables. *Otherwise,* / *Apart from that*, it might get stolen.

2 There's a small museum in the town, but *apart* / *other* from that, there's nothing worth seeing.

3 *Otherwise* / *Other than* the main sights, I can't really suggest anything.

4 There are several hotels in town which aren't too expensive. *Otherwise* / *Apart from*, there's a nice campsite on the outskirts, if you have a tent.

5 *Apart from* / *Other than* walking, you're best taking taxis as they're not much more expensive than buses.

6 I'd put on plenty of sun cream even if you're not going to sunbathe. *Otherwise,* / *Other than that*, you'll get sunburnt.

7 The Chinese restaurant in Havana Road is OK. *Otherwise* / *Other than that*, there are a couple of decent pizzerias.

PRACTICE

8 **Work in pairs or groups. Each pair or group should choose a different city or area in their country that they know fairly well. Imagine someone has written to you to ask where to stay, what to do there, etc. Make a list of all the points you might make.**

9 **Write your email. Make sure you divide the email into paragraphs as you did in Exercise 5. Use some of the expressions to introduce new subjects and the advice structures.**

2 WRITING Letters of complaint

SPEAKING

1 Work in groups. Discuss the questions.
- What things have you bought over the internet?
- Have you ever had any problems with online transactions? What happened? Did you sort it out?
- Have you ever rung a customer helpline? What was the service like?

WRITING

2 Read the letter of complaint below – without filling in the gaps. Answer the questions from Exercise 1 for the writer of the letter.

Dear Sir / Madam,

¹_____ my telephone conversation today (15th September), I am writing to complain about the digital camera I bought from your website on 18th July this year and the service I have received.

When I ordered the camera, I was informed that delivery would take two weeks, but in ²_____ , it took over a month, arriving too late for me to take it on holiday. I sent a number of emails prior to my holiday, but they were never answered.

When I finally received the camera, it was not exactly ³_____ advertised. According ⁴_____ your website, it supposedly had 100GB of memory. However, it stated on the packaging that this was only with a memory card, sold separately. I rang to complain, but I ⁵_____ told that I should have looked more carefully and was then directed to details on the website.

The main advert is misleading, especially as customers have to follow three different links to find the full information on a product. To make ⁶_____ worse, when I called your helpline, it took me half an hour to get through and when I ⁷_____ , the three-minute conversation cost me five pounds and I was told I would still have to write if I wanted to take the matter ⁸_____ .

As compensation for the late delivery and the lack of clarity on the website ⁹_____ the camera's specifications, I feel that I should be sent the missing memory card free of ¹⁰_____ .

Yours faithfully,

Jamila Benitez

3 Complete the letter in Exercise 2 with these words.

as	did	following	matters	to
charge	fact	further	regarding	was

4 Underline any phrases that you could use in any letter where you are writing to complain.

5 Work in pairs. Discuss the questions.
- Do you think the complaint is fair?
- Do you think the company will agree to the compensation? Why? / Why not?

KEY WORDS FOR WRITING

according to

We can show sources of information using *according to*.

According to *your website, it supposedly had 100GB of memory.*

In letters of complaint, we often contrast this with the reality of the situation using *however* or *but*.

However, *it was stated on the packaging that this was only with a memory card, which was sold separately.*

6 Complete 1–6 with *according to* plus a noun from the box.

consumer laws	my brother	the flyer
the forecast	the opposition	your brochure

1 It's going to brighten up by the weekend, _____ , so we're still planning to go for a picnic.

2 _____ , the government is doing everything wrong, but they're not offering any solutions either.

3 _____ this guy gave me, there's a special night at a club in town tonight. Entrance is free before ten.

4 _____ , the hotel is in easy reach of the beach.

5 I did warn him that it wasn't a good place to go, but then _____ , I know nothing!

6 _____ , the company cannot legally charge your credit card until they have sent out the goods.

7 Complete the sentences with your own ideas.

1 According to my dad, _____ .

2 According to the government, _____ .

3 According to your website, you provide a fast, efficient service. However, _____ .

4 According to your publicity, your staff are highly professional, but in reality _____ .

GRAMMAR

8 Look back at the letter and find the ways these written and spoken comments were reported.

1 Your delivery will take two weeks.

2 You should have looked more carefully. The information is on the website.

3 If you want to take the matter further, I'm afraid you'll have to put it in writing.

Passives and reporting

In letters of complaint, we often use verbs in the passive form, because we don't know the person who made the comment – or we don't see them as really responsible for the problem we are complaining about.

9 Use the correct passive form of the verbs in bold to write second sentences that report the first sentences. You will need to add other words.

1 FareAir is sorry to announce that flight 203 has been delayed for five hours.
We were informed that the flight had been delayed by five hours only minutes before we were due to board. **inform**

2 If you're not satisfied, we'll give you your money back.
I _____ full refund if I was not satisfied. **promise**

3 Postage and packaging are included.
It _____ your website that postage and packaging were included in the cost. **state**

4 Speak to the manager about it.
My husband _____ speak to the manager. **tell**

5 We can only replace it. We can't give you a refund.
I _____ replacement. They wouldn't refund the money. **offer**

6 Please could you arrive at the station 30 minutes before departure?
Everyone _____ at the station 30 minutes before departure. **ask**

7 The advert said the price was all-inclusive.
It _____ being all-inclusive. **advertise**

PRACTICE

10 Look at the advert below. Work in pairs. Make a list of things that could go wrong. Then compare your ideas in groups of four. Who had the longest list? Who has the funniest problem?

11 Choose two or three of the problems from your list and write a letter of complaint about them. Make sure you:

- make it clear what you want the company to do – offer compensation, apologise, etc.
- write in paragraphs.
- include as much language from these pages as you can.

GIFTS MAPPED OUT

Looking for a gift which will provide memories and entertainment? Why not get a personalised jigsaw puzzle based on a special place? Use the location finder on our website and we'll create a puzzle of the map or photo of the area. Alternatively, you can send us a digital photo of whatever you like. Puzzles come in three sizes – 150, 250 or 500 pieces – and are packaged in a durable presentation tin.

We also have a range of gift cards, which you can add your own messages to. Orders normally take two weeks. Guaranteed delivery for Christmas on orders received before December 15th.

3 WRITING A leaflet or poster

SPEAKING

1 **Work in groups. Discuss the questions.**

- Have you ever belonged to any organisations such as a club or society?
- What's good about being in a club? Are there any disadvantages?
- What do you think people do when they meet in these organisations? Explain why you would – or wouldn't – join each one.

a drama club	a history society
an athletics club	a debating society
a cycling club	Boy Scouts / Girl Guides
a reading club	a green activist group
a gastronomic club	a political party

WRITING A leaflet or poster

2 **Read the leaflet below that aims to persuade people to join a club. Put the paragraphs (a–f) in the correct order according to the following:**

1 Grab people's attention and say the name of club.

2 Explain more about the sport and club and what it does.

3 Persuade a wider group of people – if they have doubts.

4 Add a further reason.

5 Factual information about where, when, etc.

6 Final slogan or encouragement.

WANTED! TOUCH RUGBY PLAYERS

a Our club runs friendly games, training sessions and league matches three nights a week (Mon, Wed and Fri) from 7 till 9 at the sports centre fields. Sessions cost £2.

b Most of our teams are mixed, so it's not just for men. Nor do you have to be especially athletic or co-ordinated, because there are teams for all levels. There are also lots of substitutions during the game, so if you're out of breath, you can always rest and chat to the others on the bench.

c Come along! You'll find a warm welcome and enjoy a fantastic game.

d Feeling out of shape? Bored of working out in the gym? Looking for a sport with a great social vibe? Look no further: TOUCH RUGBY is the thing for you.

e And once you've learned how to play, it's something you can play whenever or wherever you like because it needs no special equipment other than a ball.

f Touch rugby is rugby, but with all the tackling, kicking and rough stuff taken out. You have to pass the ball backwards to your teammates as you run and try to put the ball down behind the opposing team's goal line. The defenders stop you by lightly touching your body, at which point you stop and roll the ball to another player. After every six touches, the ball is given to the opposing team. It's a fantastically easy sport and remember, all it involves is a light touch, so there's no risk of injury. It's all about running, passing and having great fun!

3 Work in pairs. Discuss the questions.

- Would you be interested in joining?
  Why? / Why not?
- Who do you know that might be interested?

VOCABULARY

4 Match 1–4 with a–d and then 5–8 with e–h.

1	an incredibly wide / a huge	a	enjoyable
2	a passionate / huge	b	range of abilities
3	hugely / tremendously	c	organised
4	superbly / really well	d	interest
5	tremendous / great	e	cheap
6	a really warm / enthusiastic	f	welcome
7	absolutely / endlessly	g	fun
8	ridiculously / amazingly	h	fascinating

5 Give six opinions using words from Exercise 4.

I think cycling is tremendously enjoyable.

The festival in my town is superbly organised.

KEY WORDS FOR WRITING

6 Complete the sentences by adding the correct words ending in *-ever*.

1 You can drop into our offices _____ you like.

2 _____ good you are, you'll find a group to suit you.

3 We'll get you into shape, _____ your fitness level.

4 _____ you live, you'll find a branch near you.

5 Why not bring a friend? _____ joins before the end of August will receive free membership for six months.

6 You can pay _____ you like, with the exception of American Instant credit cards.

7 _____ preconceptions you have about chess players, they're probably wrong!

8 _____ you are, and _____ your age, this is the sport for you.

GRAMMAR

7 Read the explanation box and decide what words have been left out in each of these examples in bold.

8 Cross out as many words as you can in the sentences without changing the meaning or making things unclear.

1 Are you planning to work abroad? This is your chance!

2 Do you worry about speaking in public? Do you get nervous in front of an audience or do you forget your words? Our course could help.

3 Have you never been to a gym before? We'll show you how the gym machines work and we'll give you support when you're training.

4 We are having a really great time. We wish you were here and we hope everything is fine with you. Karen.

5 Sara rang. She said she can't come this evening, but she will be at the meeting tomorrow.

6 I had to go out and I won't be back till 8. There's some dinner in the oven. I love you.

9 Work in pairs. Compare what you deleted. Is the subject and tense of each verb still clear?

PRACTICE

10 Work in pairs. Decide on a sport, activity or other kind of organisation you want people to join. Then discuss what you would put in each of the paragraphs, using the ideas from the leaflet in Exercise 2.

11 Write the leaflet or poster. Add a design or illustration if you like.

4 WRITING Stories

VOCABULARY Describing disasters

1 Read the sentences and decide what kind of natural disaster each one is describing.

1 The ground floor was completely under water and all our stuff was **ruined**. We were **stranded** on the roof for hours until they **rescued** us.

2 It **spread** very rapidly. Luckily, they managed to **evacuate** our town shortly before the whole place **went up in flames**.

3 It was **triggered** by a massive underwater earthquake. By the time they hit the coast, the **waves** were 30 feet high. All the villages near the beach were completely **destroyed**.

4 There'd been increasingly strong **tremors** for weeks and then it erupted one evening. All the villagers had to **flee** the area to escape the streams of **lava**.

5 It destroyed everything in its **path**. Our neighbour's house was completely **flattened**. We were incredibly lucky that we only had our roof **blown off**.

2 Use the extra information in sentences 1–5 above to guess the meanings of the words in **bold**. Translate the sentences into your language.

3 Cover Exercise 1. See how much of each description you can remember. Use the words below to help you.

1 water – ruined – stranded – rescued
2 spread – evacuate – before – flames
3 triggered – hit – waves – destroyed
4 tremors – erupted – flee – lava
5 path – flattened – lucky – blown off

4 Compare what you remember with a partner. Then look back at Exercise 1 and check your ideas.

WRITING A travel blog story

5 Read the short story from a travel blog about a natural disaster. Answer these questions.

1 Where was the writer when the disaster struck?
2 What happened?
3 How did he feel?
4 How did the locals react? What explanation did the writer give?

6 Complete the gaps in the story using these words.

active	breeze	delayed	minor
blocked	cleared	journey	slopes

BLOG   ABOUT ME   PHOTOS   CONTACT

AN EXPLOSIVE TRIP!

So we finally made it to Bali! As I write, I am sitting on a hotel balcony overlooking the beach, enjoying the early evening ¹_____ . Bet you wish you were here, eh?

The ²_____ across Java was fairly eventful – and took a few days longer than we were expecting. Believe it or not, what ³_____ things was getting caught up in a volcanic eruption!

One of the things we'd been really looking forward to doing was climbing Mount Semeru, the highest mountain on the island. It's an ⁴_____ volcano, so to be on the safe side, we found a local guide, Kencur, who knows the mountain really well. At two in the morning, we set off up the ⁵_____ in total darkness.

The first indication that something was up was a series of tremors, like a ⁶_____ earthquake. This was followed by a loud rumbling noise, like thunder, that came up from the ground as we were walking. At this point, Kencur stopped and suggested we return to our hostel. Shortly afterwards, the volcano erupted, leaving the main road out of town completely ⁷_____ by rocks and lava. We were stranded in our hostel until the roads were ⁸_____ – three days later! It was pretty scary, unlike anything I'd ever experienced before, but what really struck me was how relaxed about everything all the locals were. I guess they'd seen it all before.

7 Work in groups. Discuss the questions.

- Have you heard about any volcanic eruptions in the news over the last year?
- Have you heard about other natural disasters? Where? When? What happened?

KEY WORDS FOR WRITING

like, unlike

We often use *like* to show one thing is similar to another.

The first indication that something was up was **a series of tremors, like a minor earthquake**. *This was followed by* **a loud rumbling noise, like thunder**.

To show one thing is different to another, we use *unlike*.

It was pretty scary, **unlike anything I'd ever experienced before**.

8 Match the two parts of the sentences.

1 Siberia was a really unique place,
2 The festival was a great success,
3 I could hear trees creaking and breaking
4 Thankfully, this volcano is dormant,
5 The hailstones smashed against our windscreen
6 The mist settled over the village
7 It's unbearably humid here,
8 The rain poured down for days,

a like matchsticks as the winds came through.
b unlike anywhere I'd ever been before.
c unlike last year, when it rained non-stop.
d like an endless waterfall from the skies!
e unlike back home, where it's a drier heat.
f like a blanket of cloud.
g unlike most others in the area, which are active.
h like bullets from a machine gun!

9 Work in pairs. Complete the sentences. Then compare your ideas with another pair. Who has the funniest, the most original or the most interesting ideas?

1 Suddenly, there was a huge bang, like
_____ .

2 It was so cold that my hands were like
_____ .

3 He had a face like _____ and a voice
like _____ .

4 _____ was unlike anything I'd ever
seen before.

5 _____ was unlike anything I'd ever
heard before.

6 _____ was unlike anything I'd
tasted before.

10 Work in groups. Make comparisons between your country and other countries using *like* and *unlike*.

PRACTICE

11 Choose one of the topics below and write a story of around 250 words about it.

- a natural disaster
- extreme weather
- a crime

5 WRITING Personal statements

SPEAKING

1 Work in pairs. Discuss the questions.

- Have you ever written a personal statement? When? What for? What kind of things did you put in it? Were you pleased with it?
- How important is it to be honest when writing personal statements?
- Do you think it's OK to be funny when writing personal statements? Why? / Why not?

WRITING

2 Niran is applying to do an MBA (a Master's Degree in Business Administration) at the University of Sydney in Australia. Look at the notes he made before writing his personal statement. Then discuss the questions in pairs.

> Experience
>
> Reasons for doing course
>
> Personal qualities
>
> Education and qualifications

- What would you expect to read in each section?
- What other areas could he include?
- What do you think is the best order to put all this information in?

3 Complete Niran's personal statement below with these words.

active interest	solid grounding
competitive edge	transferable skills
invaluable insight	valuable contribution

I am applying for this course because I would like to broaden my understanding of the world of business and apply the theoretical and practical knowledge I have acquired to date. Furthermore, I feel an MBA will give me a ¹ _____ in the job market.

As a teenager, I often accompanied my uncle to his office, where I gained an ² _____ into how businesses are run. It was at this point that I decided to pursue a career in this field. My subsequent degree in Business Studies and Accountancy has given me a ³ _____ in core business skills.

I am currently doing a part-time English course in order to improve my language skills. In addition to this, I have almost completed an online computing diploma.

At present, I'm doing an internship for a media company. This experience has given me the opportunity to put into practice much of what I learned on my degree course. Despite having been at the company for only a short period of time, I still believe I have acquired a set of ⁴ _____ that I can apply to any business environment.

I am a positive, hard-working person who enjoys challenges. I believe I could make a ⁵ _____ to the course because I am up-to-date with what is happening in the business world and also take an ⁶ _____ in current affairs.

SPEAKING

4 Work in groups. Discuss the questions.

- What do you think is good about Niran's personal statement?
- Is there anything you would change or add? Why?
- Look at the list of transferable skills below. Which do you think you have? Give examples of when / how you have used them.
- Are there any of these skills you'd like to develop further?

computer skills	problem-solving skills
people skills	organisational skills
language skills	time-management skills
leadership skills	negotiating skills

VOCABULARY

Describing yourself

In the personal statement, Niran gives a description of his character. Note that he doesn't just use an adjective. He also adds a comment to exemplify or clarify the description.

I am a positive, hard-working person who enjoys challenges.

5 Match the descriptions 1–5 with the follow-up comments a–e.

1 I'm a very ambitious person
2 I am very passionate about my studies
3 I am a highly sociable kind of person
4 I'm very punctual
5 I can be very demanding

a and am determined to be a success in my field.
b and have a wide circle of friends.
c as I expect the best of people around me.
d and really love the subject.
e as I am always on time and never miss a deadline.

6 Match 6–10 with f–j.

6 I am a very positive person
7 I am a very conscientious worker
8 I am quite a creative person
9 I am quite a well-rounded person
10 I can be quite a stubborn person

f who takes pride in doing things well.
g and excel at finding innovative solutions to problems.
h who finds it hard to see other people's points of view.
i and have a wide range of interests.
j who always tries to look on the bright side.

7 Choose the five adjectives from Exercises 5 and 6 that you think best describe you. Explain your choices to a partner. Do they agree with your description of yourself?

KEY WORDS FOR WRITING

Adding information

There are several different linking words you can use to add information. Some link two sentences together and are more commonly used after full stops; others are more often used to link clauses within a sentence.

8 Look at the pairs of linking words in italics. For each pair, decide if both choices are possible or if only one is. Cross out any incorrect linking words.

1 I believe I am well qualified for the course. *In addition*, / *As well*, I have already gained considerable work experience in the field.

2 I speak fluent English and German. *Additionally*, / *In addition*, I speak very good French and basic Spanish.

3 I have read widely in the literature of the field and have relevant practical experience *too* / *as well*.

4 I am very keen on sport. I am a keen cyclist and play tennis regularly. *What's more*, / *In addition to*, I have been studying karate for the last six years.

5 *In addition to* / *As well as* being determined and ambitious, I am *also* / *furthermore* highly organised.

6 I spent a year studying Graphic Design in Canada. *Additionally*, / *In addition to this*, I have taught myself how to use specialist software such as InDesign and I *also* / *as well* have excellent web design skills.

9 Compare your ideas with a partner.

PRACTICE

10 Decide on a course of study or job you would like to apply for. You are going to write your own personal statement of around 250 words. You will need to give information about:

- your past and present education
- your work experience
- your skills and abilities

11 Plan the content of each of your paragraphs. Use the model statement on page 158 to help you.

12 Write the statement.

6 WRITING Reports

WRITING

1 Read the introduction to a report about public transport and car use and then the list of its main findings. Discuss the questions in pairs.

- What do you think the statistics would be if the report was about your city or area?
- Considering the aim of the council, which of the statistics do you think is good news and which is bad? Why?
- What action would you recommend to the council?

2 Read the summary of the findings and complete the text with these words.

examples	interviewed	mentioned	respondents
factor	long	minority	vast
favourably	majority	rated	widely

INTRODUCTION

The survey that led to this report was conducted with people in the Northsea area. It aimed to find out how people travelled and the reasons for their choices, with a view to the council developing policies to discourage car use.

Main findings:

- 75% use the car as their main form of transport.
- In the previous month, four out of five people had used some alternative – train, bus, bike, motorbike or (electric) taxi.
- 90% said they would be willing to use alternative transport to the car.
- 83% of journeys by public transport were by bus.
- Only one tenth of those surveyed felt public transport provision was good or very good.
- The main reasons cited for not using public transport were cost and inconvenience.

SUMMARY OF FINDINGS

While the findings of the survey showed that cars remain the main form of transport, there was some hope in the fact that there were high numbers of people willing to change. Only a small [1] _____ felt they would continue to use their car, no matter what.

Most [2] _____ had used buses, and the [3] _____ said they would use them more often if they were cheaper and more convenient. [4] _____ of inconvenience that were [5] _____ on numerous occasions were the lack of timetable information and buses running infrequently and failing to connect with other routes.

Even though bus travel actually compares [6] _____ to car travel, cost-wise, the perception of the [7] _____ majority of people [8] _____ was that it was more expensive. Interestingly, those using the train [9] _____ it highly, **despite** it being more expensive than the bus. This suggests comfort is also a [10] _____ .

RECOMMENDATIONS

If the council is to encourage less car use, it clearly needs to develop bus services. It should improve timetabling and make information more [11] _____ available, for example through a website. In the short term, a campaign to raise awareness of the relative costs of buses and cars – as well as increasing parking fees in the centre – could help. **However**, to make a real difference, the council needs to invest in new buses in the [12] _____ term to increase frequency and comfort.

3 Work in pairs. Discuss the questions.

- What extra information is included in the report outside the main findings of the survey?
- Do you think the summary is a fair summary of the main findings? Why? / Why not?
- Do you agree with the recommendations?

GRAMMAR

be to

In the report, you read:

*If the council **is to** encourage less car use, it clearly needs to develop bus services.*

be to + infinitive (without *to*) is often used with *if*-clauses to show a desired future result. Negatives are formed as *is not to* or *isn't to*. The main clause shows what must be done first, using *need / must / have to*, etc.

*We **must do something now if the situation is not to deteriorate** further.*

4 Write sentences with *if, be to* + infinitive (without *to*) and *need*, etc., using these ideas.

1 the government / win the next election / change their policies now.
2 we / improve our marketing / boost sales.
3 we / reduce crime / increase the number of police.
4 the company / reduce its debts / not go bankrupt.
5 the council / build more cycle lanes / encourage more people to cycle to work.
6 discourage waste / the government / introduce a tax on the amount of rubbish people throw away.

KEY WORDS FOR WRITING

while, despite, however, even though

Despite this can be used instead of *however*, and *despite the fact that* can be followed by a clause.

***Despite the fact that** I told him not to, he took the car.*

However can also come in the middle of a sentence.

*Cars are expensive to run. There are, **however**, ways to save.*

5 Look at the words in bold in the report on page 160. Then discuss the questions in pairs.

1 Which word contrasts an idea with an idea in the previous sentence?
2 Which three words help to link two parts of a sentence?
3 Which two words could be swapped round?
4 Which word is followed by a noun / *-ing* form?
5 Where are the commas in the sentences with words in bold?

6 Choose the correct words. One or two are correct in each sentence. Cross out any incorrect words.

1 *While / Despite / Even though* student numbers fell this year, the school is confident it can grow in the future.
2 Most students were satisfied with their classes, *even though / despite / however* there was a lot of noise from ongoing repair work.
3 The school doesn't have enough resources. *However / While / Despite this*, the teachers do an excellent job.
4 Profits were down last year, *despite / however / even though* having more students.

7 Rewrite the sentences using the words in bold so that your sentences mean the same.

1 Despite the government investing in buses, most people still prefer to travel by car. **even though**
2 While the cost of air travel to passengers has been falling, the cost to the environment has increased. **however**
3 Most people rated the service as poor. However, the majority also praised the quality of the food. **while**
4 Things have improved, but we're still struggling. **despite**

PRACTICE

8 You are going to write a report on improving public services in your area. First, complete the findings below with what you imagine the statistics are for your area. Then compare with a partner.

MAIN FINDINGS

_____% of people use private instead of public health services.

_____% visited their local hospital or clinic in the past year.

_____% of those who saw a doctor required no treatment.

_____ out of _____ people are currently considered overweight.

_____% of respondents felt public health was good or very good.

_____ tenth(s) of people could get an appointment with their doctor within 48 hours.

The main reasons for using private healthcare were _____ , _____ and _____ .

9 Write an introduction to the report to explain the survey and its purpose. Then write a summary and analysis based on the statistics you wrote. Finally, write a conclusion about how things could be improved.

7 WRITING Arguing your case

SPEAKING

1 Work in groups. Discuss the questions.

- Can you remember the last time you went to a zoo? Who did you go with? What did you see?
- Can you think of three reasons why keeping animals in captivity is a good thing?
- What are the alternatives to zoos?

GRAMMAR

Articles

Articles are used before nouns. We use *a / an* when we introduce something new.

*They've got **a** huge snake there – and **a** gorilla!*

*There is **a** zoo in my town, but I've never been there.*

We use *the* when we think the listener knows the specific thing we mean – because they can see it, because they know there's only one or because it's already been mentioned. When we use *the*, we often add a clause to clarify which thing we mean.

*Do you know **the** old zoo near the park? It's a bit depressing!*

We don't use articles with plurals or uncountable nouns when we talk about them in general, or if they represent the whole of a type or group (e.g. animals).

Zoos are a thing of the past nowadays, aren't they?

2 Find the five mistakes and correct them.

1 The zoos protect endangered animals.
2 When kids visit zoos, they get a chance to see lots of different animals.
3 I saw a TV programme the other day about the zoo in Singapore and it sounds like the amazing place.
4 The zoo in my town is home to the very rare kind of panda. That's the main attraction.
5 The fact that fewer and fewer people are visiting zoos these days does pose the big problem.
6 Without a funding, what will happen to all the animals housed in such institutions?
7 For me, the main issue is whether or not animals should be kept in an unnatural environment.

WRITING

3 Read the essay which has been written in response to the task: 'Zoos are not something we need in the 21st century. Discuss.' Does the writer agree or disagree with the idea of zoos? How do you know? Do you agree with this point of view?

4 Complete the gaps with *a, an, the* or nothing.

5 Work in pairs. Discuss the questions.

- What is the function of each of the four paragraphs?
- What is the function of each of the three sentences in the opening paragraph?
- In what different ways does the writer introduce ideas they do not agree with?

ZOOS ARE NOT SOMETHING WE NEED IN THE 21ST CENTURY

Over the last twenty years or so, [1] _____ fierce debate about zoos has been raging. It is often claimed that [2] _____ zoos are [3] _____ outdated form of entertainment and should be closed down. However, over recent years, there has been growing appreciation of the work zoos do both in terms of protecting endangered animals and also in terms of public education.

One argument against zoos is that they are cruel. They are seen as being a kind of prison for animals that should supposedly be left in the wild to roam free. It is also believed that zoos somehow legitimize [4] _____ idea that it is acceptable to capture animals and to keep them in [5] _____ captivity, and that this then encourages all manner of cruelty towards animals in society in general.

Nevertheless, the positive work done by zoos has become increasingly important and is surely sufficient reason for their continued existence. For instance, zoos do a lot to protect [6] _____ endangered species. Many have breeding programmes, which are essential if we want these animals to survive. A good example here are orangutans. These animals' natural environment is rapidly being destroyed and, as a result, they are on [7] _____ verge of extinction. As such, zoos represent [8] _____ final chance of survival for orangutans. Anyone that attacks zoos is, in fact, hastening the demise of these beautiful animals.

If you add to this [9] _____ excellent work many zoos do in raising awareness of the problems facing animals in the wild, then you surely have sufficient reasons for supporting [10] _____ continued existence of this endangered public institution!

KEY WORDS FOR WRITING

6 Can you find three more words or phrases that the essay writer uses to indicate what they see as weak arguments?

7 Complete the sentences with these words.

believed	common	sometimes
claimed	seen	supposedly

1 It is _____ said that animals in zoos live much longer lives.

2 Zoos are _____ enjoyable places to visit.

3 It is widely _____ that nature programmes and documentaries will gradually make zoos redundant.

4 It is often _____ that zoos perform valuable work by breeding endangered species and then returning them to the wild.

5 Animals are sometimes _____ as having no individuality or personality.

6 One _____ argument against zoos is that we don't have the right to deprive animals of their freedom.

8 Underline the parts of the sentences in Exercise 7 that you can re-use in your own writing.

9 Work in pairs. Think of ways to explain why each of the arguments in Exercise 7 might be seen as weak. Begin each sentence with *However*.

10 Compare the sentences you've written with another group. Do you agree with them? Why? / Why not?

PRACTICE

11 You are going to write an essay arguing your point of view in response to one of the following titles:

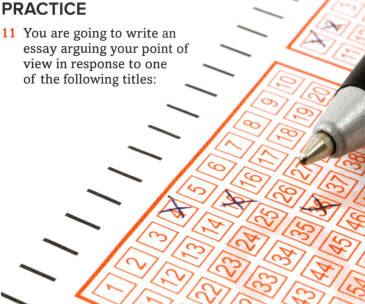

* 'Lotteries cause great harm to society and should be banned.' Discuss.

* 'Criminals need education, not prison.' Discuss.

* 'Professional sport causes more pain than pleasure.' Discuss.

* 'Staying at home for your holiday is better than travelling somewhere.' Discuss.

Work in pairs. Choose one of the titles. Discuss possible reasons why people might agree or disagree with the statement above, and then discuss your own opinions.

12 Plan the content of each of your paragraphs. Use the model essay on page 162 to help you.

13 Write your essay. Use as much language from these pages as you can.

8 WRITING Formal and informal emails

WRITING

1 Read the email enquiring about language courses in Manchester and answer the questions.

1 Why does Kathrin address the person she is writing to as *Ms*?

2 Which language does Kathrin want to study?

3 Does she have any previous experience of the language?

4 What expectations does she have of the course?

5 What five things does she ask about?

6 Why does she end with *Yours sincerely* instead of using a different ending?

To	pennylee99@chinacentre.org

Subject: Courses at the China Centre

Dear Ms Lee,

I am writing to **enquire** about the Mandarin courses **currently** offered by the China Centre.

I am planning to take a Mandarin Chinese course at elementary level sometime early next year, preferably for a period of between three and five weeks. I have studied Mandarin before, but only at beginner level, and would be looking to review much of what I **previously** studied.

As such, **I would be most grateful** if you could send me information about what courses you will be offering between January and June next year, and also let me know the prices of these courses. **Furthermore**, I would appreciate it if you could let me know what kind of **excursions** and cultural activities your centre offers. I would also like to know whether or not it is possible to invite friends along on the excursions.

Finally, **I wonder if it would be possible for you to forward me** any information you might have about accommodation in the Manchester area, as I would like to stay locally while studying.

I look forward to hearing from you soon.

Yours sincerely,

Kathrin Jacobson

VOCABULARY

Formal and informal language

The degree of formality that we use when writing to people depends on who we are writing to, how well we know them, and why we are writing. Generally speaking, more formal writing involves longer, more complex sentences, more multi-syllable words of Latin origin, fewer phrasal verbs, fewer contractions (*I've*, *you're*, etc.) and fewer abbreviations.

2 The email you read is quite formal. Match the more informal expressions below with the words or expressions in bold in the email with similar meanings.

ask	can you send me	on top of that
at the moment	hope to hear	trips
before	it'd be great	want to

3 Choose the more formal options in each of the sentences below.

1 *Cheers / Thank you* for bringing this *matter / stuff* to my attention.

2 *We are looking to / We want to* expand our team and currently have *jobs / vacancies* available.

3 *We are sorry / We regret* to *tell / inform* you that the item you *asked for / requested* is no longer in stock.

4 *If you need / Should you require* any *more help / further assistance*, please do not *hesitate / wait* to ask.

5 I *trust / hope* that this will not *be / prove* too much of *a pain / an inconvenience*.

6 *Is there any chance you could / I wonder if it would be possible for you to* provide me with copies of your *newest / most recent* catalogue?

7 *In the event of any delay / If your goods are going to be late*, we will *contact you / let you know ASAP / as soon as possible*.

8 If you are in any way *unhappy / dissatisfied* with the goods you *buy / purchase*, we *would / will* be more than happy to *offer you / provide you with* a full refund.

9 I *believe / reckon* that there are *plenty / a number* of ways in which this problem could be *sorted out / rectified*.

10 While I *appreciate / understand* the problems your company is having, I would still like to *ascertain / find out* when I might expect to *receive / get* my refund.

4 Complete this more informal email by putting one word from Exercises 2 or 3 into each space.

To j.arkwright@arkwright.com
Subject: A favour

Hi Josh,

¹ _____ this finds you well. Not sure if you're in the office at the moment or if you're away on one of your overseas ² _____ , but I just wanted to write and ask a couple of favours.

First off, can you ³ _____ me the sales figures for the last six months? Mike has ⁴ _____ me to go through them ahead of the big sales meeting in Greece next month.

On ⁵ _____ of that, I also need about 1,000 copies of the new brochure sent over ASAP. It'd be ⁶ _____ if you could courier them, actually, if it's not too much of a ⁷ _____

One last thing. Is there any ⁸ _____ you could double-check the hotel bookings for Athens and ⁹ _____ me know if there are any problems? Oh, and can you ¹⁰ _____ out what time our flights get in and ¹¹ _____ out transport to the hotel for us all?

¹² _____ for all your help on this.

Best,

Ella

PRACTICE

5 Work in groups. Discuss which of the activities below you think would best encourage team-building skills among your group. Explain your choice.

- corporate sword-fighting
- mountain climbing challenge
- creating a giant work of art
- ballroom dancing classes
- cooking a special dinner
- a quiz competition
- sailing a large yacht

6 Write a formal email to a company that offers special events for groups. Ask about the activity you most like the sound of. Find out the following information:

- which day the activity is available on
- what time it starts / finishes
- how much it costs (and if there are any discounts)
- if you can have a brochure
- if there are any age limits
- how you can book

7 Write an informal email to a colleague who works with you, using language from these pages. Make sure you include the following:

- tell them what event you have chosen and when it is
- ask them to invite everyone in the office and to tell you as soon as possible if anyone can't make it
- ask them to organise transport for the day and to send a schedule to everyone

GRAMMAR REFERENCE

1 ENTERTAINMENT

HABITS

Past

To talk about past habits, we can use the past simple, *used to* + infinitive (without *to*), or *would* + infinitive (without *to*).

*I **listened** to music all the time when I was younger.*

*I **used to listen** to music all the time when I was younger.*

*I'**d listen** to music all the time when I was younger.*

Present

To talk about current habits we can use the present simple, *tend to* + infinitive (without *to*), and *will* + infinitive (without *to*).

*I **listen** to music all the time.*

*I **tend to watch** films on demand through my TV.*

*I don't follow football much, but I **will watch** the big games.*

Will is not as common as the other forms.

Adverbs and adverbial phrases of frequency

always** / **all the time** / **constantly

normally** / **usually** / **as a rule** / **on the whole** / **by and large

sometimes** / **now and again** / **once in a while

almost never** / **very rarely** / **hardly ever** / **once in a blue moon

We also use phrases with *not as much as*.

***not as much as** … I'd like to / I want / I used to / I did before.*

Making negatives

We can make negatives with *tend to* and *used to* in different ways.

*I **didn't use to** like it very much.*

*I **never used to** listen to music at home.*

*I **tend not to go out** during the week.*

*I **don't tend to go** to the cinema that much.*

Exercise 1

Complete the second sentence so that it has a similar meaning to the first sentence using the word given. Do not change the word given. You must use between four and five words, including the word given.

1 I only go to the cinema once in a blue moon.
   HARDLY
   I _____ cinema.
2 We used to fight constantly when we were kids.
   TIME
   We used _____ when we were kids.
3 As a rule people don't read on public transport here.
   TEND
   People here _____ public transport.
4 I don't like classical music much but I sometimes go to a concert with my dad.
   WILL
   I don't like classical music much but now and _____ to a concert with my dad.
5 He was fitter before because he cycled 50 km every day.
   WOULD
   He used to _____ cycle 50 km every day.
6 I did it all the time when I was younger, but I'm not so keen on it now.
   AS
   I don't do it _____ to.

COMMON MISTAKES

- *I ~~use to~~ **usually** / **tend to** go out with friends on a Friday.*
Don't say *use to* or *used to* to talk about habits in the present.

- *I ~~was going~~ **went** / **used to go** swimming a lot when I was younger.*
Don't use the past continuous to talk about past habits.

- *I ~~would have~~ **had** / **used to have** long hair when I was younger.*
Don't use *would* to talk about character and other kinds of states.

- *I don't go **as much** ~~how~~ **as** I'd like to.*
Don't use *how* instead of *as* in comparatives.

Exercise 2

Rewrite the sentences, correcting the mistake in each.

1 I used to go and see films when they come out at the cinema because I prefer to see them on the big screen.
2 I'm tend to stay in on Friday nights, as I'm generally too tired to do anything much.
3 I don't see her as much how I used to, because we're both so busy.
4 My parents never used to go out late at night because we would live in quite a rough area.
5 I was making my own comics and films when I was younger.
6 By and large I don't use to watch TV much. There are too many ads, which annoys me.

DID YOU KNOW?

Would is actually far more common than *used to* to talk about past habits. That's because while we often introduce a topic with *used to*, we tend to give the details with *would*.

*I **used to make** my own films when I was younger. I'**d watch** famous films and get ideas and then my brother and I **would try** to make our own versions. **We'd then do** screenings for our family.*

ADJECTIVES AND ADVERBS

Adjectives

Adjectives tend to go before a noun.

*The film had a really **uplifting** ending.*

*It's quite **dull** music, if you ask me.*

Adjectives go after 'linking' verbs.

*The painting looks very **realistic**.*

*She went **red** with embarrassment.*

These verbs can be followed by an adjective on its own: *be, become, get, go, feel, grow, keep, look, remain, seem, smell, stay, sound, taste* and *turn*.

In these cases, the adjective describes the subject of the verb.

Adverbs

Adverbs go before adjectives.

*His writing is **absolutely** impossible to read.*

*It was a **strangely** moving film.*

Adverbs can come before other adverbs.

*The traffic was moving **really** slowly.*

Adverbs at the start of sentences or clauses show an opinion about the whole sentence or clause.

***Fortunately**, no-one was injured in the accident.*

*I meant to be here earlier, but, **stupidly**, I got halfway here before I realised I'd left your address at home.*

Most adverbs are formed by adding -ly to the adjective, but some adverbs have the same form as the adjective: *alive, fast, hard, late, later.*

When we use an adverb with the verbs *be, look, become, seem, get, taste,* etc., they do not describe the subject of the verb, they describe how something is done.

Exercise 1

Choose the correct option in these sentences about the paintings on page 11.

1 *Initial / Initially*, they may strike you as fairly *traditional / traditionally* portraits.
2 The young man sitting in the chair looks *calm / calmly* and is *obvious / obviously* thinking *hard / hardly* about what to write.
3 The two pieces were painted *short / shortly* before the artist's death.
4 Gabriel Metsu was both *wide / widely* admired and *reasonable / reasonably* successful during his lifetime.
5 *Unfortunate / Unfortunately*, he died at the height of his fame.
6 A strange tension and feeling of danger seems *apparent / apparently* in the two paintings.
7 Dogs in paintings were a *frequent / frequently* symbol of loyalty and trust.

Exercise 2

Complete the sentences with the adjectives in the box, changing them into adverbs if necessary.

beautiful	disturbing	funny	interesting	occasional
catchy	frequent	hard	later	recent

1 You can buy a season ticket for the museum if you're going to be a _____ visitor. It works out a lot cheaper.
2 I don't do much exercise, except for _____ going swimming.
3 I've been working really _____ to improve my English and I feel I'm making progress at last.
4 Seven is a bit early. Can't we get a _____ train?
5 _____ enough, I was just thinking about calling you when you rang.
6 If we want the book to sell, we need a _____ title to ensure that people remember it.
7 A _____ report has found that kids are being exposed to _____ high levels of violence in video games.
8 _____ , this is one of only two portraits he ever painted, but as you can see it's _____ done – a real masterpiece.

Adverb position

To show frequency, we usually add adverbs before the main verb.

*They're **always** shouting at each other.*
*I **hardly ever** go out these days.*

To show how we did something or when the action happens, we usually place adverbs after a verb.

*He was looking at me **strangely**.*
*I went to this great exhibition **yesterday**.*

Exercise 3

Rewrite the sentences with the adverbs in brackets in the correct place.

1 I download films from the internet. (never)
2 I've seen him all day. (hardly)
3 He reacted badly to the news. (fairly)
4 I'm going fishing in the week. (later)
5 To be honest, I haven't even picked up a book. (lately)

6 The car was completely destroyed, but he escaped without a scratch. (amazingly)
7 The special effects are amazing – just realistic. (incredibly)
8 They got married in 2005, but he died after. (sadly, soon)

Exercise 4

Make collocations by matching 1–9 to a–i. Use a dictionary if you need help.

1	a heated	a	after
2	loosely	b	meaning
3	a symbolic	c	treated
4	ended	d	exactly the same
5	shortly	e	discussion
6	an uplifting	f	ending
7	almost	g	out of control
8	badly	h	tragically
9	totally	i	based on a true story

2 SIGHTSEEING

RELATIVE CLAUSES

Clauses with no commas

Sometimes when we use general words like *man, place* or *thing*, we need a relative clause to make clear which man, place or thing we are referring to. When the relative clause explains this, there's no comma. These are sometimes called defining relative clauses.

He's the man.	*He's the man **that** / **who led our country during the war**.*
	*He's the man **I spoke to earlier**.*
Highgate is the place.	*Highgate is the place **where Marx is buried**.*
	*Highgate is the place **where I met my wife**.*

These kinds of sentences don't always need a relative pronoun, but if you're unsure, use one!

Clauses with commas

In other sentences, the sentence is clear and complete, but we want to add some extra information. These are called non-defining relative clauses and always need a relative pronoun.

Vaclav Havel was the first Czech president.
*Vaclav Havel, **who was also a famous writer**, was the first Czech president.*
I met my wife in Highgate.
*I met my wife in Highgate, **which is where I lived as a student**.*

DID YOU KNOW?

• We often use *which is where* instead of *where* when adding extra information.
*That's the local registry office, **which is where** we got married.*

Exercise 1

Underline the relative pronouns and add a comma where it is necessary.

That was the home of Abe and Betty Zimmerman whose son is a famous singer, Bob Dylan.

That was the home of Abe and Betty Zimmerman, <u>whose</u> *son is a famous singer, Bob Dylan.*

1 We're meeting Jaime later. You know, the guy whose brother got us the tickets for the match.
2 People lived in houses carved out of the rock most of which have been destroyed.
3 Apparently, the hotel where we're staying in Vienna overlooks the river.
4 The 19th of July celebrates the day that we gained independence.

5 It took us ages to get there by which time we were starving.
6 The first place we will stop at is the Cavern Club which is where the Beatles started out.
7 The monument honours those who died during the war many of whom came from this city.

Modifying *which* and *whom*

Look at the ways we can show the quantity or time by adding to *which* or *whom*.

People lived in houses carved out of the rock,	**most of which** have been destroyed. **some of which** still survive today. **a few of which** are still lived in.
There were ten of us on the boat trip,	**none of whom** I knew before. **many of whom** had been before.
We had a look around the old town for two hours,	**during which time** it poured with rain. **at which point** we decided to have lunch.
We will check in around 11,	**by which time** we hope the rooms will be ready. (= before 11) **after which** we will have a mid-morning snack.

DID YOU KNOW?

Many native speakers use *who* instead of *whom*.
There were ten of us on the boat trip, **most of who** had been before.

Exercise 2

Complete the sentences with these words and phrases.

at which point	most of whom	where
by which time	none of which	which
during which time	some of which	who

1 The statue was erected by Sukarno, _____ was our first president after we gained independence.
2 Next stop for us is Yekaterinburg, _____ the last tsar was executed.
3 There must have been 20 people waiting to check in, _____ were shouting at the receptionist!
4 We didn't get into town until after ten, _____ all the hotels were already booked for the night.
5 The museum houses a remarkable collection of books, _____ date back as far as the tenth century.
6 Margie and the kids spent a few hours shopping, _____ I stayed in and updated our travel blog.
7 After lunch, we went to check out the castle, _____ was very grand.
8 We looked in seven different shops and none of them had it in stock, _____ we just gave up.
9 The guidebooks, _____ I actually bothered to read at all, were soon conveniently 'lost'!

We often use a relative clause to add an opinion to the sentence we just said.

We spent a week hiking in the jungle,	**which was amazing. which was quite hard. which was my idea of hell.**

Exercise 3

Rewrite each of the pairs of sentences below as one sentence.

1 We saw Big Ben, Buckingham Palace, Tower Bridge and the London Eye. They were all amazing.
2 There were loads of recommendations on the internet. Most of them were really helpful.
3 We stayed out dancing until two in the morning. I was completely exhausted by then!
4 We spent a week in Bolivia. The election was on while we were there.
5 We spent two days in Bergen and then drove down to Stavanger. My girlfriend has family in Bergen.
6 Chen's grandfather still lives at home with the rest of the family. His grandfather is 97.

COMMON MISTAKES

- We went on the guided tour round the old town, ~~that~~ **which** was nice.
  My mum's uncle, ~~that~~ **who** I didn't really know, to be honest, used to work in the palace.
  You can't use *that* to add extra information.

- This is the stadium that ~~it~~ holds the Cup Final.
  The tour guide who ~~he~~ showed us round the castle was really funny.
  When *that* or *who* is the subject of the relative clause (*the stadium holds … / the tour guide showed …*), don't add another pronoun (*it / he*, etc.)

- Balliol is the oldest college in Oxford, many of ~~their~~ **whose** students go into politics.
  Whose replaces *their / his / Mary's*, etc., in a relative clause.

TALKING ABOUT THE FUTURE

Timetables

We prefer the present simple to talk about timetables, but the present continuous is also possible and doesn't change the meaning.
My train **leaves** at nine.   My train **is leaving** at nine.

Offers

We use *will* to offer to do something for someone.
I'll help you with that.   **I'll lend** you some money, if you want.

Decisions about the future

To talk about a decision about the future that you've already made on your own, we prefer *be going to*. The present continuous is also often possible, and doesn't change the meaning.
I'm going to study for my exams tonight.
I'm studying for my exams tonight.

To talk about a decision (or a promise or a threat) made at the time of speaking, use *will*.
Thanks. **I'll pay** you back tomorrow.
I'll call her now and see what she says.

Predictions

For predictions based on what we can see, hear, feel or on what we already know, we prefer *be going to*, but *will* is also possible.
I'm sure they**'re going to lose** the next election.
OR
I'm sure they**'ll lose** the next election.

For predictions made at the moment of speaking, we prefer *will*, but *be going to* is also possible.
You**'ll break** that in a minute!
OR
You**'re going to break** that in a minute!

You'll regret it!
OR
You're going to regret it

Arrangements

To talk about activities we have arranged with other people in the (near or foreseeable) future, we prefer the present continuous, but can also use *be going to*.

I'm meeting a friend later.
OR
I'm going to meet a friend later.

We're returning to the UK next year.
OR
We're going to return to the UK next year.

Exercise 1

Complete the sentences with the word in brackets using one of the forms given in each space.

1 *will* / present simple
   A: What time _____ you _____ work? (finish)
   B: About five, most days.
   A: OK. Well, I _____ you outside your office around quarter past, then. (meet)

2 present continuous / *be going to*
   A: I _____ Mary later. Do you want to come? (meet)
   B: No. I've got an exam tomorrow, so I _____ some revision tonight. (do)

3 present simple / *will* / present continuous
   A: I _____ some friends after the cinema. Why don't you join us? (meet)
   B: I might do. What time _____ the film _____ ? (end)
   A: Half eight.
   B: Right. Well, look. I _____ you later to confirm one way or the other, OK? (text)

4 *be going to* / *will* / present continuous
   A: I'm so excited about this trip. I can't wait. Paris _____ amazing. (be)
   B: When _____ you _____ ? (leave)
   A: Thursday. That reminds me, actually. I need to book a cab to the airport before I forget.
   B: I _____ you there, if you want. It's not a problem. (drive)

5 *will* / *be going to*
   A: I'm quite tired now, so I _____ exhausted by the end of the day! (be)
   B: You _____ , I'm sure. A bit of hard work never killed anyone. (survive)

Things we don't think will happen

To talk about things we don't think will happen, use *be not likely to* or *be (highly) unlikely to*.
She's not likely to change her mind.
It's highly unlikely to make any difference.

Things we see as (almost) inevitable

To talk about things we see as (almost) inevitable, use *be bound to* – or *be likely to*.
It's bound to be sunny in July.
We're quite likely to lose. Half our side is injured.

Things that we expect to happen

Use *be due* to talk about the times that things should happen.
The bus is due (to arrive) in five minutes.
When is the baby due?

Exercise 2

In each sentence, decide if both options are possible. If not, choose the correct option.

1 *I'm working / I'm quite likely to work* late tonight, but *I'll call / I'm calling* you when I'm done.
2 *I'm going to go / I'll go* and do the Maracana stadium tour tomorrow. I booked it online.
3 Turn the gas down. The food *burns / is going to burn*!
4 *It's going to / It's bound to* cause problems if they go ahead with the redevelopment plan.
5 *I don't think he'll / He's highly unlikely to* accept the offer, but I guess it's worth asking.
6 *I'll give / I'm due to give* you a lift to the airport, if you like.
7 He's *going to / bound to* fail. He just hasn't done enough work this term to pass.
8 We *have / are having* a little get-together at our place on Sunday, if you fancy coming.
9 *I'm due to fly / I'm flying* to Rome on March the 6th to attend a conference.

3 THINGS YOU NEED

EXPLAINING PURPOSE USING *SO*, *IF* AND *TO*

Use *so* to show that the second part of the sentence is a potential result of the first. The word *that* can be added after *so*, but doesn't have to be.

DID YOU KNOW?
So (that) is often followed by *can*.
*Do you want to borrow a torch **so (that) you can see** where you're going outside?*
*Pass me a cloth **so (that) I can grip** the lid of this jar better.*

We use *if*-clauses (*if* + noun + verb in present tense) to talk about possible situations in which certain things might be necessary.
*This is useful stuff to have **if you need** to remove stains.*
*Hang it up with a nail **if you can't find** anything else.*

We use *to* + infinitive (without *to*) to explain the purpose of doing things, why we need something or what something is for.

DID YOU KNOW?
You can also say *in order to* + infinitive (without *to*). This is more common in formal writing.
*I'm just going out **to buy** a few things for the house.*
*A cable is required **(in order) to connect** the device to the computer.*

Exercise 1

Complete the sentences by adding *so*, *if* or *to*.

1 Have you got a dustpan and brush _____ I can clean up this mess I've made?
2 I must buy some wire _____ hang this up with.
3 _____ you want to put those shelves up properly, you'll need a drill.
4 You'll need an adaptor _____ you're going to use your laptop in the States.
5 Put some cream on _____ protect yourself from the sun.
6 What are those things you wear on your knees _____ you do skateboarding or something like that?
7 You should put a plaster on your foot _____ stop your shoes cutting into your skin.
8 Can I borrow your stepladder _____ I can change the light bulb in the hall?
9 Have you got a clip or something _____ keep these papers together?

Exercise 2

Complete the sentences using _so_, _if_ or _to_ and the ideas in brackets. You may need to add some extra words.

1 We need some matches or something _____ the stove. (light)
2 Maybe you should wrap some tape round where there's a crack _____ . (it / not / leak)
3 You'll need wire cutters _____ that – not scissors. (you / want / cut)
4 Have you got something I can stand on _____ this light bulb? (I / can / change)
5 Can't you just use some string _____ it? (tie it together / and / make / a handle / you / carry)

SHOULD AND _SHOULD HAVE_ (SHOULD'VE)

We use _should (not / never)_ + <u>verb</u> to give general advice, suggestions or criticism about a present situation.

You **should** <u>see</u> complaints as an opportunity to improve.
We **should never** <u>give</u> terrorists what they want.
We **should** <u>go</u> and try that new pizzeria that's just opened round the corner.

We use _should (not / never)_ + have + <u>past participle</u> to show a criticism or regret about a past action.

He **should have** / **should've** <u>checked</u> the shoes at the point of sale.
They **shouldn't have** <u>parked</u> here. They've blocked me in.

Exercise 1

Complete the two dialogues with the correct form of _should_ and the verbs in brackets.

A: You ¹ _____ bowling with us. We had a great time. (come)
B: Well, you ² _____ me so late. I couldn't rearrange things. (tell)
A: I know. Sorry. Maybe we ³ _____ next week sometime. (go)

A: The neighbours kept me awake last night again.
B: Really? Maybe you ⁴ _____ them next time. (report)
A: I have already, but the police didn't want to do anything.
B: They ⁵ _____ them at least. (come and warn)
A: I guess they felt they had more important things to do.
B: Did you tell them how often it's happening?
A: Not really. Maybe I ⁶ _____ so calm when I spoke to them. (be)
B: Yeah, maybe.
A: I don't know. Maybe we ⁷ _____ . (just move)
B: Yeah, but you ⁸ _____ . It's just wrong! (have to)

DID YOU KNOW?

Use _should be -ing_ to refer to a current unfinished situation.
Stop distracting me. We **should be working** not chatting.

Use _should have been -ing_ to refer to an unfinished / interrupted action in the past.
It was his own fault he crashed. He **shouldn't have been driving** so fast!

Exercise 2

Choose the correct option after _should_.

1 The new system has been a disaster. We should _have tested_ / _have been testing_ it properly before we introduced it.
2 With so much unemployment, the government shouldn't _cut_ / _be cutting_ jobs like it is.

3 Apparently, she was sacked because she was seen in a shopping mall when she should _have worked_ / _have been working_.
4 It's his own fault he got into trouble. He shouldn't have _texted_ / _been texting_ while the teacher was talking to the class.

COMMON MISTAKES

We should ~~to~~ go. We're late.
I should ~~travelling~~ be travelling there now, but I missed my bus.
He should ~~took~~ have taken it back to the shop sooner.
They should ~~of~~ have had it fixed by a professional.
Always follow _should_ with a form of the infinitive (without _to_).

Exercise 3

Rewrite the sentences, correcting the mistake in each.

1 I'm sorry it's a bit late. I should rang you earlier, but I forgot.
2 They should of try to sort it out instead of blaming me.
3 When you take it back, you should to ask for some kind of compensation.
4 I sometimes think I should never go to university because I didn't enjoy it much and I have a huge debt now.
5 It's terrible I have to work tonight. I should celebrating my birthday with my friends!

4 SOCIETY

SO AND SUCH

In the part of the sentence describing the cause, use _so_ before an adjective or an adverb or before words like _few, little, much_ or _many_. Use _such_ before a noun, an adjective + noun and before _a lot of_ + noun. Remember that you don't have to start the result clause with _that_ – especially in spoken English.

It was **so** expensive in Moscow, we couldn't stay there long.
There's **so** much traffic, it's quicker to walk sometimes!
**So** few people had bought tickets **that** they decided to cancel the event.
They did **so** badly in the elections **that** their leader resigned.
It was **such** a surprise **that** I just didn't know what to say!
The ride was **such** a laugh **that** we went on it six times.
There's **such** a lot of rubbish on the streets, it makes me angry.

DID YOU KNOW?

Few and _many_ go before plural, countable nouns (_people / families_, etc.) and _much_ and _little_ go before uncountable nouns (_crime / damage_, etc.).
There's **far too much** crime and **too few** people doing anything to change things.

Exercise 1

Choose the correct option in sentences 1–8. Then match them with a–h at the top pf page 171.

1 Our situation sometimes looks _so_ / _such_ bleak,
2 He was involved in _so_ / _such_ a terrible public scandal,
3 The government have lied _so_ / _such_ many times,
4 Food prices have gone up _so_ / _such_ quickly,
5 The earthquake caused _so_ / _such_ widespread damage,
6 _So_ / _Such_ few women are having babies these days,
7 They've got _so_ / _such_ poor hospitals,
8 There's _so_ / _such_ little crime now,

a there have been riots in the street markets.
b that most kids can't even get basic health care.
c they're actually making police officers redundant!
d I've just lost faith in them.
e the government's introduced tax breaks for big families to boost the birth rate.
f that it's hard not to feel pessimistic about the future.
g that tens of thousands are feared dead.
h that in the end he was forced to resign.

Exercise 2

Complete the sentences by adding *many*, *much*, *few* or *little*.

1 There's so _____ poverty in the world that surely tackling that has to be our main goal.
2 So _____ people bothered to vote that the election results are almost meaningless!
3 So _____ people turned up to vote in the election, there were long queues at the polls.
4 So _____ new jobs have been created that there are actually a lot of posts which are unfilled.
5 So _____ research has been done into the problem that it's hard to say what's causing it.

COMPARATIVES WITH *THE* ..., *THE* ...

We show correlations using the following basic patterns:
the + comparative + noun / pronoun (+ verb), *the* + comparative + noun (+ verb).

The more affluent the area is, **the nicer** the cars are.
The bigger you are, **the more difficult** it is to find nice clothes.
The more roads there are, **the more people** use their cars and **the more pollution** there is.

Note: we sometimes leave out the nouns and use *more / less / fewer* as pronouns.

The more I earn, **the more** I buy. (= more money, ... more things)
The less I know, **the better**. (= less information)

Exercise 1

Complete the sentences with one word in each space.

1 _____ richer the country, _____ lower the birth rate.
2 The better educated people _____ , the _____ money they are likely to earn.
3 The stronger _____ economy, the _____ unemployment there is.
4 The hungrier people are, the _____ desperate they tend to be _____ the more conflicts _____ will be.
5 The happier people are, the _____ illnesses they _____ .

Common patterns in conversation

We often use these short patterns, especially in conversation:

The sooner, the better   The faster, the better
The bigger, the better   The fewer, the better
The simpler, the better   The more, the better

Exercise 2

Write a short reply to each question using *the ..., the better*.

1 What size boxes do you want?
2 What kind of camera are you thinking of buying?
3 When do you want this done by?
4 How do you want your coffee?
5 How many people should we invite?

5 SPORTS AND INTERESTS

SHOULD(N'T) HAVE, COULD(N'T) HAVE, WOULD(N'T) HAVE

Use *should have (should've)* + past participle to show you think something in the past was a good idea, but didn't happen.
*We **should have phoned** you. We forgot. Sorry.*

Use *shouldn't have* or *should never have* + past participle to show you think something that happened wasn't a good idea.
*You **shouldn't have hit** him. It was wrong of you.*

Add a comment using *would have (would've) / wouldn't have / would never have* + past participle to show a certain past result.
*It's your birthday? You should've said. I **would have bought** you a present.*
*I should've gone more slowly. I **wouldn't have made** that mistake.*

Add a comment with *could have (could've) / couldn't have / could never have* (Or *might have / might never have*) + past participle to show possible past results.
*They should've acted sooner. They **could have saved** his life.*
*They should've asked for help. They **could never have done** it on their own.*
*He shouldn't have substituted the striker. They **might have won**.*

Exercise 1

Choose the correct option.

1 It's his fault. He *should have / would have* dealt with the problem sooner rather than leaving it so long.
2 The fire was my fault. I *shouldn't have / wouldn't have* left the gas on while I was out.
3 It's my own fault. I *should have / would have* warmed up more before I started playing. I *wouldn't have / couldn't have* strained my back if I had.
4 I blame the players. They got knocked out because they *wouldn't have underestimated / underestimated* the opposition. They *should've / would've* taken the game more seriously.
5 He *should have / would have* talked it through first. He *might not have / might've* got himself into so much trouble.
6 The game was pretty awful, but I suppose it *would have been / might have been* worse – we *could have / wouldn't have* lost.

DID YOU KNOW?

We often follow *would have / wouldn't have* with a clause starting with *but*.
*We **would have won, but** we had a goal that wasn't allowed.* (= that's why we didn't win)
*I **wouldn't have said** anything, **but** he asked me how you were.* (= that's why I spoke)

Exercise 2

Complete sentences 1–4 with the correct form of *would* and the verb in brackets. Then complete 5–8 with the correct form of *could*.

1 I _____ here earlier, but the traffic was terrible. (get)
2 She _____ to come, but it was impossible. She had so much work. (like)
3 I _____ him forgetting normally, but I'd told him twice that it was really important. That's why I was so angry. (mind)
4 I _____ him, but he'd invited me to his party, so I felt I had to! (invite)

5 It could have been worse. He _____ his neck. (break)

6 It could have been worse. They _____ you when they grabbed your bag. (hurt)

7 It could have been worse. She _____ her wallet stolen too. (have)

8 The storm was bad, but it could have been worse. It _____ a lot more damage than it did. (do)

THE PRESENT PERFECT CONTINUOUS AND SIMPLE

Present perfect continuous

The form of the present perfect continuous is *have / has + (not) been + -ing*.

It's used to talk about actions, intentions or feelings that started in the past and are still going on now. It emphasises the fact these things happened regularly or continuously.

I've been knitting for six months now. (= a regular activity and I still do it)

I've been meaning to go round and see him. (= a continuous intention, but I haven't seen him)

He's not been feeling well. (= continuous feeling and he is still ill)

Present perfect simple

The present perfect simple is *have / has + (not) + past participle*. It is used to talk about actions or events completed at some point before now, but with a connection to the present.

I've put on five kilos since January. (= five kilos is complete)

That's the third double fault I've served. (= three completed before I said this)

The following verbs are rarely used in the continuous form: *be, believe, belong, cost, exist, fancy, hate, have* (= possess)*, know, like, love, prefer, seem, understand.*

I've always fancied going to the Caribbean but I've never had the chance.

We've known each other for years.

Exercise 1

Match the sentence halves. Then say why the present perfect continuous is used in 1–4 and the present perfect simple in 5–8.

1 She's been trying to call you all morning,
2 I've been meaning to ask Luis if he could help me,
3 I've been putting off going to the dentist for ages,
4 She's been thinking about dropping out of the course,
5 I've asked my landlord to fix the shower loads of times,
6 I've only met him once before,
7 I've never really fancied going skiing.
8 I've heard that song so many times recently,

a but he still hasn't done it! It's really annoying.
b but I just haven't found the right moment to ask.
c but your phone has been switched off.
d I don't know why. I guess it's not my kind of thing.
e I'm a bit sick of it.
f as she's been struggling to keep up with the work.
g but he seemed like a really nice guy.
h but it's so painful I guess I should have it looked at.

DID YOU KNOW?

Of all the tenses in English, the present perfect continuous is used less than 0.5% of the time!

When talking about 'how long', fluent speakers prefer the continuous form, but we can use the present perfect simple to talk about duration with little difference in meaning.

I've been teaching here for six years now.
I've taught here for six years now.

The present perfect simple is commonly used with the adverbs *yet, already, always, never, ever* and *just.*

I haven't decided what to do yet.
They've already asked Bill – and he said no.
She's always done her best at school. (and she still does)
I've never liked swimming in the sea. (and I still don't)
I've just managed to get hold of some tickets for the game.

With the present perfect continuous and simple, we use:
since to show when an activity, intention or feeling started.
I've been playing since I was a kid.

for to show the period.
She's been trying to call you for the last hour.

phrases like *all morning / all day / all year* when it is still the same morning, day or year.
I've been planning to visit them all week / month / year.

Exercise 2

Complete the sentences with one word in each space.

1 I've been working there as a volunteer _____ over six years now.
2 I haven't seen him _____ morning. He must be off work.
3 She's been seeing a counsellor _____ the accident.
4 I've _____ been interested in golf. I don't know why, really, because I like other sports like rugby.
5 Don't tell me what happened! I haven't seen the highlights _____ and it's more exciting when you don't know the score.
6 I've _____ seen that film, but I wouldn't mind seeing it again. It's brilliant.
7 I've _____ loved playing cards – ever _____ I was a child.

COMMON MISTAKES

• *I've ~~been writing~~ written twenty emails today.*
Don't use the continuous form with specific numbers (unless all twenty emails are unfinished!).

• *I haven't seen him for six years ~~ago~~.*
Don't use *for* with *ago*. (You can say *The last time I saw him was six years ago.*)

• A: *Have you ever been hang-gliding?*
B: *I have, actually. I ~~'ve been~~ went with a friend last year.*
Use the past simple with past time phrases like *last year.*

6 ACCOMMODATION

MODIFIERS

absolutely / very / really

We got ~~very~~ absolutely soaked. (or very / really wet)
It was ~~absolutely~~ really hot. (or absolutely boiling)
Don't use *very* with extreme adjectives like *soaked, boiling, great, awful, enormous* that already have the meaning of 'very'. Use *absolutely* or *really*. Don't use *absolutely* with normal adjectives like *hot, cold,* etc. Use *very* or *really*.

too

Oh it was ~~too~~ really incredible. I loved it. (or absolutely incredible)
It was ~~quite~~ a bit too hot for my liking. I can't do much in that heat.
It was miles too hot for my liking. I simply couldn't go outside.
Too always shows you DON'T like something or it's a problem.
If it's a small problem use *a bit / a little too*. If it's a big problem use *much / miles too*.

a bit / quite / fairly

The food was ~~a bit~~ **quite** nice, but maybe **a bit** bland.

A bit makes negative adjectives weaker. It is not used with positive adjectives.

We can use *quite*, *fairly*, *pretty* and *rather* with both positive and negative words.

Modifying nouns

It was **a complete** waste of time.

It was **a bit of** a nightmare.

It was **a bit** dull. There were **hardly any** activities.

To modify nouns, use *a bit of* or adjectives like *real, complete, slight* or *hardly any, almost no*.

hardly / almost

We ~~hardly~~ did **almost** nothing all day apart from lie on the beach.

Hardly is a negative and goes with *any / anything*, etc.

Almost goes with *no, nothing, don't, didn't*, etc.

Exercise 1

Cross out the incorrect modifiers in *italics*. In some cases, both words or phrases are correct.

1 The town we stayed in was *a bit / quite* dull, but the surrounding area was *very / absolutely* stunning.
2 We *hardly / almost* had any rain the whole time we were there, but there was *a bit / a bit of* a chill most days.
3 The place gets *absolutely / really* packed with tourists in August and there are *hardly / almost* no vacancies in the hotels in the summer.
4 The place was a *real / really* tourist trap and everything was *absolutely / very* expensive. I'm sure the locals don't go there much.
5 It was *pretty / fairly* isolated. There were *hardly / no* houses nearby.
6 The beach was *fairly / a bit* near, but it was *quite / a bit* too far to walk to.

DID YOU KNOW?

We can show that something is less than *quite / a bit* by using *not very*.

It was **quite** good. I enjoyed it.

It was**n't very** good. I wouldn't recommend it.

It's **a bit** expensive. I'm not sure I can afford it.

They're **not very** expensive. Anyone can afford to get one these days.

Fluent speakers also say *not that expensive* or *not particularly expensive*.

Exercise 2

Complete the second sentence so that it has a similar meaning to the first sentence using the word given. Do not change the word given. You must use between three and four words, including the word given.

1 This coffee is really weak.
   STRONG
   This coffee _____ .
2 It was unbearably hot in the tent.
   ABSOLUTELY
   Inside the tent it _____ .
3 The town centre was almost deserted at night.
   HARDLY
   There _____ the town centre at night.
4 Personally, I'd prefer it if the music wasn't so loud!
   TOO
   The music's _____ for my liking.

5 There was hardly anything to do during the day.
   ALMOST
   There _____ to do during the day.

HAVE/GET SOMETHING DONE

Have/get something done is a passive construction. We use it when the person who did an action is unknown or unimportant. *Have/get something done* focuses on both the object and the person that the object belongs to. Compare:

My bike **was stolen** from outside the shop. (= the focus is only on my bike)

I **had** my bike **stolen**. (= the focus is on the bike <u>and</u> on the fact that I was the victim)

Get is more common with some verbs, *have* with others. There are no rules for this. The best way to learn is by seeing examples. Look at how the structures are used in different tenses:

It was a mess! They **were having** some work **done** on the roof.

I **should have** my hair **cut**.

I **had to have** my picture **taken** for the college website.

I'**m going to get** my hair **dyed** blond.

I'**d never have** my hair **cut** that short! It wouldn't suit me.

Exercise 1

Complete the conversations by reordering the words in italics.

1 A: *of / straightened / getting / thinking / hair / I'm / my*. I'm sick of this hairstyle.
   B: Really? I'd love to have curly hair like you.
2 A: *photo / get / should / framed / that / you*. It's really nice.
   B: Do you think so? Maybe I will, then.
3 A: The dentist said *have / going / the / taken / to / have / I'm / to / tooth / out*. I'm dreading it.
   B: I can imagine. I hate going to the dentist, but what choice do you have?
4 A: Someone broke into the car and *stolen / their / had / they / all / and / money / passports* .
   B: Oh no! That's awful. So what did they do?
5 A: I'm going to have to stop the car. The engine's overheating.
   B: I told you *should / we / have / it / had / checked* before we left.

Exercise 2

Complete sentence b using a *have* (or *get*) passive structure, and any other words necessary, so that it has a similar meaning to a.

1 a Our luggage was stolen from our hotel room.
   b We _____ from our hotel room.
2 a Don't touch that gate. It's only just been painted.
   b I _____ so be careful you don't touch it.
3 a My car is at the garage at the moment, being repaired.
   b I _____ at the moment.
4 a They should send someone to repair the air conditioning in here.
   b They really ought to _____ .
5 a I usually do my weekly shop online and they deliver it to my house.
   b I usually do my weekly shop online and _____ to my house.

7 NATURE

NARRATIVE TENSES

The past simple

The past simple describes finished events – often ones that follow each other. These events can be linked together using words such as *and*, *and then*, *after that*, *after*, *before*.
*We **pulled over** and **waited** for the rain to stop and then we **continued** our journey.*

The past continuous

The past continuous shows an action was at the same time as another, but was unfinished or interrupted – often by a verb in the past simple.
*I **met** my wife when we **were** both **living** in Slovakia.*
*I **had** an accident while I **was driving** to work.*

The past perfect simple

The past perfect simple describes an action finished before a previously mentioned action or before the story began.
*I'd only **answered** two questions by the time he **finished**.*
*When I **got** to work, I realised I'**d left** my keys at home.*

DID YOU KNOW?

Continuous tenses are sometimes used to emphasise the duration of an activity. Notice the time phrases.
*It **was raining the whole time** we were there.*
*We **were waiting for hours** for the fog to lift.*

Exercise 1

Choose the correct option.

1 The thunder was so loud I *couldn't / can't* get to sleep.
2 The sun was burning hot and I got really sunburned because I *was forgetting / had forgotten* to put any cream on.
3 I *got / was getting* caught in a storm when I was walking home, so I stopped in a café until it'd blown over.
4 It *got / was getting* dark, so we decided to go home while we could still see the path.
5 The roads were really treacherous because the snow *was melting / had melted* a bit the day before and had then frozen overnight.
6 I went away on holiday and when I *had got back / got back* I found that slugs had eaten all the flowers in my garden!
7 The fog *was coming down / came down* suddenly and we got completely lost and had to phone for help.
8 It absolutely poured down in the morning and by the time we arrived, the campsite still *didn't dry out / hadn't dried out*, so the whole place was a mudbath.

PARTICIPLE CLAUSES

Participle clauses can follow a noun. They define the noun in the same way that relative clauses do. Clauses that use present participles (the *-ing* form) have an active meaning and clauses that use a past participle have a passive meaning.
*… a range of dishes **featuring** the insects* (= a range of dishes **that feature** the insects)
*… experiments **aimed at** combating illnesses* (= experiments **that are aimed at** combating illnesses)

Exercise 1

Complete the sentences using the correct form of the words in brackets.

1 The suffering _____ by vivisection is just horrendous. (cause)
2 Supplies are slowly starting to reach the areas worst _____ by the flooding. (affect)

3 There have been calls for a ban to be placed on beef _____ from any areas affected by mad cow disease. (import)
4 The low numbers of young people _____ part in sport or _____ regular exercise continues to be a cause for concern. (take, do)
5 The government has promised to help rebuild all the properties _____ in the recent forest fires. (damage)
6 City Farms is a new project _____ by the local council and aimed at putting kids in contact with animals. (fund)
7 The police have said that some of the animals _____ from the laboratories could well be carrying diseases. (free)
8 The group _____ the protests has issued a statement _____ all forms of hunting. (lead, oppose)

8 CRIME AND PUNISHMENT

SHOWING DEGREES OF CERTAINTY WITH MODAL VERBS

Uncertain

When we use *could* or *might* to give an opinion or speculate about something, we show we think it's possible, but are not completely sure.
*It **could be** worse. We **could be** out there in the rain.* (= It's possible for it to be worse)
*She **might have known** her attacker.* (= It's possible she knew)
We can also use *may* instead of *might*, especially in more formal writing.
*Police believe that high speed **may have played** a part in the crash.*

Certain

When we use *must* or *can't* to give an opinion or speculate about something we show we are certain it's true, even if we have no direct evidence/experience.
*It **must be** at least six o'clock.* (= I think it is six because we left at five and we have been travelling for a long time)
*It **must have been** awful.* (= I imagine it definitely was)
*She **can't have seen** the sign.* (= I imagine she didn't see it, because there were no other causes I can think of)

DID YOU KNOW?

We don't usually use *must* in the negative when it means *imagine / guess* – it's far more common to use *can't*.
*It ~~mustn't~~ **can't** be more than fifteen years old.*

Present and past infinitives

Remember verbs that go with modals are always in an infinitive form.
*It **can't be** easy, doing three jobs at a time.* (= I'm sure it isn't)
*He **must earn** a lot of money because he's always going on holiday.* (= I'm sure he earns)
If we want to refer to a past event, use a past infinitive: *have +* past participle
*It **can't have been** easy when he was growing up, being so poor.*
*I **must have dropped** it somewhere.*

Exercise 1

Complete each sentence by adding *can't, must, can't have* or *must have*.

1 It _____ be very nice, finding out you're being cheated on!
2 It _____ be great, getting to travel all over the world.
3 It _____ been difficult, only seeing your kids once a month.

4 He's been working thirteen-hour days for weeks. He _____ be exhausted.

5 This doesn't look right. I think we _____ taken the wrong turning earlier.

6 He tore his knee ligaments. It _____ hurt like mad!

7 It _____ be easy for her, bringing up six kids on her own.

8 I _____ left the door unlocked, because there was no sign of them breaking in.

9 Given the time of the murder, she _____ done it. It _____ been someone else.

10 Your glasses _____ be somewhere. You _____ looked very hard!

DID YOU KNOW?

As we saw with *should* and *would* (page 170), we can use a continuous form of the verb after *must, can't, might*.

*She **can't be earning** much if she's only doing cleaning work.* (present)

*We should get off the phone. He **might be trying** to call now.* (present)

*I didn't time it, but I **must've been waiting** for over an hour.* (past)

*He **shouldn't have been smoking** in there.* (past)

Exercise 2

Complete the second sentence so that it has a similar meaning to the first sentence using the word given. Do not change the word given. You must use three or four words, including the word given.

1 The police believe it's possible the thieves got in through an open window.
   MIGHT
   The thieves _____ through an open window, according to the police.

2 I can't see how they did it other than knowing someone in the bank.
   MUST
   They _____ in the bank in order to do it.

3 I'll check she's not waiting for us outside. It's possible she is.
   MIGHT
   She _____ outside, so let me go and check.

4 I very much doubt the painting is worth a lot.
   BE
   If you ask me, the painting _____ a lot.

5 I'm sure it took ages to write the report as it's so detailed.
   TAKEN
   That report _____ to write, given it's so detailed.

6 He can't have enjoyed it because he came home early.
   MUST
   He _____ boring because he came home early.

NOUNS AND PREPOSITIONAL PHRASES

We often add prepositional phrases to nouns to define the nouns more. Usually, there is only one possible preposition that can be used after a particular noun, although sometimes alternatives are possible. We just have to learn which prepositions can be used with which nouns.

After the prepositions, we use either a noun or a gerund (*-ing*) form of a verb.

*The main **problem** with <u>prisons</u> is that we place too much **emphasis** on <u>punishing</u> prisoners and don't pay enough **attention** to <u>rehabilitation</u>.*

Exercise 1

Complete the sentences with the noun + preposition combinations.

access to	awareness of	decrease in
addiction to	ban on	involvement in
anger about	damage to	recipe for

1 Police have arrested a leading politician for his _____ a corruption scandal.

2 The singer Manny Biggs has admitted himself into a rehabilitation centre for treatment for his _____ drugs and alcohol.

3 The government is considering a complete _____ the ownership of guns.

4 Better _____ the internet could help solve many of the problems that currently affect the third world.

5 The demonstration against rising prices of water turned into a riot, resulting in widespread _____ cars and buildings.

6 There has been some _____ the police handling of the incident last week in which a man was shot.

7 Can you give me the _____ that soup you made?

8 There's actually been a big _____ the incidence of street crime over the last few years.

9 Nowadays, there's much greater _____ the need for recycling and energy conservation.

Prepositions and meanings

Different prepositions can add different information to the noun.

*a book **of poetry*** (= it contains poems)
*a book **about organised crime*** (= the subject is crime)
*a book **by Gabriel García Márquez*** (= the author is Márquez)
*a book **for Christmas*** (= the reason you give the book)
*a book **with pictures*** (= a feature of the book)
*an impact **on unemployment*** (= what the impact affects)
*the impact **of the policy*** (= where the impact comes from)

It's possible to have two prepositional phrases.
*There is a lot of concern **among parents about rising crime**.*

The prepositions that follow nouns often depend on the verbs used before the nouns. For example:
give a lot of attention to the problem
deflect attention from the real problem

Exercise 2

Choose the correct preposition in each sentence.

1a I'm afraid there's no room *in / for* the class for another desk and chair.

1b We've got room *in / for* one more person in our car.

2a Police have discovered a terrorist threat *of / to* the president.

2b The airport has increased security because of the threat *of / to* terrorism.

3a What's the name of that film *with / about* Jet Li that came out last year? He was great in it.

3b It's a really interesting film *with / about* gun crime.

4a The police have set up a meeting *about / with* the local residents *about / with* burglaries in the area.

4b The survey looked at attitudes *towards / among* young people *towards / among* politics.

5a There's a demonstration *against / of* racism being held next week.

5b The students are going to put on a demonstration *of / for* what they've learned at the end of the course.

9 CAREERS AND STUDYING

CONDITIONALS WITH PRESENT TENSES

We use present tenses in the conditional if part of sentences to talk about things that are true now, are generally/usually true or are likely to happen in the future. We can use a range of different structures in the result clause.

to talk about general truths	**If** I ask about doing other stuff, he **tells** me to be patient.
to talk about definite future results	**If** they invest more in education, it**'ll help** the economy.
to give advice	**If** it's that bad, you **should think about** leaving!
to express possibility	**It might get** better **if** I just **give** it a bit more time. **If** I get this promotion, I **can buy** a place of my own.
to make offers / promises	**I'll give** you a hand **if** you need help filling in the forms.
to talk about plans	What **are** you **going to do if** you don't get the promotion?
to express obligation	**If** you want to get in, **you have to get** really good grades.

Exercise 1

Make if sentences using the ideas below. Use the words in bold to decide which structures to use in the result clauses.

1 you fail three subjects / repeat the whole year   **obligation**
2 not feel well / take a day off sick   **advice**
3 ask my uncle for a job / the worst comes to the worst   **possibility**
4 I / be in big trouble / report not finished by Friday   **definite result**
5 things not get better at work / hand in my notice   **plan**
6 you're struggling / do my best to help   **offer**

Present tenses in if clauses

We can use the present simple / continuous or the present perfect simple / continuous in if clauses.

I get paid extra **if I work** overtime. (= always / whenever)

If you're having problems (= now / at the moment), you can always talk to me.

If you've finished that (= already), could you make me a coffee?

You can't concentrate properly **if you've been working** too hard (= from the past to now).

Exercise 2

Choose the correct option in each of the if clauses.

1 If you haven't heard / haven't been hearing from them soon, maybe you should call them.
2 You should take some time off if you aren't feeling / haven't felt well.
3 We might all lose our jobs if the company loses / has lost any more money next year.
4 If you work / have been working here for more than two years, they have to give you a month's notice if they want to get rid of you.
5 If everything goes / is going according to plan, I'm going to go and work abroad for a year.

CONDITIONALS WITH PAST TENSES

In if-clauses, we use the past perfect simple / continuous for imagined past situations. We use the past simple / continuous for imagined present situations. In result clauses, we use would (not / never) + have + past participle for imagined past results and would (not / never) + verb for imagined present and future results. We can use might in the same way. Might shows less definite results.

Imagined past

It **would** probably **have been** a different story if I**'d been doing** it on my own!

(= I wasn't doing it on my own. That's why I enjoyed it.)

If it **hadn't been** for her I **might never** even **have heard** about the job.

(= Because of her, I heard about the job.)

Imagined present / future

Even **if they doubled** my money, **I wouldn't want** to work near a beach again.

(= They won't offer me more money to do that job, which is good, because I don't want it!)

Mixed present and past

If **I wasn't** in the army, **I would never have gone** somewhere like Haiti.

(= Because I am in the army, I was able to go to places like Haiti.)

Exercise 1

Complete the text with one word in each space (didn't, hadn't, etc., count as one word).

If it hadn't [1]_____ raining that day I might [2]_____ have seen the advert. I usually cycled to work, but that day it was pouring down and I was late, so I took the metro. I was working for a TV company at the time and it was good, but I saw this ad and it said 'Imagine if you ³_____ in your job for the rest of your life, how ⁴_____ you feel? ⁵_____ you think you'd contributed to the world? Would you ⁶_____ made your mark?' It really made me think and it led me in a completely different direction. I became a nurse. I liked the TV work, but I don't think it ⁷_____ have been as rewarding, even if I ⁸_____ continued to do it. I doubt I'd ⁹_____ so happy now if it ¹⁰_____ been for that ad.

Exercise 2

Complete sentence b so that it has a similar meaning to a.

1 a I'm amazed you didn't get angry when your boss said that to you.
  b If my boss _____ that to me, I _____ furious.

2 a Our present success is a direct result of all your hard work.
  b If it _____ for all your hard work, we _____ as successful as we currently are.

3 a I was very nervous in the interview. Maybe that's why I didn't get the job.
  b If I _____ more confident in the interview, I _____ the job.

4 a I know him better than you and I can tell you now: that was a stupid thing to say to him.
  b If you _____ him as well as I do, you _____ that to him!

5 a The money's terrible. I only stay because I find the work really rewarding.
  b To be honest, if I _____ the work so rewarding, I _____ my notice tomorrow.

10 SOCIALISING

THE FUTURE PERFECT

Form

The future perfect is formed using *will / won't* + *have* + past participle.
They **will have done** all the painting before the weekend so we can move in then.
Can I give you it on Friday? I **won't have finished** it by Thursday.

Time references

We usually have a time reference with the future perfect such as *before the weekend*, *by Thursday*. The most common phrases begin with *by*: *by this afternoon*; *by the time we get there*; *by the end of the year*; *by then*.

Before

The future perfect shows how an action will be complete before that time. Compare:
I**'m going to write** my essay on Thursday. (... so don't disturb me on Thursday!)
I **will have written** my essay by Thursday. (... so let's go out on Thursday!)

Less certainty

We can also use *should* or *might* instead of *will* to show less certainty.
I **should have finished** by about six or so, but I'll call you if I haven't.
The government say they're going to change the law after the next election, but they **might have left power** by then!

Exercise 1

Choose the correct option.

1 *I'll have lived / I'm going to live* here for two years in June.
2 *I'm going / I will have gone* to Estonia on Thursday morning. So can we make it Tuesday or Wednesday?
3 It's absolutely pouring down now, but they said it'll *ease off / have eased off* during the afternoon.
4 Hurry up! The film *will probably have started / will probably start* by the time we get to the cinema.
5 *I'm helping / I'll have helped* a friend move house tomorrow, but *we're finishing / we should've finished* by five, so call me then.
6 It said in the paper that by the time you're 60, *you're going to spend / you will have spent* nine whole years watching TV! How depressing is that?

COMMON MISTAKES

• If they ~~will have fixed~~ **have fixed** the car, I can drive you to the airport this evening.
  I'll call you when I ~~will have finished~~ **have finished**.
Don't use *will* in phrases with time adverbs (*when, until,* etc.) or *if*-clauses.

DID YOU KNOW?

We often use the future perfect to say what we think has almost certainly happened before now.
They**'ll have left** by now. (= I'm 99% sure they have left)
They **won't have left** yet. (= I'm 99% sure they haven't left)
It **won't have landed** yet. (= I'm 99% sure it hasn't landed)
You **won't have heard** of it. (= I'm 99% sure you don't know it)

QUESTION TAGS

Question tags are formed using an auxiliary + a pronoun.
If there is an auxiliary verb (*have* or *be*) then the question tag is made with the auxiliary verb.
For positive sentences, use negative tags.
*It was a great game, **wasn't it**?*
With negative statements, use a positive tag.
*The meeting shouldn't take too long, **should it**?*
If the main part of the sentence doesn't have an auxiliary verb, the question tag uses an appropriate form of '*do*'.
*Terry lives near there, **doesn't he**?*
Positive tags are often used to make polite requests.
*You couldn't save my place in the queue, **could you**?*
We also use these tags:
*Let's start, **shall we**? (polite way to make suggestions)*
*Pass me the salt, **will you**? (makes commands more polite)*

DID YOU KNOW?

We don't add question tags to questions.
Are you doing anything this weekend ~~aren't you~~?
Do you want to go and get something to eat ~~don't you~~?

Exercise 1

Decide which two sentences with tags are correct. Rewrite the other four so they are correct.

1 A: Would you like a coffee, wouldn't you?
  B: No, I'm fine, thanks. I've just had one.
2 A: You knew him quite well, isn't it?
  B: Yeah, we went to college together.
3 A: You couldn't lend me a pound, could you?
  B: Sorry, I haven't got any change on me.
4 A: You weren't at the last class, you were?
  B: No. I was ill. Did I miss much?

5 A: Lovely weather, isn't it?
  B: Fantastic.
6 A: Haven't you heard of One Direction, have you?
  B: No. Why? Should I have?

DID YOU KNOW?

Other tags are becoming common in spoken English, although some people think they sound uneducated.

You know where the cathedral is, **yeah / right**?

It's really good, **no**?

Exercise 2

Replace *yeah?, right?* **and** *no?* **with more formal tags.**

1 You've been to university, ~~no?~~ *haven't you?*
2 It's a fantastic place to visit, no?
3 You know where to go, right?
4 We're going to meet them later, yeah?
5 He shouldn't be here, right?
6 They can't come tomorrow, right?

11 TRANSPORT AND TRAVEL

UNCOUNTABLE NOUNS

Here are some common uncountable nouns. Many may be countable in your language.

accommodation	information	progress
advice	litter	research
behaviour	luck	scenery
chaos	luggage	traffic
equipment	money	trouble
experience	music	weather
furniture	news	work

Many concepts or abstract nouns are uncountable: *peace, wealth, motivation, happiness.*

With uncountable nouns we often use the following quantifiers: *some, no, plenty of, not much, (not) enough, a good / great deal of, hardly any, (not) any (at all), little, more, less.*

Many nouns can be both countable and uncountable. There is often a difference in meaning.

fruit: *We grow all our own fruit.* (= general fruit to eat)
     A tomato is actually a fruit! (= one kind of fruit)

Exercise 1

Choose the correct option.

1 Can I get *a coffee / coffee*, please? Black, one sugar.
2 She's upset. She just needs a bit of sympathy and *understanding / an understanding*.
3 That was *a really lovely dinner / really lovely dinner*.
4 They have *a very happy marriage / very happy marriage*.
5 It's important to have *understanding / an understanding* of the local culture when you travel.
6 Have you had *a dinner / dinner* yet?
7 I don't drink *a coffee / coffee*. It makes me too hyper!
8 *Marriage / A marriage* is less important than it used to be.

Exercise 2

Decide which six sentences are incorrect. Then rewrite them correctly.

1 My hairs are getting really long. I need a haircut.
2 There are lots of accommodations in the town.
3 They breed sheep on a big farm out in the countryside.
4 There weren't that many peoples in class today.

5 The news this week are so depressing!
6 Sorry I'm late. I had some troubles with my car.
7 The tourist board gave me some really useful advices.
8 I forgot to bring any paper with me today.

EMPHATIC STRUCTURES

There are two common patterns we use to emphasise how we feel. In these patterns, *What* and *The thing that* mean the same thing and work in the same way.

What The thing that	annoys me irritates me worries me amazes me 's great 's really scary I find strange I love I can't stand etc.	is	that … when … the fact that … the way … the amount of … the number of … -ing … etc.

We can use the same pattern to talk about things that happened in the past.

The thing that amazed me **was** *the fact that* people stopped for pedestrians at crossings.

What I found strange **was** *that* there were so few people there.

Exercise 1

Complete sentence b using the word in brackets, and any other words necessary, so that it emphasises the feeling in a.

1 a The amount of pollution they have there is really worrying.
  b The thing _____ of pollution they have there. (worries)

2 a I find it strange that people prefer to drive rather than walk or cycle.
  b What _____ that people prefer to drive rather than walk or cycle. (find)

3 a When people get on the train while you're trying to get off, it really annoys me.
  b What _____ getting on the train while you're trying to get off. (annoying)

4 a The government increased the prices on the buses and it made people angry.
  b What _____ that the government put up the price of bus tickets. (angered)

5 a Being able to travel around the world with my job is great.
  b What _____ able to travel round the world. (love)

We can also change the word order in sentences using *It*.

Having to wait around in the airport between flights **is** *really boring.*

It's *really boring having to wait around in the airport between flights.*

Notice when we start with *What / The thing that*, we must link with *is / was*. There is no linking verb when we start with *It*.

What *angers me most* **is that** *the government is failing to do anything about pollution.*

It *really angers me* **that** *the government is failing to do anything about pollution.*

Exercise 2

Complete the sentences with your own ideas about the topic in brackets.

1 It drives me mad _____ . (air travel)
2 What I loved doing most _____ . (your childhood)
3 The thing I find most frustrating _____ . (learning English)
4 It's great _____ . (school)
5 It worries me _____ . (society)

12 HEALTH AND MEDICINE

SUPPOSED TO BE -ING AND *SHOULD* FOR TALKING ABOUT THE FUTURE

be supposed to be -ing

When we have arranged and organised something for the future, we usually use the present continuous or *be going to*.

I**'m meeting** a friend later. We**'re going to** see a film.

We**'re going** to the beach on Sunday. Do you want to come?

If we now can't or don't want to do what was arranged, we use *be supposed to be -ing*. We usually add an explanation or excuse to explain why not.

I**'m supposed to be meeting** a friend later, but I think I'm going to cancel. I'm feeling a bit rough.

We**'re supposed to be going** to the beach on Sunday, but I'm not sure we will now. The weather forecast is dreadful.

should / shouldn't

Should and *shouldn't* show we have a positive feeling or expectation about a future event.

It **should** be good (= I think it will be good). *I'm sure you'll have a great time.*

He **shouldn't** find the exam too difficult (= I don't think he'll find it hard). *I'm sure he'll pass.*

DID YOU KNOW?

We don't use *should* / *shouldn't* when we expect something bad.

I'm afraid the injection ~~should~~ is going to / will be painful and you ~~should~~ might be sore for a few hours afterwards.

~~You shouldn't like it~~ I doubt you'll like it.

Exercise 1

Choose the correct option.

1 I'll give you some antibiotics for the infection. It *should / shouldn't* clear up in a few days.
2 I'm *going / supposed to be going* away tomorrow, so I won't be in the office.
3 I'm just popping out to pick up my prescription. I *should / shouldn't* be long.
4 My brother's got to have some dental work done. It *should / is probably going to* be quite expensive.
5 We're *supposed to be having / having* a meeting tomorrow, but there are so many people off with flu that I think we'll have to cancel it.
6 I've e-mailed instructions on how to find us. It's quite a distinctive building as well, so you *shouldn't have / you're not supposed to be having* any difficulties.
7 *I doubt anyone will be / There shouldn't be anyone* in class today because of the bus strike.
8 Look at the weather! It's awful and the kids are *supposed to be playing / going to play* tennis today.

DETERMINERS

Determiners are words that go before nouns to show which or how many things you mean. They also show if we are talking about something in general or a specific thing or person. Some determiners such as *the, no, any* or *my, your,* etc. can go before any kind of noun, but others are only used with singular nouns or plurals or uncountable nouns.

Only before singular nouns

a, an, another, each, every, this, that

Before uncountable nouns

much, little	(only uncountable)
this, that	(also singular nouns)
some, most, all, other, more, less	(also plural nouns)

Before plurals

these, those, several, many, few, fewer	(only plurals)
some, most, all, other, more, less	(also uncountable)

DID YOU KNOW?

A lot of people say that *less* should not be used with plurals and you should use *few* instead. However, increasingly native speakers use *less* with both plurals and uncountable nouns.

Determiners and *of*

We don't usually use *of* with determiners unless it's with: another determiner

*most **of** the people questioned; both **of** my parents*

a pronoun

*neither **of** them; all **of** us*

Negatives

no, none and *neither* are determiners with a negative meaning, so avoid using them with the negative form of verbs.

There ~~isn't no~~ cure.

There's no cure. OR **There isn't any cure.**

~~None of my friends aren't~~ married.

None of my friends are married. OR **All of my friends are single**.

DID YOU KNOW?

We can replace a determiner + noun with a pronoun:

I liked both jokes.	*I liked both.*
Those shoes are nice.	*Those are nice.*
I'll ask the other students.	*I'll ask the others.*
Is this my book?	*Is this mine?*
There was no food left.	*There was none left.*

Exercise 1

Rewrite the sentences, correcting the mistake in each sentence.

1 Most of patients are here because of stress.
2 There's been a case of meningitis at the school but it hasn't spread to others students.
3 Each the three operations lasted about five hours.
4 I didn't like neither of the two treatments, personally.
5 Every doctors I saw failed to diagnose me properly.
6 They said they had none record of my appointment.

13 LIFE-CHANGING EVENTS

THE PAST PERFECT SIMPLE AND CONTINUOUS

The past perfect simple

The form of the past perfect simple is *had* + past participle. We use it to emphasise single actions or events that happened before a past time or event that has been mentioned. The past perfect simple is often used to talk about how many times something happened. It often goes with the words *by the time, before, after, already, always* and *never*.

*He'd had a couple of big rows with his boss **before he decided to leave**.*

*You know why he got sacked, don't you? He'd been late every day for a week **before it happened**!*

The past perfect continuous

The form of the past perfect continuous is *had been* + *-ing*. It is used to talk about actions, intentions or feelings over a period up to the time of a particular event in the past. It is often used to talk about how long something happened for. It is often used with expressions that show duration such as *for a while* and *for ages / months / years*.

***We'd been thinking about** moving **for a while** and then one day I went past this house that was for sale and just fell in love with it.*

Note that certain verbs tend not to be used in the continuous forms. These include *agree, be, believe, depend, disagree, doubt, forget, hate, like, love, mean, mind, owe, prefer, realise.*

Exercise 1

Choose the correct option.

1 A: So what made you decide to become a zoologist?
   B: I'd *always been / always been being* interested in science and I'd *always wanted / always been wanting* to work with animals, so it just seemed like a sensible choice.
2 I *had looked / had been looking* for work for ages, and I'd *had / been having* a few interviews, but nothing came of any of them, so in the end I took the first thing I got offered.
3 Me and my brother *hadn't got / hadn't been getting* on for quite a few months, so in the end I decided it was time to move out and get a place of my own.
4 I'd *asked / I had been asking* her out three or four times before, but *she'd always said / she'd always been saying* no, so you can imagine my surprise when she finally said yes!
5 He'd *talked / been talking* about taking up a sport for years, but *he'd never done / he'd never been doing* anything about it, so I was quite surprised when he actually started running.

DID YOU KNOW?

While past perfect forms emphasise that something happened before another event in the past, after using one we often then go back to using basic past forms when we add more details.
A: *Were you surprised when they split up?*
B: *No. They'd been arguing a lot anyway and then she found out that he was having an affair.*
*I was fired because **I'd complained** about the boss. When he found out about it, he **called** me to his office and **fired** me on the spot.*

Exercise 2

Complete the sentences with the correct form of the verbs in brackets. Where both the past perfect continuous and past perfect simple are possible, use the continuous form.

1 We _____ for it for ages, but it still _____ as a bit of a shock. Once the kids _____ finally _____ , the house _____ so quiet and empty. It'll take some getting used to! (plan, come, go, seem)
2 He _____ the lottery for years and _____ never _____ anything at all, so you can imagine how much of a shock it _____ when he _____ he _____ £100,000. (do, win, be, hear, win)
3 We _____ from Batumi to Tbilisi and we _____ for a few hours when my husband suddenly _____ he _____ the door unlocked! We had to turn round and go all the way back again! (drive, go, remember, leave)
4 It was quite odd, really, because she _____ everyone for ages how much she _____ retiring, but then once she finally _____ it was like she just _____ how to fill her days and she _____ getting really depressed. (tell, look forward to, stop, not / know, start)

BE ALWAYS / CONSTANTLY -ING, WISH AND WOULD

Habits and behaviour

We usually use the present simple to talk about habits.
*He's so soft. He **lets** her get her own way all the time.*

However, we use the present continuous + *always / constantly* to emphasise that a habit never stops or has no exceptions.
They're so aggressive. They're always getting into fights.
She's so spoilt. She's constantly getting what she wants!

Be always + *-ing* usually shows you find something annoying, but it can also emphasise unusual things you like.
*He's very romantic. **He's always buying** me roses and writing me poems and things like that!*

Use *I wish* + *would(n't)* + verb to show you want people to behave differently.
***I wish** the kids **would help out** more. (They don't usually)*
***I wish** he **wouldn't shout** so much. (He shouts a lot)*

Character

Use *wish* + *he / she was(n't)* or *were(n't)* to describe how we want people's character to be different.
***I wish he was / were** less strict. He punishes us too hard.*
***I wish she wasn't / weren't** so lazy. She never does anything.*

COMMON MISTAKES

- *She's such a slob. She ~~is never doing~~ never does any exercise.*

Don't use the present continuous to emphasise things that never happen.

- *I wish he ~~isn't~~ wasn't so mean.*

Use the past simple to talk about a current characteristic.

- *I wish he ~~would have~~ had shorter hair* OR *I wish he would cut his hair.*

- *I wish he ~~would be~~ was happy.*

Don't use *wish* + *would* to talk about character or appearance. Use the past simple.

Exercise 1

Find six sentences which have mistakes. Then rewrite them correctly.

1 I wish he wouldn't tidy up sometimes. He's so messy!
2 He's so stubborn. He's never admitting he's wrong!

3 He's so manipulative. He always trying to make me feel guilty.
4 They're constantly talking and disrupting the class.
5 I wish he is more assertive and that he'd defend himself a bit more.
6 She's so cheerful. Always she is smiling and laughing.
7 I wish they wouldn't argue so much. It's upsetting.
8 I really wish her not to go on about her boyfriend all the time. It just gets very boring.

Exercise 2
Write full sentences using the ideas below.
1 He / constantly / interrupt her / when / she / talk
2 I wish / she / play her music so loud / while / I / try / study
3 I wish / he / speak to me as if I / child
4 I really wish he / so mean / and that he / buy the cheapest thing all the time
5 They / always / joke / and / mess around

14 BANKS AND MONEY

PASSIVES
We use passives to focus attention on who or what an action affects and when it is unclear or unimportant who performs the action. We form passives using the verb *to be* + the past participle.
*My wages **are** usually **paid** into my account on the 22nd. (present simple)*
*A new security system **is being installed** at the moment. (present continuous)*
*Your new card **was sent out** to you last Monday. (past simple)*
*They said cash withdrawals **were being made** in Morocco. (past continuous)*
*The cheque **has been cleared**, but you will be charged for this. (present perfect simple)*
*I suddenly realised I**'d been tricked**. (past perfect simple)*

In passive sentences, we often don't mention who performs the action, because it's understood or it's unknown / not important. In passive sentences, if we want to show who or what performed the action, we add information using *by*.
*I **was offered** yet another credit card **by my bank** last week!*
*The dollar **has been strengthened by the news**.*

DID YOU KNOW?
We use the *be* + *-ing* form of the passive after certain verbs and after prepositions.
*He strongly **denied being involved** in the scandal.*
*I have absolutely **no interest in being sold** insurance!*
*I'm **scared of being ripped off**!*

Note: intransitive verbs (verbs that don't have an object) are never used in the passive form. These include *become, happen, die, lack, rise, fall, wait, arrive, cry, disappear.*

Exercise 1
Complete the sentences with the correct passive form of the verb in brackets.
1 The computer's very slow this morning, I'm afraid. The system _____ at the moment. (update)
2 I pay all my bills by standing order, so the money _____ automatically at the end of every month. (send)
3 It would appear that your overdraft limit _____ repeatedly _____ over recent weeks. (exceed)
4 I spoke to someone yesterday and they told me the money _____ already _____ . (transfer)

5 My credit card _____ three times yesterday and I'd like to know why. (reject)
6 We can't accept this cheque, I'm afraid. Look, it _____ yet. (not / sign)
7 It's not my fault! Up until last week, all my correspondence from the bank _____ to the wrong address. (forward)
8 According to our records, the letter _____ to you on the 28th of last month. (send)
9 We have all your details and you _____ as soon as a decision _____ . (contact, make)

WISH
The verb *wish* refers to hypothetical things: things we want, but which are impossible. As such, it is followed by past forms.

wish + past simple
The past simple is used to refer to current situations that can't be changed.
*I **wish I was** better with money. I'm always in debt.*
*I sometimes **wish I had** a car, but I can't afford one.*

wish + could
We use *could* to refer to abilities we would like.
*I **wish I could help**, but I've got people over for dinner.*
*I sometimes **wish we could stop** working, but we can't.*

wish + would
We use *would* to refer to habits (see page 166) or to people, organisations or things that are 'refusing' to do something.
*I **wish the government would** invest in schools more.*
*I **wish he wouldn't waste** his money the way he does.*
Don't use *mustn't* with *wish*, use *didn't have to*.
*I **wish I ~~mustn't~~ didn't have to go**, but I've got to work.*
Use *hope* and present tenses for future possibilities, not *wish*.
*I **hope interest rates go up** soon. I have a lot of savings.*

wish + past perfect
The past perfect simple or continuous refers to regrets about the past and to things in the past we now want to be different.
*I **wish I'd invested** the money instead of spending it.*
*I **wish we'd never sold** that painting. We sold it for £6,000 and it's worth ten times that figure now.*

wish + could have (done)
We use *could have (done)* to refer to past possibilities.
*I **wish I could have done** something, but it was impossible.*
*I really **wish I could have gone**, but I was just so busy.*

Exercise 1
Complete the sentences with the correct form of the verb in brackets.
1 A: I wish I _____ fill in my tax return! (not have to)
   B: Isn't it worth getting an accountant?
2 A: I wish we _____ about it earlier. (think)
   B: Oh well. We didn't.
3 A: I wish the government _____ taxes. (cut)
   B: Yeah? I think we should be paying more!
4 A: I wish I _____ my holiday abroad months ago. (book)
   B: I bet! It's so expensive now that our currency has collapsed.
5 A: I wish I _____ . It sounds like you had a great time. (can come)
   B: Yeah, we did. Still, next time, yeah?

LINKING WORDS

and, when, after, then, afterwards, after that

And, when and *after* join two events within a sentence. *Then,* *afterwards* or *after that* connect two ideas across separate sentences, unless preceded by *and* or *but*.

*Wash the chickpeas **and (then)** put them in water to soak.*

*Wash the chickpeas. **Afterwards** / **After that** / **Then**, put them in water to soak.*

once, until

Once can mean *after*. It's often followed by perfect tenses.

***Once** the onions **have turned** brown, take them off the heat.*

Until shows what happens up to a particular point in time.

*Fry the onions slowly **until** they are brown.*

for, during

Use *for* to show duration.

*Boil the broccoli **for** just three minutes.*

Use *during* with a noun to show when another event happened.

*He had a phone call **during** dinner and had to leave.*

as, so

As can mean *because*. It follows a cause and links to a result.

*Cook it on quite a low heat, **as** you want to make sure the meat is soft and tender.*

So (that) can explain the reason for doing an action.

*Marinate the meat for an hour **so (that)** it doesn't dry out.*

although, despite, however

Although and *despite* link contrasting ideas within a sentence. *However* usually shows the ideas in one sentence contrast with those in the sentence before. (see Writing 6, page 161)

in case, provided, unless, otherwise

In case is used to show that you are prepared for something that might happen.

*I'll email you the recipe later **in case** you forget how we did it.*

Provided can replace 'if you make sure'.

*It's fairly easy to do **provided** you give yourself enough time to prepare everything.*

Unless means 'if … not'.

*You can't really cook **unless** you love eating!*

Otherwise often starts a new sentence and shows the result if we don't do something.

*Make sure you follow the instructions. **Otherwise**, it could all go horribly wrong!*

Exercise 1

Complete the sentences with appropriate linking words.

1 I don't buy these biscuits very often _____ I find them so addictive. _____ I've had one, I have to finish the whole packet!

2 He let the milk boil over, _____ the fact that I asked him to keep an eye on it, and _____ I had to clean up the mess!

3 I'll pack some snacks _____ we get hungry, _____ you won't have to bring anything.

4 Leave the beans to soak _____ at least six hours. _____ , they'll be almost inedible.

5 They'll cook whatever you want _____ you order in advance and you can eat as much as you want _____ you burst!

PATTERNS AFTER REPORTING VERBS

Some reporting verbs often followed by infinitive (with *to*):

agree	claim	intend	pretend	refuse
arrange	decide	offer	promise	threaten

Some reporting verbs often followed by *-ing*:

admit	consider	deny	involve	recommend
avoid	continue	imagine	miss	suggest

Some reporting verbs often followed by person + infinitive (with *to*):

advise	encourage	invite	remind	urge
ask	force	persuade	tell	warn

Some reporting verbs often followed by a preposition + *-ing*:

be accused of	admit to	be criticised for	be forgiven for
apologise for	rely on	be blamed for	
confess to	insist on	worry about	

Exercise 1

Choose the correct option.

1 In the end, the waiter offered *giving / to give* us the starters for free as we'd been waiting so long!

2 I was going to have the chicken soup, but the waiter persuaded me *trying / to try* the pumpkin ravioli instead.

3 The doctor recommended *to cut down / cutting down on / me to cut down on* red meat as far as possible.

4 My mum always used to force me *eat / eating / to eat* my greens when I was a kid.

5 I can't imagine *to work / working / work* in one of those places where they kill animals. It must be horrific.

6 A new campaign is being launched today, urging people *to not waste / don't waste* food.

7 The company eventually confessed to *use / using* out-of-date ingredients in their products.

8 We should consider *give / to give / giving* free samples out in order to attract more customers.

9 Since I left home, I've really missed *to have / having / to have* dinner cooked for me every night.

10 The government have been criticised for *not to do / don't do / not doing* enough to combat food fraud.

DID YOU KNOW?

Many verbs have more than one preposition and/or pattern. Sometimes this doesn't change the meaning:

*He **admitted causing** the problem.*

*He **admitted to causing** the problem.*

Sometimes it does change the meaning:

*Officials **blamed** the outbreak of the stomach virus **on** a local restaurant.*

*Officials **blamed** a local restaurant **for causing** the outbreak of the stomach virus.*

A good dictionary will provide information on verb patterns.

16 BUSINESS

THE FUTURE CONTINUOUS

The future continuous is used to refer to an existing future arrangement or plan when you want to talk or ask about a new action that will now happen during this arrangement or as a consequence of the decision.

I'll be popping out to the café in a while. (= existing arrangement / plan) *Can I get you anything?* (= new action when I pop out)

I'll be talking to the area manager later, so I'll raise your concerns with her.

Will you be seeing Max later? I promised I'd get this report to him today. (and you could take it when you go)

Exercise 1

Match the existing plans 1–8 to the follow-up comments a–h.

1 Will you be translating the website content into any other languages?
2 Your order will be going out today by special delivery,
3 They'll be launching the product in the US first,
4 When's she going to be starting her new job?
5 Will they be taking any new staff on during the summer?
6 I'll be going past the canteen,
7 Will you be using the computer later?
8 He'll be retiring in the summer,

a so it should be with you first thing tomorrow.
b Because I must remember to ring and wish her luck.
c Because that could be one way of breaking into some overseas markets.
d so we won't have to put up with his moaning for much longer.
e Because I'll watch that film I missed last night if you're not.
f so I might buy one when I'm in New York next month.
g Because I'll apply if they are.
h so I'll get you a coffee, if you like.

DID YOU KNOW?

We can use *going to* instead of *will* with no change in meaning.

They're going to be launching the product in the US first, so I might buy one when I go there.

will be -ing and time phrases

The future continuous is also used to talk about something that will be in progress at a particular time or over a particular period of time in the future.

I can't make Friday. I'll be attending a conference in Bolton.

That's a good question. I'll be talking about that later on.

You're not going to be doing any sport for a while after the operation.

EXPRESSING NECESSITY AND ABILITY

Replacing must with forms of have to

If we'd done more market research, we wouldn't have had to redesign it so soon.

It's a risk investors are going to have to take.

This is the third time this month I've had to talk to you about this.

I sold my car last month, so I've been having to take public transport to work since then.

Most respondents claimed they had had to make sacrifices for the sake of their career.

This device allows you to share files without you having to rely on a computer.

Having to get up so early for my new job has been quite difficult.

force and make

When something creates an obligation for someone to do something, use *force* or *make*.

The negative feedback that we got forced us to look at the design again.

If we'd done more market research, it would've made us think about our product a bit more.

Replacing can with forms of be able to

This deal means I'll finally be able to give up my day job and focus entirely on the business.

We'll soon be able to generate our own electricity.

Over the last few years, we have been able to keep ahead by developing new products.

In the end, we were able to fulfil all our orders before Christmas.

Being able to speak another language has made a huge difference to my life.

I'd love to be able to code computer programmes.

enable, allow, let

When something gives you the ability or permission to do something use *enable, allow* or *let*. Note that *let* is not followed by *to*.

The loan will enable / allow us to buy more stock.

The development will let us cut costs massively.

Exercise 1

Complete the second sentence so that it has a similar meaning to the first sentence using the word given. Do not change the word given. You must use between two and five words, including the word given.

1 We've been able to step up production thanks to the new investment.
   ENABLED
   The new investment _____ up production.
2 With this device, you can monitor how much electricity you're using.
   LETS
   The device _____ how much electricity you're using.
3 It's great being self-employed. I don't need to be nice to people I don't like!
   BE
   The best thing about working for myself is not _____ nice to people I don't like.
4 We've reached the factory's capacity, so we can't expand at the moment.
   WON'T
   Without a new factory, _____ expand.
5 They only found out because he forced me to tell them.
   MADE
   They wouldn't have found out if he _____ them.
6 We had to abandon the project in the end.
   FORCED
   We _____ abandon the project in the end.

DID YOU KNOW?

We can use *force* in the passive instead of *have to*.

The company had to / was forced to close down its main plant.

INFORMATION FILES

FILE 1

Unit 1 page 11 **SPEAKING**

Student A

Some of the following language might also help:

> The painting shows …
> In the background / At the back of the picture, you can (just) see …
> In the foreground / At the front of the picture, there is …
> To the right / left of the (man) …
> In the (bottom / top right hand) corner of the painting, you can (just) see …

FILE 4

Unit 14 page 125 **CONVERSATION PRACTICE**

Student A

For three conversations, you are the customer.

1 You want to open a new account.

3 You want to take out a loan – decide how much.

5 You want to transfer some money overseas.

For three conversations, you are the bank clerk.

2 Student B wants to apply for an overdraft. You can do this, but there will be a charge.

4 Student B wants a new cash card. You can't produce one now. One can be sent out within two weeks.

6 Student B thinks they have been the victim of fraud. They do not have insurance and the bank can't refund any losses.

COMEDY

Comedy in Booker's terms does not necessarily have to be funny. As with the other plots, this is about story development.

1 The main characters are bound to get together, but can't see it: they have apparently different characters or viewpoints; they're from different classes; they're with a 'wrong' partner, etc.

2 This confusion becomes worse through further misunderstandings, events or new rival characters.

3 Something happens to reveal the truth. Characters become aware of their true selves. Baddies are punished. The right couple gets together or marry.

Common features: people disguise themselves (including men as women and vice versa) or pretend to be someone different, or a meeting is arranged but the wrong person comes.

Stories: *Beauty and the Beast*; *Twelfth Night*; *Cyrano de Bergerac*; *You've Got Mail*

RAGS TO RICHES

This is the story where a quiet or 'weak' character with a special talent becomes a hero or great success.

1 The main character is in poverty or bullied by a dark character.

2 The hero's talent is revealed and they have some initial success.

3 A crisis happens. Everything goes wrong and it seems they can no longer reach their goal. This may be an accident; a dark character asserting their power, the weakness of the hero or an obstacle in society.

4 Some event helps them find new strength to overcome the problem.

5 They achieve complete success, marry the 'prince', or become the 'king'.

Note: Some rags to riches stories are 'true', but when told, the account still follows this pattern.

Stories: *Cinderella; Aladdin; The Pursuit of Happyness; The Blind Side*

FILE 5

Unit 6 page 57 READING

| To | Jacksonjane@shotmail.ml |
| Subject | Re: Surprise, surprise! |

Hi Jane,

Hope this address still works for you. I bet this is a bit of a surprise! It's my fault, of course. I realise I've isolated myself a bit. If you're annoyed with me and don't want to know or respond, then fair enough. Anyway, it was just to let you know that I'm going to be over in England soon and it'd be really good to get back in touch – and introduce you to my wife and new son, Huang Fu. See picture attached. Email me.

Ben

FILE 6

Unit 16 page 147 SPEAKING

Pair A

1 a special brush which lets you brush your hair and remove knots without pain

2 a program that can edit your online profile and delete any embarrassing or potentially career-damaging information

3 a chain of specialist chocolate stores

Discuss how you'll present each product. Give each one a name. Think of the retail price and how much profit you'll make on each one. You might want to explain how each one works and why it's better than competitors – if there are any. Think about how much money you want Pair B to invest and why. What stake of the company will you give them in exchange? Negotiate if they offer you something.

When the other pair present their products, ask questions about the product, the market, how much they will be earning in a year / two years / three years, etc. If you like the product, offer to invest in their company. Negotiate what percentage of the company you want in return – and specify any other conditions.

Student B

TRAGEDY

Tragedy shows a good person's fall from grace. It follows this pattern:

1   The main character is successful but not fully satisfied. An opportunity to fulfil their dreams presents itself, but it involves a bad deed.

2   The hero gets away with their crime and enjoys the rewards.

3   Problems arise – something threatens to reveal the bad deed or end the hero's period of success. The hero commits a further evil act to protect themselves.

4   Forces gather against the hero and their life runs out of control.

5   The hero is destroyed either by committing suicide or by a relative of the victim seeking revenge.

Stories: *Macbeth; Carmen; Breaking Bad; Black Swan*

VOYAGE AND RETURN

A hero becomes a better person through a visit to another world. It follows this pattern:

1   The hero has a flawed character, for example: immature, restless, foolish, unkind or arrogant – and through some incident is transported into a strange new world.

2   At first they find the new world exciting and fascinating.

3   The hero encounters a problem which makes them see a dark side to the new world.

4   The hero experiences the world as a nightmare and feels trapped and looks for a way out.

5   The hero manages to escape and returns to the world, often with new insight and as a better person.

Stories: *Gulliver's Travels; Alice in Wonderland; Big; 17 Again.*

Student B

1   There are two cows chatting in a field. The first cow says. 'This mad-cow disease is really worrying. They say it's spreading fast.' The other cow replies. 'It doesn't bother me – it doesn't affect us ducks.'

2   A doctor is consulting a colleague. 'I have this patient who is suffering form a Jimbomba – it's a rare tropical disease. It's very contagious.'

'Ah yes. Interesting, I had a patient who suffered from that some years ago?'

'Really? What should I do?'

'I recommend a diet of pizzas and pancakes.'

'Pizzas and pancakes. That's a pretty radical solution. Will it really cure them?'

'Probably not, but it's the only food that'll fit under the door.'

3   'Doctor, Doctor, I'm on a diet and it's making me really irritable. Yesterday I actually bit someone's ear off.'

'Oh dear! That's a lot of calories!'

Student B

You work for Right Car Rentals. Student A is going to collect a car they have booked online from you.

Decide if you have any special offers this week.

Point out that the car runs on diesel not petrol.

Try to sell some extras – you get 15% commission if you do!

Decide how much to charge for the following extras:

• GPS

• Additional insurance to cover damage to tyres and windscreen

• Comprehensive insurance to cover damage to the vehicle, injury or loss of life, theft of property, etc.

• A baby seat (for children under 2) or a booster seat (for children from 2 to 8)

• Cover for any additional drivers

Group B

WORK ON RESEARCH LAB HALTED

Building work on an animal research laboratory funded by Oxford University has been stopped following several months of threats and harassment by members of extremist animal rights groups. The company involved in the construction of the lab has pulled out of the project amidst fears for the safety of both site workers and the firm's board members.

The £18 million centre was intended to allow experiments aimed at combating illnesses such as cancer, heart disease and diabetes to be carried out. The project has attracted negative publicity since it was first announced, with demonstrations against it being held quite regularly. Recently, however, it seems that a small radical group opposed to the use of animals in any kind of scientific research has launched a campaign of intimidation. Only last week, the addresses of university staff were published online, leading to concerns that they might now be targeted.

Animal rights groups see vivisection as cruel, unreliable and unnecessary. However, leading scientists have claimed that the research the lab aims to do will provide invaluable insights into the treatment of all manner of illnesses. Work on the building will apparently resume once new builders have been found.

UNLIKELY RECIPE FOR SUCCESS

A Mexican restaurant in Dresden, Germany seems to have found the secret of success: maggots! Since adding a range of dishes featuring the insects to their menu, Espitas restaurant claims to have been almost constantly fully booked.

Despite being a popular source of protein in many countries, in Germany maggots are more commonly associated with decay and death. This didn't stop restaurant owner Alexander Wolf from adding the insects to his menu earlier in the year. Apparently, the initial idea was little more than a joke, but the response was overwhelmingly positive. 'Most are disgusted, but try them out of curiosity or for a dare', noted Mr Wolf, 'and are amazed at how good they taste. Many people come back again, and usually bring more friends with them'.

The restaurant now offers everything from maggot salads to maggots in ice cream, fried maggots with corn and cactus to maggot cocktails. Interestingly, all the maggots are imported from Mexico, as German maggots are not deemed tasty enough.

Following on from recent successes, Mr Wolf now plans to introduce other traditional Mexican dishes such as ant eggs and grasshoppers.

a hammer

a drill

a saw

a torch

a stepladder

a nail

a screw

toothpaste

a rope

wire

a pan

a cloth

a dustpan and brush

a mop and bucket

glue

a corkscrew

a tin opener

a lighter

a rubber

Tippex

a stapler

scissors

clips

Sellotape

washing powder

a needle and thread

an iron

clothes pegs

a charger

a ruler

a plaster

a bandage

FILE 8

Unit 12 page 110 **SPEAKING**

Student C

1 A hypochondriac went to the doctor. 'Doctor. You've got to refer me to a consultant. I've got liver disease.' 'How could you possibly know that?' replied the doctor. 'There's no discomfort and no outward signs of illness with liver disease.' And the patient says, 'You see! Those are my precise symptoms.'

2 A man went to his doctor for a check-up. After examining the man, the doctor said, 'Well, I've got some bad news and some good news. The bad news is you've got hepatitis, but the good news is you've also got Alzheimer's, so you'll forget all about it!'

3 'Doctor, Doctor. Have you got something for a bad headache?'

'Of course. Just take this hammer and hit yourself on the head. Then you'll have a bad headache.'

FILE 12

Unit 16 page 147 **SPEAKING**

Pair B

1 a key ring that is fitted with a balloon that automatically inflates on contact with water

2 a special Caribbean sauce for barbecues

3 a special box for shoes that enables you to remove smells instantly

Discuss how you'll present each product. Give each one a name. Think of the retail price and how much profit you'll make on each one. You might want to explain how each one works and why it's better than competitors – if there are any. Think about how much money you want Pair A to invest and why. What stake of the company will you give them in exchange? Negotiate if they offer you something.

When the other pair present their products, ask questions about the product, the market, how much they will be earning in a year / two years / three years, etc. If you like the product, offer to invest in their company. Negotiate what percentage of the company you want in return – and specify any other conditions.

FILE 13

Unit 14 page 125 **CONVERSATION PRACTICE**

Student B

For three conversations, you are the bank clerk.

1 Student A wants to open an account. You need to see sufficient relevant ID.

3 Student A wants to take out a loan. You can't lend this much to someone with such a bad credit rating.

5 Student A wants to transfer money overseas. This is fine, but there will be a 5% commission charge.

For three conversations, you are the customer.

2 You want to apply for an overdraft. Decide how large.

4 You have lost your card and need a new one.

6 According to your bank statement, 1500 euros were withdrawn from your account last week in Belgium. You've never even been to Belgium!

FILE 14

Unit 3 page 27 **CONVERSATION PRACTICE**

Student B

Look at the four situations below. Think about what you need to ask your partner for in each of these situations.

1 You've got some new shoes which are rubbing on the back of your heels and you don't want your heels to get sore and bleed.

2 On a picnic, the tab on the top of a tin/can has broken off so you can't open it easily.

3 A screw on your glasses has come loose and the arm of the glasses has fallen off.

4 You need to change a light bulb, but you can't reach the light even if you stand on a chair.

FILE 16

Unit 15 page 134 **VOCABULARY**

almond	mint	tomato	grapes	broccoli	plum
raisin	turnip	hazelnuts	octopus	parsnip	coconut
trout	courgette	parsley	eel	rosemary	fig
ginger	orange	kidney bean	lentils	sweet potato	sweetcorn
oyster	peach	cabbage	pumpkin	radish	celery
pepper	fennel	spring onion	chilli	salmon	beetroot

FILE 15

Unit 12 page 110 **SPEAKING**

Student A

1   A priest was asked to inform a man with a heart condition that he'd just inherited $10 million. Everyone was afraid the shock would kill him. So the priest went to the man's house and said, 'Joe, what would you do if you were left $10 million in a will?'

    'Well, Father, I'd give half of it to my church.'

    At which point, the priest dropped dead!

2   A man in a bar falls off his stool. Some guys decide to be nice and help him home, so they pick him up off the floor, and drag him out the door. On the way to the car, he falls down three times. When they get to his house, they help him out of the car and he falls down four more times. They ring the doorbell, and one says, 'Here's your husband!' and the man's wife says, 'Where are his crutches?'

3   'Doctor, Doctor. I think I need glasses.'

    'You certainly do, Sir. This is a hairdresser's!'

FILE 18

Unit 3 page 27 **CONVERSATION PRACTICE**

Student A

Look at the four situations below. Think about what you need to ask your partner for in each of these situations.

1   The strap on your bag has broken.

2   You've dropped your ring and it's rolled under a cupboard and you want to try and get it out.

3   You've dropped a bottle of oil on the floor and it's smashed.

4   You knocked over a flower vase in the house you're staying in and a bit of it has broken off.

FILE 19

Unit 11 page 99 **CONVERSATION PRACTICE**

Student A

You are going to collect a car you have booked online. It's a small family car with a little bit of space in the boot. You are travelling with your partner (who might do some of the driving) and your five-year-old daughter (who hates being in cars).

The car rental assistant may try to sell you some extras.

Ask about them and decide if you want them or not.

Think of three other questions you will need to ask.

FILE 17

Student B

Some of the following language might also help:

> The painting shows …
> In the background / At the back of the picture you can (just)
>   see …
> In the foreground / At the front of the picture there is …
> To the right / left of the (man) …
> In the (bottom / top right hand) corner of the painting you
>   can (just) see …

AUDIO SCRIPTS

UNIT 1

▶ TRACK 1

1 Yeah, at the weekends, of course. I go shopping, go to the cinema, go clubbing sometimes. I don't tend to during the week, though, because I've got to get up early for school and I've got homework, and basically my parents prefer me to stay at home.

2 Yeah, all the time. My headphones are glued to my ears! I like all kinds of stuff as well – rock, pop, even some classical.

3 Not as much as I'd like to, because I really love it – especially musicals. I mean, I do go now and again, but the seats are so expensive I can't afford to go more than a couple of times a year.

4 Very rarely, to be honest. I guess I might in the summer – if it's very hot. I find it a bit boring, just going up and down the pool. It's not really my kind of thing – and I'm not very good at it either.

5 Probably less than I think I do, if you know what I mean. It's always on in the background, you know, but I don't pay much attention to it most of the time. I will watch a big game if there's one on and the occasional film, but apart from that, most of it's rubbish.

6 Yeah, I guess so. I usually play football on a Wednesday and I go running now and again. I generally cycle to college as well – unless it's raining.

7 No, not as a rule. I tend to watch films on demand through my TV at home. Oh, and I download quite a lot of stuff too.

8 Not as much as I used to. I was addicted to this online game for a while until my parents banned me. I'd sometimes play for five hours a day! I play other games now, but my parents control it a bit more.

▶ TRACK 2

1 I don't tend to during the week, though.

2 Yeah, all the time! My headphones are glued to my ears.

3 Not as much as I'd like to, because I really love it.

4 Very rarely, to be honest. I guess I might in the summer.

5 I don't pay much attention to it most of the time. I will watch a big game, if there's one on.

6 Yeah, I guess so. I usually play football on a Wednesday and I go running now and again.

7 No, not as a rule. I tend to watch films on demand through my TV at home.

8 Not as much as I used to. I was addicted to this online game, until my parents banned me. I'd sometimes play for five hours a day!

▶ TRACK 3

1 It does nothing for me. It's quite boring, quite dull.

2 It's one of those tunes that's very easy to remember – very catchy.

3 It's hilarious – just really, really funny.

4 It didn't do much for me. It's typical big-budget Hollywood – very commercial.

5 I can't explain it. It's really strange – really weird.

6 It's just too much for my liking – really over-the-top.

7 You can't stop reading. It's so exciting, so gripping!

8 It's good, but it's quite upsetting – quite disturbing.

9 It's a really inspiring story, really uplifting.

10 Don't go and see it! It's dreadful, absolutely awful.

▶ TRACK 4

A: So what kind of things do you do in your free time?

B: I guess films are the main thing.

A: Really? Do you go to the cinema much then?

B: Oh, all the time. I mean, I go at least once a week, but I'll often go two or three times!

A: Wow! That is a lot!

B: Yeah. I mean it depends what's on.

A: Right.

B: What about you? Do you go much?

A: Now and again, if there's something I really want to see, but I'm happy just to watch at home.

B: Really? But if you're watching an action movie with all the special effects, don't you want to see it on the big screen?

A: Yeah, I guess, but, to be honest, I'm not that keen on action movies.

B: Really? I mean, what about *X-Men*? Or *The Hunger Games*, stuff like that?

A: Yeah, *The Hunger Games* was OK, I suppose, but I'd rather see other things.

B: Actually there was this great Korean film on TV last night – *Oldboy*.

A: Oh yeah, I started watching it, but I turned over.

B: You didn't like it?

A: Not really. It was so over-the-top. That scene where he eats the live octopus! I don't know. It was all a bit too weird for my liking. Didn't you find it strange?

B: I guess it *is* a bit, but that's what I like about it. They actually did an American remake of it, but I prefer the original – I've seen it loads of times.

A: Really? As I say, it's not really my kind of thing. I prefer a good drama. So what other films are you into?

B: Oh, all sorts. I mean, I'm really into action films and stuff like that, but I'll watch most things really. As I say, I go most weeks, so, you know …

A: Have you seen *Long Walk to Freedom*?

B: Yeah. Have you?

A: No, but I've heard it's good. I was actually thinking of going to see it.

B: You should, I was in tears by the end.

A: Really? I thought it was supposed to be a feel-good movie.

B: No, it is, it is. It's really inspiring, really uplifting – he's just such an incredible character. Honestly, it's brilliant.

A: I'll check it out then.

▶ TRACK 5

1 A: I'm really into 60s music. The Beatles, The Stones, stuff like that.
   B: Yeah? It's not really my kind of thing. It's more the kind of stuff my dad listens to.

2 A: Do you like Tarantino? I love his films.
   B: He's all right, I guess, but I'm not that keen on his films. They're a bit over-the-top for my liking.

3 A: Have you ever read any Paulo Coelho? His books are fantastic.
   B: I've read one. It was OK, I guess, but it didn't really do that much for me, to be honest.

Now, if you follow me through into the next room, we come to two paintings by a 17th century Dutch artist who was both widely admired and reasonably successful during his lifetime. Born in Leiden in 1629, Gabriel Metsu moved to Amsterdam around 1655 and produced over forty major works. Sadly, though, he died at the age of 37, at a time when his career was going particularly well, and since then he has been rather forgotten, which seems a bit of a shame, to be honest.

These two pieces were meant to be hung together as companion pieces. In the painting on the left, a young man is writing a letter and on the right, we see a young woman reading a letter. The viewers are supposed to understand that he is composing a love letter to her, and that here she is digesting it. On the surface, these may look like fairly conventional, fairly realistic pieces, but look more carefully and you soon realise they are actually very open to interpretation.

The man appears to be a member of the upper middle classes, and his surroundings create the impression that he's well travelled: through the open window, we can see a globe in the room behind him and there's an expensive Turkish rug on his table. To his right, there's an Italian-style landscape hanging on the wall, which suggests he's a man of the world. Meanwhile, the woman, who is also expensively dressed, seems to belong more to the domestic world. Painted in bolder colours, she looks calm and content as she reads.

However, not everything is as it first appears. Beneath the surface of the calm domestic world lies trouble. In the foreground of the painting, we see a tiny thimble – the small china cup you wear on your finger to protect it while you are sewing. Obviously, the woman was so excited to receive her letter that she jumped up in the middle of her needlework. To the right of the picture, we see the woman's maid pulling back a curtain, behind which we see two ships on a stormy sea. This could well be a symbol of the difficult, stormy nature of love, especially when partners are separated. Look carefully and you'll notice too that the servant has another letter to deliver – presumably to the man shown here.

Even he, depicted in darker, more subtle shades, is a victim of the fires of the heart. The rich red of the carpet and the bright light pouring in through the window suggest he has a heated mind. The underlying message now seems painfully clear: passion can lead to chaos!

▶ **TRACK 7**

1 Famously, van Gogh sliced his ear off.
2 Unfortunately, it couldn't be restored.
3 Incredibly, he was only nine.
4 Obviously, some people will just think it's weird.
5 Hopefully, some will like it.
6 Initially, Picasso's work was quite realistic.
7 Frankly, they were stolen.

▶ **TRACK 8**

A: It's basically about this guy who's a weatherman and he has to report on this annual festival. It's a small town, and he's living in LA and is now a city boy so he thinks the place is silly, and he's quite arrogant. On top of that, he's been covering the story for several years and he's bored with it.
B: Well, it would be boring.
A: I guess. But he's kind of laughing at them.
B: At who?
A: The people in the town and the whole festival.
B: Right.
A: Anyway, he does the story and that night he has a date with this woman, but it's a complete disaster and he goes back to his hotel and you know, he can't wait to get back to LA.

B: Right.
A: Anyway, the next day he wakes up, and he hears the same song as he'd heard the previous day. And as the day goes on he realises, basically it is exactly the same day.
B: He's gone back in time?
A: Well, not exactly because what happens is the next day he wakes up and it's the same day again, and the same the next day and the next.
B: He's stuck?
A: Exactly, and when he first realises, he kind of enjoys it, because he, er, he can, can improve each day to avoid, like, the things he didn't like. And so, for example, his date with the woman improves. And then he realises he'll never actually ever get together with the woman because he always has to start the same day. Then, and then he gets depressed and tries to commit suicide but even when he kills himself he wakes up again repeating the same day and it's like a living hell.
B: Sounds a bit depressing.
A: No, it's hilarious, really funny.
B: OK. So how does he escape? I guess he does.
A: To be honest, I forget now, but he does and you know they all live happily ever after, but it's great.

UNIT 2

▶ **TRACK 9**

af**flu**ent	run-<u>down</u>	house
grand	**stun**ning	soar
de<u>pri</u>ved	**tren**dy	knock <u>down</u>
hideous	up-and-<u>com</u>ing	steer <u>clear</u> of
<u>high</u>-rise	be <u>based</u>	<u>ren</u>ovate
his**tor**ic	date <u>back</u> to	
rough	<u>do</u>minate	

▶ **TRACK 10**

M = May I = Ivana

M: What a lovely day!
 I: Yeah, it's nice, isn't it? It's been a really warm autumn.
M: So, where are we?
 I: Well, the bit we've just been through, with all the high-rise blocks, is what we call New Belgrade. It's the big up-and-coming area as all the new businesses are relocating here. And I don't know if you can see it or not, but just behind us, over to the right, is the Arena, which is where all the big concerts and sports events are held. It's one of the biggest entertainment venues in Europe.
M: Yeah, I think I did catch a glimpse of it.
 I: You might've seen it on TV – it's the place they held the Eurovision Song contest.
M: Oh, right. To be honest, I'm not really that keen on Eurovison. It's not really my kind of thing.
 I: No? Well, I guess you never win these days! Anyway, now we're crossing over the River Sava into Old Belgrade.
M: Wow! The river looks wonderful.
 I: Yeah, it's great. In the summer, we often go out on little boats or have dinner down by the waterside.
M: Oh, that sounds lovely. And what's that big bridge over there?
 I: That's the Ada Bridge. It's quite new, actually. It only opened a few years ago.
M: It's very impressive.
 I: It looks even better when it's lit up at night.
M: Mmmm.

I: And just down there, there's a little street called Gavrila Principa Street, which is where Manakova Kuca – Manak's House – is located. It's an ethnological museum and it houses an amazing collection of old national costumes and embroidery and stuff.

M: OK. I'll check that out if I have time. What's that building over there?

I: Oh, that's St Mark's Church.

M: Wow! That's a stunning building. How old is it?

I: Not that old, actually. It was built in the late 1930s or something, but it's on the site of a much older church. It contains the tomb of Stefan Dusan, who was perhaps the greatest Serbian emperor ever.

M: Oh, OK.

I: And if you want to walk around here later, you're quite close to the Kalemegdan Fortress, one of the most historic buildings in Belgrade. There's the Victor Monument up there as well, which was erected after the First World War. It's one of the city's most famous landmarks.

M: Right. Well, I'll have to remember to take my camera with me up there, then.

I: And now we're coming up to Dedinje, which is one of the more affluent parts of the city. It's where all the celebrities and the old aristocratic families live – and a lot of the embassies are based here as well.

M: The houses certainly do look very grand.

I: Yeah, they're amazing.

▶ TRACK 11

1

We're proud to announce that this year we're opening a new wing dedicated exclusively to Asian art. It's taken us over a decade and nearly a hundred million euros to put it all together, but we've been extremely lucky in that we've received some very generous donations, without which none of this would've been possible. The extension is perhaps the most significant and innovative architectural addition to the building in our history. Officially, it's due to open in a couple of months, and having overseen the collection, I can tell you with some confidence that it'll be a sensation.

2

A: But we don't need it.

B: Yeah, but it's just such a lovely thing. And anyway, if we only ever bought things we actually really need, we'd hardly ever buy anything. Just think of it as a piece of art for the house.

A: Yeah, maybe, I guess … but where are we going to put it?

B: I don't know. We'll find somewhere, I'm sure. It could go in the kitchen perhaps. Or the living room?

A: It's just asking for trouble. It's bound to get broken. The kids will smash it or the dog will run past and knock it over.

B: Oh, come on! That's not likely to happen. You're worrying about nothing. And anyway, I like it.

A: Fine. Suit yourself. Get it then. How much do they want for it anyway?

3

They've just opened this new exhibition of old military vehicles, which is supposed to be really good. It opens at ten, so I'm going to go down there tomorrow morning and have a look at that. I'm not sure if it's free to get in or not, though. I guess you might have to pay, but that's OK. I'm sure it'll be worth it. Don't know if tanks are really your thing or not, but if they are then you might fancy coming along. Just thought I'd suggest it anyway. Give me a bell back when you get this and let me know.

4

A: Oh, man! I think I'm gonna faint!

B: You shouldn't have gone on that ride.

A: Well, it looked quite tame, but all that spinning around has made me dizzy. Oh, I need to sit down.

B: Wait there. I'll go and get you a glass of water.

A: Thanks. I'm so embarrassed.

B: Don't worry about it. Just learn your lesson for next time.

5

The club is applying for planning permission to expand the current site by some 20,000 seats – and we're launching a campaign to block this. For many years now, on match days, there have been both transport and anti-social behaviour problems in the area, and we believe that any expansion is bound to worsen the situation. We understand the club's desire to boost its income, but we don't believe that all other alternatives have yet been explored. We've nothing against the club in itself, but we're firmly opposed to any development that'll result in further tensions between supporters and local residents.

▶ TRACK 12

1 This year we're opening a new wing dedicated exclusively to Asian art.
2 The kids will smash it.
3 It opens at ten.
4 I'm going to go down there tomorrow morning and have a look at that.
5 I think I'm going to faint.
6 I'll go and get you a glass of water.

▶ TRACK 13

1 There are bound to be problems when the new system is introduced.
2 I think we're due to arrive at something like twenty to ten.
3 If he keeps doing things like that, something bad is bound to happen sooner or later.
4 He is due to appear in court on the 31st of the month.
5 Your mum's bound to worry about you while you're away. It's only natural.
6 She can't travel at the moment as she's due to give birth any day now.
7 It is technically possible to get a visa to travel there, but it's not likely to be easy.

REVIEW 1

▶ TRACK 14

1 It's going to boost the club's income.
2 I'd listen to his stuff all the time when I was younger.
3 I'm sure it'll be worth it in the end.
4 It's likely to present a huge challenge in the coming years.
5 It's due to be completed in 2020.
6 It might take years to repair the damage.

UNIT 3

▶ TRACK 15

Conversation 1

A: What's the name of that stuff you use to put posters up?

B: Can you be a bit more specific?

A: Yeah, sorry, I mean that stuff – it's a bit like chewing gum or something, but it doesn't actually feel that sticky.

B: What? You mean Blu-Tack?

A: Yeah! Is that what they call it?

Conversation 2

C: It's, um ... what do you call those things climbers use? They're made of metal. They're like a hook.

D: What? You mean the thing you use to connect yourself to the rope?

C: Yeah, they have a sort of clip thing that opens and shuts. You see people using the small ones as key rings sometimes.

D: Yeah, yeah. I know exactly what you mean. I don't know! Do they have a special name? Aren't they just clips?

▶ TRACK 16

A: I brought you a present.

B: Wine?

A: No! I know you don't drink. No, it's Californian grape juice. I had some at a friend's the other day and it was really delicious.

B: Really?

A: Apparently, they have all sorts of varieties.

B: Yeah? Well, thanks! Shall we have some now?

A: Sure! Have you got a corkscrew?

B: Ah, that's a point, actually. I'm not sure I have, actually. Let me have a look. There's so much stuff in these drawers. Most of it's rubbish. I really should clear it out. Mmm. I don't think there's one here. Can't you use a knife?

A: I don't think so.

B: You need a stick or something to push it down. Would a pencil do?

A: It wouldn't be strong enough.

B: What about a wooden spoon? You could use the handle.

A: Yeah, that should do. Let's see ... Oh no!

B: Oh, it's gone everywhere!

A: Sorry! Have you got a cloth?

B: Yeah. I think we need a mop and bucket as well.

A: Sorry.

B: Don't worry about it. These things happen. You might want to rub some salt into that shirt or it'll leave a stain.

A: Really?

B: Well, it works for other things.

▶ TRACK 17

1 When it arrived and I put it on, it didn't fit.

2 When I took it out of the box, I found the screen was scratched.

3 When I tried to put it together, I realised it had a bit missing.

4 It was supposed to be for sensitive skin, but it gave me spots.

5 When I filled it the first time, I realised it had a leak.

6 I only wore it for a week and the strap came off.

7 They fell apart after a month. The soles came off!

8 When I got home and tried them on I realised the back pocket was ripped.

▶ TRACK 18

[Part 1]

Presenter: Hello. Welcome to *Rights and Reason*. On today's show, we'll be discussing the importance of dealing with customer complaints in the globalised world; the government's proposed new laws on data protection and privacy; and we'll be giving advice on the hazards of buying a second-hand car.

Our first item came out of a post on the *Rights and Reason* web page from a Chinese listener, Fei Han. Fei is a visitor to Britain from China and three weeks ago he bought a pair of shoes in a well-known store. When he opened the box at home, he discovered one of the shoes had an insole missing. Fei says he put off going back to the store because he was worried about his poor English and didn't want the stress. In fact, he says he even thought about keeping and using them, but unsurprisingly, found them too uncomfortable to walk in. So eventually he took them back. And this is where the problems really started.

The assistant told him it wasn't company policy to sell insoles separately and that he should have checked the shoes at the point of sale. He was even accused of losing the insole himself! The assistant said he could only prove this wasn't the case by checking the CCTV cameras after the store closed that day. Fei left a contact number, but heard nothing and went back three days later. After explaining the situation again to a different assistant, the store manager was called and Fei was finally offered a new insole. Unfortunately, when he got home he discovered it was the wrong size, at which point he gave up! The incident has clearly left Fei feeling let down and questioning whether this poor treatment was due to him being a tourist. Now, to discuss this case and the wider implications for customer services, we have John Squire from the Institute of Customer Care.

▶ TRACK 19

[Part 2]

P = Presenter JS = John Squire

P: Welcome John. So what do you think of this case?

JS: Yes. Thank you. I mean, clearly Fei shouldn't have been treated like that and given the final outcome, the company hasn't achieved anything by it. It's almost a case study in what NOT to do.

P: And do you think this happened because he was foreign?

JS: Well, possibly, I'm sad to say, but we also know that this can be because of a deeper problem in the company. A culture can develop within companies where it is assumed the customer is at fault or is trying to cheat the company by complaining. That then stops the assistant listening to the issue and thinking about it rationally.

P: OK. So are you saying the customer is always right?

JS: No, no. Not at all. There are instances of serial complainers who try to exploit companies, and of course sometimes the customer *is* at fault. However, you should *start* from the view that they do have a valid point and allow them to speak. Listen. Consider what the customer wants. What's the cost of resolving the situation — even if you *do* have a doubt? I mean, in Fei's case even if he was lying — and who on earth loses *part* of their shoe — how much would replacing that insole cost?

P: Indeed. And there's a bigger cost to poor care, isn't there? Your institute's produced some interesting statistics on this recently – I mean it's cheaper to keep customers.

JS: Absolutely. Estimates suggest the cost of retaining a customer is a fifth of the cost of getting new customers, and customers are actually four times more likely to use or recommend a service again if a problem is sorted out efficiently.

P: Isn't that the issue with tourists, though? They're one-time customers, so why bother?

JS: Yes. Well, I think that's an incredibly narrow view. Many of these stores are global brands and tourists make recommendations at home. They may also have friends who are local to the UK store, but I think even if that wasn't the case, it still shows a wrong attitude. You know, not all cultures share this approach to complaints. In Japan, they are often made in the spirit of improving a service rather than seeking compensation. We say all companies should see complaints in this way – as a gift. For every person who complains, there'll be 25 who are also dissatisfied, but who said nothing. A person who complains has made an effort. They are providing valuable feedback and reveal how you can improve products and services. If that complainant is foreign, think that they may have additionally overcome embarrassment about their language abilities, like Fei. Companies often pay to get feedback and here they're getting it for free! In short, the message is: take customer care seriously whoever the person is, and train your staff to do it well.

P: John Squire, thank you very much.

UNIT 4

▶ TRACK 20

A: So what do you think of your president?

B: Oh, I can't stand him. He's so arrogant.

A: Really? Whenever I see him on TV, he comes across as being fairly well-intentioned.

B: Ah, it's all marketing. You hear some people say he's boosted our reputation in the world, whatever that's supposed to mean, but he's done nothing for people like me. In fact, he's just put up tuition fees for students.

A: I know. I saw. It's €8000 or something a year now, isn't it?

B: More than that!

A: Really! I don't know how you manage. The cost of living is so high in your country.

B: Tell me about it! I'm going to be so far in debt by the time I graduate, I'll be paying it back for years.

A: Is it easy to find a job there?

B: Well, this is it. Unemployment's shot up recently. It's really worrying. If you ask me, they've been so concerned with supposedly 'green' laws like banning plastic bags, they've totally ignored the economy and now it's a complete mess.

A: So, when's the next election? Can't you vote against them?

B: It's next year, but I'm not going to vote.

A: No?

B: No. They're all as bad as each other. The opposition are so busy fighting among themselves that they're not going to make any difference.

A: I know what you mean, but there must be someone worth voting for. I mean, like our government has done a few controversial things – stuff I didn't agree with – but, you know, they've done good things as well. I mean, the economy's really booming.

B: Yeah? Maybe I should think about emigrating there after uni.

A: You should. Honestly, there's such a skills shortage that companies are paying really good money now. They're desperate for people.

B: You don't think the language would be a barrier?

A: Not necessarily. Quite a few multinationals have set up there recently and they all use English. And anyway, you'd pick our language up after a while. They've actually done a lot to cut back on bureaucracy too, so it's much easier for foreigners to get work than it used to be.

B: Yeah? I'll have to think about it. It'd be nice to escape my debts, anyway!

▶ TRACK 21

A: I don't know how people can make ends meet.

B: Tell me about it! I can only just get by and I've got a good job.

A: The job market is so competitive at the moment.

B: I know what you mean, but if you're prepared to be flexible there's plenty of work.

A: The pace of life is so fast here.

B: I know! It's exhausting. I feel like I spend my life just rushing around.

A: There's so much crime, you can't go out at night!

B: Yeah, maybe. Mind you, it's not like that everywhere. If you avoid certain areas, it's perfectly safe.

A: They haven't done anything to boost tourism.

B: Yeah, I know what you mean. Mind you, look what they've done to improve poor areas. That's great.

A: This country is so bureaucratic!

B: Tell me about it! I had to fill in four forms in three different places to get a work permit!

▶ TRACK 22

1

The government will today launch a new initiative aimed at getting vulnerable young people off the streets and into hostels. The move is a response to growing concern about the number of teenagers sleeping rough on the streets of the capital, many of whom, it is feared, are in danger of becoming involved in drugs and other criminal activity.

2

A senior executive at one of the country's leading law firms is today almost half a million euros richer after winning her case against her employers, McLintock and Rice. Judith Fenton had claimed she was denied promotion as a direct result of telling colleagues she was pregnant. The court ruled in her favour and she was awarded compensation of €487,000.

3

Police are today conducting investigations after a young Asian student was attacked near the city centre by a group of white youths late last night. The attack was captured on CCTV and a senior policeman has announced he believes it may well have been racially motivated. The nineteen-year-old victim is still being treated in hospital and is believed to have suffered several broken bones.

4

A tiny pressure group has claimed victory over one of the country's richest men. Multi-millionaire Ronald Stamp had been planning to build a hotel and entertainment complex on a privately owned beach on the north-east coast. However, following protests by local residents, the group Save Our Seaside took legal action to prevent what they claimed would amount to 'vandalism on a huge scale' – a claim that was yesterday upheld in court.

5

A woman from East Sussex last week became the country's youngest grandmother. At the age of 29, Tracy Bell is now the proud granny of a baby boy, Kevin. Bell's daughter, Caroline, aged fourteen, said she had initially been too scared to break the news to her mother, and had waited until a doctor had confirmed she was indeed pregnant. Mrs Bell, however, seems resigned to the situation, stating that as she is already bringing up five children, one more will make little difference.

▶ TRACK 23

A: Did you see that thing on the news about that woman who's been suing the firm she works for?

B: I was just reading about that, actually. She won, didn't she?

A: Absolutely. It was shocking what happened to her. It was such typical double standards!

B: Well, maybe. But it was a lot of money. I'm not so sure about it all, to be honest. If you ask me, if you're in that kind of situation, you have to decide what you want. Either you try and get promoted or you focus on having kids. You can't have everything in life, can you?

A: That's such rubbish! You can't really believe that. This is the twenty-first century! Surely a woman's allowed to have children and a career!

▶ TRACK 24

1 It was shocking what happened to her.
2 It just seems a bit excessive.
3 Mind you, it was a lot of money.
4 It makes you wonder what's gone wrong with the world.
5 It was such typical double standards!
6 That's good news for a change!
7 I don't know how they manage.
8 At least they're doing something about it at last!
9 You can't have everything in life, can you?
10 It's a bit of a worry.
11 It's lucky it was caught on film.
12 That kind of thing shouldn't be tolerated.

REVIEW 2

▶ TRACK 25

1 It was so bad it really undermined his reputation.
2 You use a sort of brush thing to clean it.
3 When I switched it on I found it had a fault.
4 You should've asked them to fix it.
5 The lower child mortality is, the lower the birth rate.
6 It was such typical double standards.

UNIT 5

▶ TRACK 26

Conversation 1

A: What are you up to later?
B: Oh, I'm going to a belly dancing class.
A: You're doing what?
B: Belly dancing. You know, like …
A: Yeah, I know what it is. I just had no idea that you did that.
B: Well, I don't really. It's actually the first class.
A: Oh, OK. So why belly dancing?
B: I've been thinking about doing something to get a bit fitter and I've never liked sport particularly. I find jogging and swimming and stuff like that a bit boring, you know – and then I saw this class advertised and I thought it'd be fun.
A: Yeah, I guess so. I should really do something as well. I've put on five kilos since January.
B: Really? It doesn't look it. You've got a lovely figure.
A: Well, I don't feel like I have! And I'm really unfit. I had to run for the bus this morning and it took me about ten minutes to get my breath back!
B: Well, why don't you come with me?
A: I don't know. I think I'd feel a bit self-conscious.
B: Come on! You can't be worse than me. I'm totally uncoordinated! It'll be a laugh.
A: Well, maybe.

Conversation 2

C: Are you around this weekend at all?

D: No, I'm going to a fencing workshop all day Saturday.
C: You're going where?
D: This fencing workshop. It's like a master class with this top Russian fencer.
C: Wow! I didn't even know you did fencing. How did you get into that?
D: Oh, we actually used to do it at school. In PE, we had the option to try out all kinds of sports and I just really got into it, and then I joined a club, and then I started competing a bit more seriously, you know.
C: I had no idea. Well, what about Sunday? I'm going to have a wander round the flea market in the morning.
D: To be honest, I think I'm just going to have a lie-in and chill out at home. I'll be exhausted after Saturday.
C: Fair enough. Just the thought of doing that kind of exercise makes me sweat!

Conversation 3

E: What're you doing this evening? Do you fancy meeting later?
F: No, I can't. I've got my … um … my, um, knitting group tonight.
E: You've got what?
F: My knitting group.
E: Since when?
F: I've been doing it for about six months now. I took it up because I was giving up smoking and a friend suggested doing it. She said it'd give me something to fiddle with instead of cigarettes, so I joined this group and it's been really good. I feel so much healthier now and I actually really like the knitting. I just find it very, very relaxing.
E: OK, but isn't it just full of old women, this group?
F: No, not at all. Well, I mean, I am the only man, but most of the women are quite young.
E: Ah.
F: What? What's 'Ah' supposed to mean?
E: Nothing.

▶ TRACK 27

1 You run how far?
2 You do what?
3 You went where?
4 She's into what?
5 You got up when?

▶ TRACK 28

1 I shouldn't have said anything.
2 We should've gone somewhere else.
3 It could've been much worse than it was.
4 It couldn't have come at a worse time.
5 It wouldn't have made any difference.
6 I would've scored that!

▶ TRACK 29

C = Chloe, M = Molly, K = Kyle

M: I must go and send my cousin an email in a minute.
C: Oh, OK.
M: I've been meaning to go round and see him, because he's not been well, but Kyle's a bit reluctant to drive me round there because it'd mean spending time with my uncle.
C: Really? What's wrong with him?
K: He's just mad, that's all.
M: He's not, he's just …
K: Annoying?

M: No!

K: Crazy? Exhausting?

M: Chloe – just ignore him. Kyle – you can be so horrible sometimes.

K: Listen, Chloe, the last time we went to see him he had a thing about handstands. We were sitting outside a café, just having a coffee and chatting, and he suddenly just got up and did a handstand – right next to all the tables! He kept it up for about half an hour!

C: That does sound a bit odd. How old is he?

M: About 50.

C: 50!

K: I told you! He's crazy.

M: He is not! He's just one of these people who can't sit still. I mean, he's always loved sport and when he does something new, he really gets into it. Like he took us ice-skating once. Do you remember?

K: How could I forget?

M: I mean, we were exhausted after about an hour, but he just kept on skating – and we watched him going round and round for another hour.

K: It was like he'd just completely forgotten we were there! And what about the hang-gliding?

C: Hang-gliding?

M: Yeah, he used to go hang-gliding. Obsessed with it, he was. He went practically every weekend for about three years.

K: Until he had an accident. He fell something like 1000 metres without a parachute.

C: You're joking!

M: No, it's true.

C: So what happened?

M: Well, he'd borrowed someone else's glider for some reason, and they didn't have a parachute, but he went up anyway. And he was caught in really bad weather and the hang-glider broke and he fell.

C: And he wasn't badly injured?

M: Well, he went through some trees, which broke his fall. He had hairline fractures in his shoulder and his neck and some minor cuts and bruises but basically he was OK. He was incredibly lucky he didn't die.

C: Absolutely!

K: Anyway, then we saw him about three weeks later roller-skating in the park, even though he still had his neck in a brace!

C: But he did give up the hang-gliding after that?

M: Not exactly, no. He tried it once more – to overcome any fear. I mean, he just wanted to prove to himself he could do it, but since then ... no. The last few years he's been really into windsurfing. He's actually always liked it – he did it when he was younger – but the last few years, that's been his main obsession. He lives on the coast, so he goes nearly every day.

C: Right. I'm starting to think Kyle might be right!

K: And you haven't heard all of it. For the last few months he's been rubbing lemon juice into his skin and his hair every day! He says it gets rid of dandruff and he was going on and on about how amazingly healthy it is.

M: OK, OK! It's true. He is a little bit mad, but he's a nice guy and he's fun to be with.

K: In small doses!

1 Have you managed to buy the tickets?
2 I've been calling all morning.
3 I've been meaning to for ages.
4 Why has Wayne decided to leave?
5 He's been thinking about it for a while.
6 She's always been good at sports.

UNIT 6

Conversation 1

A: Have you ever been to Hungary?

B: Yeah, I went to the Sziget Festival a couple of years ago.

A: You went where?

B: The Sziget. I don't know if I'm pronouncing it right, but it's an enormous music festival in Budapest. It's held on this island in the middle of the Danube.

A: Oh right. So where did you stay?

B: We camped on the festival site. It was a bit of a nightmare, actually, because it absolutely poured down while we were there. The whole place was flooded and we got absolutely soaked – tent, sleeping bags, everything. And it was so muddy, everything got filthy. It was crazy.

A: Couldn't you stay somewhere else?

B: Well, we actually did in the end. We met these really nice Hungarians who lived in the city and they put us up for a couple of nights.

A: Wow, that was generous! So would you go again?

B: Absolutely. We had a great time, in spite of the weather. I hardly slept the whole time we were there. There was so much going on.

Conversation 2

A: Did you go away in the holiday at all?

B: Yeah, I went to Turkey.

A: In August? Wasn't it a bit hot?

B: It was absolutely boiling, but then I love the heat – and you get quite dry heat there.

A: I guess. So did you enjoy it?

B: Yeah, it was brilliant. We stayed in this absolutely amazing place on the south coast – right on top of the cliffs, overlooking the ocean.

A: Sounds nice.

B: It was. Wait, I've got a picture of it somewhere on my mobile.

A: Let's have a look. Wow! Look at that sunset. That's stunning!

B: I know. It was like that nearly every night.

A: That's great. Were there any other places nearby? It looks as if it's in the middle of nowhere.

B: It was a bit isolated, yeah. It was a few kilometres along this narrow track to the nearest village – well, town – but they had a minibus to take people there in the morning and to bring them back in the evening.

A: Wasn't that a pain, having to rely on the bus? Didn't they run more often than that?

B: No. It was a bit annoying, but considering how cheap the place was, you couldn't complain. And there was a little beach near the hotel. There was a little path between the cliffs – and the beach was almost deserted, which was lovely.

A: I'm not surprised. Sounds like hard work.

B: It was a bit of a struggle climbing back up, but it was worth doing once.

A: I guess. It doesn't sound like my kind of thing though.

▶ TRACK 32

1a It was *quite **near*** the beach, which was good.

1b It was ***quite** near* the beach but I was expecting it to be nearer.

2a The beach was a *bit **crowded*** so we didn't go there much.

2b The beach was a ***bit** crowded* but there was still enough room to relax in.

3a The surrounding area's *fairly **nice***. It's very green and it's nice to hire a bike.

3b The surrounding area's ***fairly** nice*. There are a few factories, which kind of spoil it.

4a The food was *pretty **good***, which I wasn't expecting.

4b The food was ***pretty** good*, although it was a bit too oily for my liking.

▶ TRACK 33

Conversation 1

A: I have a booking under the name of Bergen.

B: Hmm. I'm sorry sir. We have no record of any reservation.

A: That can't be right. I spoke to someone just over a week ago.

B: Well, did you receive a confirmation by email or text?

A: Should I have?

B: That's our normal procedure, yes.

A: No. I haven't had anything.

B: Well, I'm afraid there's nothing I can do.

A: Haven't you got any rooms available?

B: I'm afraid not.

A: Oh, that's great, that is.

Conversation 2

C: Hello. I was wondering if you could help. My room's not very warm. Is there any way I can turn down the air-conditioning?

D: I'm afraid it's all controlled centrally.

C: Can't you do anything about it? I mean, you seem to have it on full blast. It's absolutely freezing!

D: I'm sorry, but we haven't had any other complaints about it.

Conversation 3

E: What do you mean you're not going to give us our deposit back?

F: Look at the state of the place. It's filthy!

E: Well, it wasn't particularly clean when we moved in.

F: And what about the washing machine? That'll need to be replaced.

E: That's hardly our fault. It's ancient. It was already falling apart – and I hardly think it's worth a whole month's rent.

F: Well, it's the combination of things. When you take everything into account – the stuff which is broken and missing, the mess – it all adds up.

E: What? To over a thousand pounds? You're taking the mickey! I can't believe you think we're going to pay that! It's ridiculous!

Conversation 4

G: I warned the landlord that boiler was a health hazard again and again.

H: I know. I remember you telling me ages ago.

G: They promised to fix it, but they just kept putting it off. Honestly, I'm furious about it!

H: I'm not surprised. Still, you were right to have it checked and to get it repaired. I mean, you could've suffocated while you were sleeping.

G: Well, you hear about carbon monoxide poisoning all the time, don't you?

H: It doesn't bear thinking about.

G: The thing is, though, I'm completely out of pocket now.

▶ TRACK 34

One often hears that something was a culture shock – most often when people arrive in a new country, but also when they enter other kinds of new environments. However, it is usually described as being similar to jet lag – something which you experience for a couple of days and then get over – all you need is a good night's sleep! The reality is, however, that undergoing any big change – whether it's moving house, changing jobs or going to university – will bring about a 'culture shock'. Far from being a single event which is quickly forgotten, it is a process which may take several months – even years – to fully recover from. Psychologists more commonly call this process 'acculturation' and highlight four distinct phases that nearly everyone goes through. These are elation – the joy and wonder you first have, where everything is so new and different; resistance – when things settle into a routine and you start to see everything which is bad in your new situation. You look back through rose-coloured glasses on your life before the change. This resistance is then followed by the transformation phase, where you swing more to the other extreme and start looking down on your previous existence and its culture. You may refuse to mix with people you used to know or who speak the same language. You might put them down when you do. Finally, people reach a state of integration, where cultural differences are acknowledged and accepted and people appreciate both their own heritage and their new life.

That's the ideal situation, according to psychologist Perry Graves.

'Everyone goes through the initial stages, but not everyone finishes the complete cycle. This can cause problems because they often don't recognise the phases of acculturation. For example, some people drop out of university in their first year, saying they don't relate to the middle class values or that it has nothing to do with reality and so on. In reality, these opinions are actually a symptom of the resistance stage. In other cases, people get stuck in a transformation phase, which may stop them moving on to new experiences or lead to them cutting themselves off from their roots, from people they've known for years and years. That can lead to a deep sense of unhappiness and to feelings of frustration.'

REVIEW 3

▶ TRACK 35

1 I've been meaning to go there for a while.

2 She's had her hair done.

3 I shouldn't have put it off for so long.

4 It was a bit of a nightmare to be honest.

5 You should've told me. I could've dealt with it.

6 I've been struggling to keep up.

UNIT 7

▶ TRACK 36

1 The thunder was so loud!

2 I thought I was going to pass out!

3 I thought I was going to freeze to death!

4 When we left it was fine.

5 It was pouring down.

6 because it was so strong

7 I was afraid of skidding.

8 The whole place was flooded.

▶ TRACK 37

A: We got caught in this incredible storm on our way to visit friends in Rome.

B: Yeah?

A: Yeah, it was amazing! One moment we were in sunshine, the next we saw like a line on the road ahead and we drove through it and it was hail! Incredible – these enormous hailstones just started bouncing off the car! They were as big as golf balls. Honestly, they were hitting the car so hard, they nearly broke the windscreen.

B: Really?

A: Well, maybe I'm exaggerating a bit, but they were pretty big and it was pretty scary.

B: I bet.

A: And then the lightning started. It was lighting up the whole sky. In the end, we pulled over to the side of the road till it all blew over.

B: Right.

A: And then it cleared up again – almost as quickly as it'd started.

B: It's amazing, isn't it? It actually reminds me of a time I was in Sardinia. We were visiting this little village somewhere, the name of which escapes me. Actually, I guess we should've realised because it'd been boiling all day – very humid and sticky – and then in the evening we were just taking a walk along the beach – you get this great view across the bay to Alghero.

A: Uh huh.

B: And anyway, suddenly we saw this incredible forked lightning across the bay followed by a faint rumble of thunder, and it just continued. It was so spectacular, we were just, like, transfixed watching it because, you know, it was still dry where we were. It was amazing – I could've watched it for hours, but then suddenly it started spitting and then just two seconds later the heavens opened and it started pouring down.

A: Oh no.

B: And of course we hadn't brought an umbrella or anything, so we just ran to the nearest café we could find, and honestly, it can't have been more than a minute but we got absolutely soaked. I must've poured something like a litre of water out of my shoes.

A: Incredible.

B: I swear – sitting there in the café I think it was the wettest I've ever been!

▶ TRACK 38

1

A: Oh dear! Those don't look very healthy.

B: I know. I bought them to cheer up the flat a bit. You know, a bit of colour and greenery, but they just look depressing now! It's strange. I've been watering them every day.

A: Maybe that's it. The soil's probably too wet. I think it rots the roots.

B: You're joking! You mean I'm drowning them?

A: I guess so!

2

C: What are these flowers? They're lovely.

D: They're terrible!

C: Why? What do you mean?

D: They're just so invasive! They take over the whole place. None of the other plants can survive – and they're really difficult to get rid of as well.

C: But they look so nice.

D: Yeah, but they're not native to this country and they're destroying the local varieties.

C: That's too bad. I still like them, though.

3

E: I wanted to take them something to say thank you for having me to stay and so I bought some flowers.

F: Fair enough.

E: Anyway, I handed them over and you know that feeling when you suddenly realise you've accidentally upset someone, yeah? She kind of gave me this tight smile and nodded, but, you know, they were quite a big bouquet.

F: You kind of expect something different, yeah?

E: Exactly. Anyway, she said something to her husband and he took them away and there was a bit of an awkward silence and then we just carried on with the evening.

F: How weird!

E: Yeah. I thought so, but then I was telling someone about it and they told me people there only give those flowers when someone's died!

F: Oh no!

E: It was like I was cursing her or something – hoping she'd have a funeral!

4

G: You're going to do what?

H: Gather mushrooms. Isn't 'gather' right?

G: Yeah, yeah – gather, pick whatever. It's just, I don't know, I've never met anyone who does it.

H: No? Everyone does it here in Poland. Why don't people do it in Britain?

G: Well, it's dangerous, isn't it? Don't you worry about picking the wrong one and poisoning yourself? Some of them are lethal, aren't they?

H: We're brought up doing this. We know from when we're children what's OK and what's not. And it's good – you feel more connected with nature. Last time we went we saw a deer – really close.

G: Yeah? Wow! It sounds great.

5

I: Here, take this. It should help.

J: What's in it?

I: It's just a herbal tea my gran makes. It's basically fennel seeds and leaves with a touch of lemon and honey. She swears by it.

J: I've never had fennel.

I: It's nice. It's got an aniseedy kind of taste. It's great. It'll really settle your stomach.

▶ TRACK 39

1a There's an insect that attacks the roots of the tree, causing it to die.

1b There are many problems affecting the country, but the root cause is the poor education system.

2a I have several tomato plants on my balcony, but they're not doing very well.

2b The film is basically about the police trying to find out where the bad guy has planted a bomb.

3a She worked as an actress for years without much success, but since winning the Oscar her career is blossoming.

3b The best time to go is in spring because of all the blossom on the trees.

4a Most people agree that the economic crisis stemmed from mistakes made by the banks and the high level of private debt.

4b If you cut the stems of the flowers under water, apparently the flowers last a lot longer.

5a We've had quite a lot of stormy weather recently, which has kept us indoors most of the time.

5b I'm not surprised they're breaking up. They had a very stormy relationship – always fighting.

6a They had floods of complaints when it was first sold because it didn't work properly.

6b With all this rain, there've been quite a lot of floods.

7a I bought some seeds to grow some herbs in my kitchen, but I haven't planted them yet.

7b It's just the seed of an idea at the moment. I haven't really got very far developing it.

UNIT 8

▶ TRACK 40

Conversation 1

A: How was your holiday?

B: Fine – apart from getting robbed.

A: Oh, you're joking! What happened?

B: Well, it was stupid, really. I should've been more careful. I was sitting in a café and these lads came up to me with a map asking for directions. I said I didn't understand and they walked off. Then I suddenly realised my bag was gone.

A: Oh no!

B: I'd left it under my chair and one of them must've grabbed it while they were talking to me.

A: That's terrible! Did it have much in it?

B: Fortunately not. My purse was in my pocket.

A: Still, it can't have been very nice.

B: Yeah, it was a bit upsetting, but I didn't let it spoil the holiday.

A: Well, that's good.

Conversation 2

C: Who was that on the phone?

D: It was the bank. They wanted to know if I'd spent $800 in Manila.

C: Manila? That's like 5,000 kilometres away!

D: I know. I guess someone must've got hold of my card details somehow.

C: Sure, but how did they manage to get it half way round the world?

D: Apparently, they have machines which can swipe the card and grab all your details, then they just sell the details to whoever over the web.

C: Right. So have you got any idea when it happened?

D: No. I mean, it could've been when I bought those new trainers on the internet, but then again it might equally have been in the local supermarket.

C: You reckon? Maybe you should just pay for everything in cash.

D: Yeah, right! That's not very practical!

C: I'm just saying. Anyway, what about the money? Will you get it back?

D: Yeah, they said it's fine.

C: That must be a relief.

D: It is.

Conversation 3

E: Er, what are you reading?

F: Oh, it's just about all these animals and stuff they've seized this year.

E: Oh right.

F: No it's incredible. Look at this picture.

E: Oh my word – that's awful. There's a whole elephant! Why would you want a whole stuffed elephant?

F: I don't know, but it says it's worth two hundred thousand, so someone with more money than sense.

E: … and a large living room.

F: Exactly. Get this, though. Apparently, they raided a motel room and they found this guy with two live crocodiles in the bathroom and a lion in the back of a van outside.

E: No!

F: Yeah!

E: Imagine if someone had gone in to clean the room.

F: It'd be a bit of a shock. Do you think he was transporting them together?

E: It sounds like it. I suppose he must've drugged them. They'd fight otherwise.

F: I guess. Who do you think would win?

E: I'd say the crocodile. Didn't you say there were two of them?

▶ TRACK 41

1 That's dreadful! Was anyone killed?

2 That must've been awful! Were you OK?

3 Oh no! Did they take anything very valuable?

4 That's dreadful! What were the parents thinking?

5 What a shame! Were you insured?

6 That's terrible! Did you report it to the police?

7 You're joking? Do they know who did it?

8 It's awful! What must his family be going through?

▶ TRACK 42

There's nothing unusual in the idea that a film star should have learned their trade in the theatre. What is remarkable, though, is when that theatre is based in a prison – and the film star is a convicted murderer serving a life sentence, only able to film on day release from jail.

Aniello Arena is not your average film star. He came into the public eye following his leading role in director Matteo Garrone's 2012 film *Reality*. In the film, Arena plays Luciano, a fish seller whose family encourage him to audition for the local version of the reality TV show *Big Brother*. After doing so, his obsession with achieving fame slowly turns into something far darker. He gradually descends into madness and comes to believe that his whole life has become part of some elaborate screen test.

Reality explores how the entertainment industry can offer hope to the hopeless, but also suggests that the new life it seems to promise is ultimately an illusion. Obviously, it is possible to see parallels here with the real-life experience of Aniello Arena, as the world of crime also sells dreams that rarely, if ever, come true.

Arena grew up in one of the poorer quarters of Naples and drifted into crime at a young age. He was jailed in the early 1990s for the murder of three members of a rival gang, though to this day, he insists he is innocent of the offences, while freely acknowledging his criminal past.

His initial involvement with acting came about when he first encountered the work of the Fortezza Theatre Company in prison. Established in 1988 by Armando Punzo, the group stage both classic and contemporary plays, with all roles played by prisoners. The company are based in the notorious Volterra prison, where they put on performances, but they have also toured the country. Punzo claims to see potential in the prisoners that maybe they are unaware of themselves. He believes that through drama, inmates have the opportunity to look inside themselves and deal with questions they would not otherwise attempt to address. This drama therapy has proved so successful that it has been exported to the jail of Roumieh, near Beirut in Lebanon.

▶ TRACK 43

In many ways, the story of the Fortezza Theatre Company and the drama therapy it offers is in keeping with certain current trends. While public opinion often demands longer sentences and harsher conditions for those inside – hard manual labour and so on – research actually seems to suggest that if reoffending rates are to be cut, then a more enlightened approach gets the best results. Whilst an average of between 70 and 75 per cent of prisoners released across Europe go on to commit crimes again, in Denmark, Sweden and Finland, the average rate is 30 per cent. In Norway it's a mere 20 per cent. So what are the Scandinavians doing differently?

Well, from the perspective of many Norwegians, the main problem with prisons is that we place too much emphasis on punishing prisoners and don't pay enough attention to rehabilitation. Norway has no death penalty and a maximum sentence of just 21 years, and as a result embraces the fact that prisoners will one day be released back into society.

The Norwegian approach to prison is best exemplified by Bastøy, the nation's only island jail. Here, prisoners are given personal responsibility and meaningful work – and have to deal with all the challenges this involves. As well as developing literacy skills – crucial given that being unable to read or write is often cited as one of the reasons why young people get involved in crime – prisoners are also able to learn everything from IT skills to skills such as carpentry or plumbing. All of this helps to ensure they are employable on their release and thus less likely to fall back into crime. In addition, on Bastøy prisoners are able to meet and interact with normal members of society, further aiding their rehabilitation. As shocking as such liberal attitudes may seem to many, the results are so incredible that perhaps it is time for wider exploration of their implications.

REVIEW 4

▶ TRACK 44

1 Someone might have got hold of your details.
2 They must've broken in through the back door.
3 There's no point trying to look for them.
4 It was pouring down and then it turned to hail.
5 I got soaked because I'd forgotten to bring a coat.
6 I was standing there and this guy came up to me and grabbed my bag.

UNIT 9

▶ TRACK 45

Part 1

M = Melissa R = Richard

M: So how're you finding your job? Is it going OK?
R: Oh, it's all right, I suppose. It's not what I want to do long term, though.
M: No? How come?
R: Oh, it's just so menial! I'm not using any of the skills I learned at university – and my boss is just dreadful! I seem to spend most of my time running round making him cups of tea and photocopying things and if I ask about doing other stuff, he just tells me to be patient and then starts going on about

how he did the same when he started at the company.
M: Well, maybe it's true.
R: Oh, I don't know. I was talking to this girl who joined at the same time as me and she said she was learning loads in her department – being really stretched, apparently. It makes me think it's maybe more about me!
M: Oh, I am sorry! If it's that bad, maybe you should think about handing in your notice?
R: I don't know. I guess it might get better if I just give it a bit more time.
M: Well, you'd think so. I mean, it is a big company, isn't it?
R: Mmm, but maybe that's it, you see. Maybe it's a bit too big. Anyway, I can't see myself staying there long term.
M: No? Well, if you do decide to make a move, you're bound to get lots of offers.
R: I don't know about that, but it's nice of you to say so!
M: It's true!

▶ TRACK 46

Part 2

M = Melissa R = Richard

R: Well, anyway. What about you? How's your job going?
M: Oh, you probably won't want to hear this, but it's great, yeah. It's going really well.
R: Well, I'm glad at least one of us is happy, anyway!
M: Yeah, it's amazing. I've been getting loads of on-the-job training – and they've been letting me go into college one day a week as well, to improve my skills. It's been really stimulating. I've also been meeting clients quite a bit. Oh, and I gave my first big presentation last week.
R: Wow! Sounds amazing. Did it go OK?
M: Yeah, it went brilliantly. I've got my first business trip coming up next month – to New York. And I'm applying for promotion at the moment too.
R: Really? Already? Do you think you'll get it?
M: Hopefully, yeah, but you never know, do you?
R: Oh, you're bound to. From the sound of it, you're their star employee. I can just see you in five years' time, running the entire firm.
M: Ha!
R: And if the worst comes to the worst, I'll end up knocking on the door of your office, begging you for a job!

▶ TRACK 47

1 I doubt it. I'm not qualified enough.
2 I might. Stranger things have happened!
3 Probably not – but it's worth a try.
4 Hopefully. I really need the money!
5 I'm bound to. They're desperate for new staff at the moment.

▶ TRACK 48

Over the last half a century or more, delivering newspapers after school has been the first point of entry into the world of work for countless young people. Yet today, the paper boy is fast becoming a dying breed. For the first time, there are more adults delivering newspapers in the United States than young people. The steady shift from youth carriers to adults over the last few years is down to a number of factors: newspapers want deliveries to take place in the mornings rather than afternoons after school hours, and more adults – particularly retired people – are grabbing the opportunity to earn some extra income to supplement their salaries or pensions. There are also those who blame the economic boom of the early noughties – families could afford to buy more things for their kids, and so many kids settled for the comfort of a sofa and PlayStation rather than take to the streets to earn pocket money. Many delivery companies say adults are more reliable and provide a better service, but there are those who are saddened by the changes. Bud Keynes, managing director of the Milwaukee Herald: 'Doing a paper route when I was thirteen was my first experience of business. It taught me responsibility, how to manage my time and communicate with people. More than once, I got soaked or froze to death, or got chased by dogs, but it was character-building. Too many young people these days enter what is a very competitive job market lacking those basic business skills that you get from being a carrier.'

▶ TRACK 49

1 If I was better at maths, I would've studied physics.
2 I would never have become a CEO if I hadn't worked hard.
3 You might've noticed if you'd been paying more attention.
4 If I hadn't met her, I'd probably still be living at home.
5 If I'd heard something, I'd tell you.
6 I'd go with you if I could, but I can't.

▶ TRACK 50

Hello. Welcome everyone. For those who don't know me already, I'm Kimi from Finland, and I'm here studying Economics as part of the student exchange programme. Today I'm going to talk about PISA. So, hands up everyone who has heard of PISA. OK. Lots of you. Now, hands up everyone who thought I was talking about the Italian city with a leaning tower? OK – well, I'm afraid you're wrong. No – this PISA is the Programme for International Student Assessment, which is used to compare education systems round the world.

So, what I'm going to do today is take a closer look at this project. I'll begin by explaining how PISA works. I'll then move on to look at and comment on some of the results, before going on to conclude that, from a Finnish perspective, the results from PISA are not necessarily the most helpful way of measuring success.

▶ TRACK 51

OK. Basically PISA consists of three tests in Maths, Science and Reading, organised by the Organisation of Economic Co-operation and Development – OECD for short. The tests were first run in 2000 and are set every three years. Currently, around half a million fifteen-year-olds from 65 different countries take part. Each test is marked out of 800 and the average marks for each country's students gives the country's rank. The idea is that to compete economically, you need to improve education.

So, moving on to the results, the table here shows a selection of countries from the last PISA test for Maths. As you can see, China's almost 100 points ahead of my country, Finland. Such a big difference may be down to better education, but it may also be because of the kinds of kids who were tested. Unlike all the other countries, China's students all came from a single city, in this case, Shanghai.

More importantly, focusing on rank is a problem. Finland, for example, has fallen from being best in 2000. I have seen some headlines here saying 'the miracle is over' and 'plunging' standards. But there were only 40 countries taking part in 2000, not 65, and our score has actually dropped by just three percent – not exactly 'plunging'. When you look at percentages instead of points out of 800, you may also note that although we are 22 places and 37 points ahead of Russia, that's actually only about four percent.

So should we care about PISA? I guess it's good to have an independent test, but I don't think we should change our education to get better marks in it. These marks don't really tell you what education is like. In South Korea, kids typically study twelve or more hours a day, and we sometimes do half that! I know where I'd prefer to study. And does it really matter in terms of the economy? Qatar is the richest country in the world, but comes almost bottom of the table. In short, I think we should decide what we as a country want from education and avoid comparisons.

▶ TRACK 52

What I'm going to <u>try</u> and do to<u>day</u> // is take a look at Mc<u>Don</u>ald's <u>rec</u>ent per<u>for</u>mance.// I'll be<u>gin</u> / by <u>commenting</u> on their <u>sales figures</u> / for the last <u>five</u> years. I'll <u>then</u> move on to some recommen<u>da</u>tions // about how the company could im<u>prove</u> things / in the <u>years</u> to <u>come</u>.

UNIT 10

▶ TRACK 53

N = Nina, L = Linda, V = Vita

N: So how much longer have you got?
L: Three more days. By four o'clock Friday we'll have finished every single one. I can't wait!
V: Me neither. The Physics one yesterday was a nightmare.
L: I know! I'm sure I failed it.
N: You must be sick of it all.
V: I am. If I revise much more my head's going to explode!
L: Just keep telling yourself: three more days, three more days.
N: So shall we go out and celebrate on Friday, then?
V: That sounds like an excellent idea.
L: Yeah, I'd be up for that as well. Do you have anywhere in mind?
N: I thought that Equinox might be fun.
L: Where's that?
N: Oh, don't you know it? It's the big disco on the main square in town. It's great.
V: If you like that kind of place! I have to say, it's not my kind of thing. I can't stand the music down there and besides – it's full of horrible guys.
N: Oh! I thought it was OK when I went there, but if you'd rather go somewhere else, that's fine by me.
L: Well, personally, I'd quite like to get something to eat at some point, if that's all right with you.
V: Yeah, that sounds good. Any thoughts on where?
L: Well, Rico's is always a good bet.
V: Oh, it's such a rip-off, that place. Last time I went there, I spent something like €60. Can't we go somewhere cheaper?
N: How about that Brazilian place near the station?
V: Guanabara? Yeah, that'd be fine with me. Linda?
L: Yeah, whatever. I'm easy. They have music later on down there, don't they?
N: Yeah, they do salsa after ten.
V: It sounds ideal. So what time do you want to meet? Seven? Seven thirty?
N: I'm working till six and it'd be nice if I could go home first, so could we make it eight? I'll have had time to get changed and freshen up a bit by then.
V: Yeah, fine.
N: And I'll phone and book a table – just to be on the safe side.
L: OK. I'll ring a few other people and see if anyone else is up for it – and see you down there.
N: OK. Brilliant. Bye.
V: Bye.

▶ TRACK 54

Conversation 1

A: Sorry, but you couldn't pass me the salt, could you? Thank you. They look nice.

B: They are. They're lovely. Have you tried that aubergine dip? It's delicious.

A: Hmm. I have to say, I'm not that keen on aubergines. There's something wrong with them as a vegetable.

B: You're joking! Aubergines – they're the king of vegetables! Although strictly speaking, of course, they're technically a fruit.

A: Mmm.

B: They're so versatile. You can fry them, grill them, have them mashed, stuffed, barbecued …

A: Right.

B: Did you know that they used to use the skin as a dye? The Chinese apparently used to polish their teeth with it!

A: Fascinating. I can see I've not given aubergines a proper chance. Anyway, listen. Sorry, but I've just seen my friend Mercedes. I must just go and grab her. I've been meaning to talk to her all evening. Bye!

Conversation 2

C: So how do you know Niall?

D: Who?

C: Er … the person whose party this is.

D: Oh right. Well, he's like the friend of a friend of my flatmate. I don't know why I'm here, really. I feel a bit left out. My flatmate dragged me here because she thought she wouldn't know anyone – and now she's met someone. Oh – that's her over there, with that blond guy. I think I might just go. How do you know Niall anyway?

C: I'm his fiancée! You did know this is a party to celebrate our engagement, didn't you?

D: No, actually I didn't. Congratulations, though! It's a great party.

Conversation 3

E: I'm glad I'm not the only person who couldn't stand it any more.

F: Tell me about it! It was so stuffy in there, wasn't it? You could hardly breathe.

E: Yeah. They need some air conditioning or something.

F: The speaker wasn't exactly helping either, was he? I thought I was going to fall asleep at one point there.

E: Yeah, he's very dull, isn't he? I think I might just go and grab a coffee instead of going back in.

F: That sounds like a good idea. Do you mind if I join you?

Conversation 4

G: Is this the queue for the toilet?

H: I'm afraid so.

G: I love your top.

H: Oh, thanks.

G: It's quite unusual. Where did you get it?

H: I actually picked it up in a second-hand clothes stall. It was only five pounds.

G: Really? That's fantastic! I never bother looking in places like that. I mean, there's a second-hand place near me, but the stuff in there always looks in pretty poor condition. That looks brand new, though.

H: I think it's quite old actually, but the stall I got it from is just fantastic – just really nice stuff.

G: Mind you, it's so difficult getting stuff in my size.

H: I can imagine. It must be hard. I've got a friend who's maybe your height and she's always moaning about it as well. That dress is lovely, though.

G: It's great, isn't it? I actually just found this place online. Oh look – it's your turn.

Conversation 5

I: Sorry, but I couldn't help overhearing. Did you say you've just come back from Accra?

J: Yeah. Why? Do you know it?

I: Yes, quite well, actually. I spent two years there back in the 90s.

J: Wow! What were you doing there?

I: My husband was based at the embassy there, so …

J: Really? It must've been quite different back then. It's a real boom town at the moment.

I: So I've read, yes. It was relatively quiet when we were there and the infrastructure was still very much a work in progress, but we loved it. We met some wonderful people there and were able to see a bit of the countryside as well. I'm sure it's changed a lot, though.

J: For sure. It's attracting a huge amount of inward investment. In fact, my firm is planning to open an office there, so I was over there sorting that out.

I: Oh, that's great. I'm really pleased to hear it. Anyway, sorry. I didn't want to stop you chatting.

▶ TRACK 55

1 A: Miserable weather, isn't it?

   B: Yeah, awful. It's been like this for weeks now, hasn't it?

   A: I know. I can't remember when I last saw the sun.

2 A: You don't remember me, do you?

   B: It's Yuka, isn't it?

   A: No. It's Naomi.

3 A: Excuse me. You haven't got a light, have you?

   B: Yeah. Here you go.

   A: Thanks.

   B: You couldn't lend me a pound, could you?

   A: No, sorry.

4 A: You missed the class on Monday, didn't you?

   B: There wasn't one, was there? The school was closed for the holiday, wasn't it?

   A: No. Mind you, you didn't miss much. It was quite boring.

   B: Well, to be honest the whole course is a bit disappointing, isn't it?

5 A: I love that jacket. It's from Zara, isn't it?

   B: No, I got it from a shop called Monsoon.

   A: Really? You wouldn't happen to have the address, would you?

   B: No. Sorry. I honestly can't remember.

REVIEW 5

▶ TRACK 56

1 If you're struggling to cope, maybe you should delegate more.

2 I guess things'll improve once I get the hang of the new system.

3 If the worst comes to the worst, you'll just have to hand in your notice.

4 It was a shame all that food went to waste, wasn't it?

5 If it hadn't been for her, I wouldn't be where I am today.

6 With anyone else I would've felt awkward, if they'd said that.

UNIT 11

▶ **TRACK 57**

A = Assistant, C = Customer

A: Hi. How can I help you today?

C: Hi. I reserved a car online. Here's my voucher and my driving licence.

A: Yep. OK. Let's have a look. Right. We have your car ready, but we're running a special offer this week. You can upgrade to the next range for just two euros a day, so you could have an estate car if you like.

C: It's OK. We don't have much luggage.

A: Are you sure? It's a bit more powerful as well.

C: No, I think something smaller – more fuel-efficient – is OK.

A: Fine. You ordered GPS, yes?

C: That's right.

A: OK. Would you like our additional insurance cover for damage to tyres and windscreen?

C: Isn't that already included in what I paid for online?

A: No. I think it's in the small print – and this is only three euros extra a day.

C: What are the chances of anything going wrong?

A: Well, it's up to you, but better safe than sorry, isn't it?

C: I suppose so. OK, then. It is quite cheap.

A: Fine. Can I just have your credit card? That's for the insurance, the cost of the fuel and also your deposit on the car – which is returnable when you bring the car back.

C: Right, so should I return the tank full?

A: No, there's no need, but it is full now. It's diesel, by the way.

C: OK.

A: So could you just sign where I've marked with a cross? You may want to check the car as well before you leave. There are some scratches here and here, and a small dent in the rear door.

C: OK. Great.

A: Have a good trip.

▶ **TRACK 58**

A = Assistant, C = Customer

A: Hello. Right Car Rentals.

C: Oh hello. I wonder if you can help me. My name's John Farnham. I was in this morning and picked up a car from you.

A: Oh hello, Mr Farnham. How's it going?

C: Not that well, to be honest. I'm actually calling because we have a problem with the car. I was driving along the motorway and something flew up at the windscreen and cracked it.

A: Oh, I am sorry to hear that. How bad is it?

C: Quite bad. It's a very big crack. I'm uncomfortable driving with it like this.

A: OK. I totally understand. You'll need to ring our breakdown service. The number's written in the book that came with the car.

C: Oh, OK. I'll do that now. How long do you think they will be?

A: We guarantee they'll be with you within four hours.

C: Four hours? Is that really the best you can do?

A: Well, it's usually less. Still, at least you got insurance!

▶ **TRACK 59**

1 A: The taxi fare to your hotel will be €100.
   B: €100? That's expensive!

2 A: The cheapest ticket we have left is $875.
   B: $875? If that's the cheapest, I dread to think how much the most expensive is!

3 A: Our flight leaves at five in the morning.
   B: FIVE IN THE MORNING! That's going to be a killer!

4 A: It's a bit old, but it's a nice car! I could let you have it for 1500.
   B: 1500? I was thinking more like 150, personally!

5 A: If you just wait at the station, I should be able to get there within an hour or two.
   B: AN HOUR OR TWO? It'd be quicker for me to walk!

6 A: I'm afraid the contract does state that there's a €50 penalty if you return the car more than an hour late.
   B: €50? Where on Earth does it say that?

▶ **TRACK 60**

S = Sanjar L = Lily

S: Lily. What's up? You look really fed up!

L: I just got a parking ticket!

S: Oh no! That's so annoying! Where were you parked?

L: Just round the corner. But what's really irritating is the fact it happened when I'd actually gone to look for change for the machine.

S: You're joking!

L: No! I parked my car and then I suddenly realised I only had notes. There was no-one around, so I went off to a shop to get change and when I got back …

S: That's terrible. Didn't you see who gave you the ticket?

L: I did look, but they'd vanished. They can't have been there long. I think they must've run away to avoid any arguments.

S: Probably! Couldn't you appeal?

L: It's not worth it. In the end, it's basically my word against theirs.

S: I know. You'd never win that one. How much is the fine?

L: £80! *And* I got a speeding ticket the other day after I got flashed by a speed camera! That was another 80 – and three points on my licence.

S: Oh Lily! Poor you! They're so strict on these things.

L: But it's so over-the-top. I mean, I was only doing three or four miles over the speed limit. What annoys me is the fact that people who are essentially honest are treated like criminals for these little things.

S: I know! And it's not as though people drive that fast here. You should go to Iran. You take your life in your hands driving there. People, they go so fast, but really close behind you and they don't use their brakes. They just flash their lights!

L: Ooh! It's horrible when people do that. I don't know about Iran, but I have to say, I drove through Paris last year and that was terrifying. There were like six lanes and everyone was swerving in and out of the lanes. I got cut up a couple of times and I had to brake, but then people were sounding their horns at me!

S: You see! That kind of thing doesn't happen so often here. People really are more polite here. The thing that amazed me when I first came here was the fact that people actually stopped for pedestrians at crossings. That hardly ever happens back home! You have to be really careful not to get run over.

L: It can't be that bad, can it? Drivers here can be very inconsiderate and I've had plenty of people swearing at me in London.

S: Believe me! It's nothing compared to Tehran. Sometimes there you're not even safe on the pavement! People ignore stop signs, go through red lights. Honestly, it's anarchy!

UNIT 12

▶ TRACK 61

Conversation 1

M = Michelle, J = Joop

M: Hello.

J: Oh, hi Michelle. It's me, Joop. Listen. I'm just ringing to say we're not going to make it to the restaurant later. Kaatje isn't feeling very well.

M: Oh dear. What's up?

J: Well, actually, she had a bit of a panic attack earlier while we were out.

M: You're joking!

J: No. We were in this shop and she suddenly started breathing strangely and sweating and stuff.

M: Oh no! Is she all right now?

J: Yeah, she's OK. She had a little sit down and it passed, but she'd rather stay in tonight. She told me to say how sorry she is.

M: Don't be silly! Tell her there's no need to apologise and I understand.

J: Thanks. I will.

M: What brought it on? Do you know?

J: Well, she's been under a lot of pressure at work recently, so it's probably that. She won't admit it, but it's been affecting her quite badly. She's not been sleeping well for a while, you know.

M: That's quite worrying. Has she been to see anyone about it?

J: No, not yet. Actually, we're supposed to be going away for a few days next week, but now I don't know whether we should stay here and get an appointment or leave it till we come back.

M: Well, maybe all she needs is a break.

J: Mmm. Maybe.

M: I know you're worried, but if it's only a few days … . Why don't you see how she is when you get back?

J: I guess.

M: Anyway, send her my love and tell her I'm thinking of her.

Conversation 2

C = Caitlin, N = Nina

C: Hello. Nina? Hi. It's me, Caitlin.

N: Hi! Where are you? I was expecting you at six.

C: Yeah, sorry, but Lachlan's had some kind of reaction to something he ate. We're in Rome hospital.

N: You're joking! Is he all right?

C: Yes, yes. He's fine now. He's with the nurse and they're running some tests to try and find out exactly what he's reacting to.

N: No! So what actually happened, then?

C: Well, we were in the middle of lunch and he suddenly said he was feeling a bit weird. And then all of a sudden his lips just started swelling up and he was really struggling to breathe.

N: That sounds terrifying. Is he all right now, though?

C: Yes, yes, honestly. We rushed him to the hospital – someone from the restaurant actually took us – and they dealt with him very quickly. He had an injection to reduce the swelling and they gave him oxygen to help him breathe.

N: Oh, Caitlin. You sound so calm. It must've been awful.

C: Well, I was panicking at the time, but everyone here has been so good to us. Anyway, listen, they're going to keep him in overnight – to be on the safe side.

N: Oh, right.

C: Sorry. I know we're supposed to be coming to the concert tonight.

N: Don't be silly! Lachlan's health is much more important than a concert. When do you think you'll get here tomorrow?

C: It shouldn't be too late. The doctor's going to come at nine, so if he says Lachlan's OK to leave, we should get to yours by lunchtime.

N: OK. Well, listen. Give him a hug from me and don't worry about rushing to get here tomorrow.

▶ TRACK 62

1 I'm supposed to be revising for my exams tonight.
2 We're supposed to be playing tennis later.
3 I'm supposed to be cooking for my family tonight.
4 She's supposed to be arriving at around nine this evening.
5 We're supposed to be getting married next month.

▶ TRACK 63

The incredible boom in medical tourism over the last few years has been one of the more interesting side effects of globalisation. For quite some time already, we've been used to the idea of medical staff moving from country to country, while more recently many hospitals have also started outsourcing record keeping, and the reading of X-rays, to developing countries in an attempt to cut costs. However, what's remarkably new is the ever-increasing numbers of patients from developed western countries who are opting to go abroad for treatment.

It's estimated that, before too long, over six million Americans and over 100,000 Britons will be travelling overseas for private medical or dental work, all done at knock-down prices. Countries such as Mexico, Jordan, Malaysia, India and Thailand all stand to benefit from a trade expected to soon be generating over four billion dollars a year. The question arises, however, as to whether this is a genuine win-win situation.

▶ TRACK 64

P = Presenter, DF = Damian Frisch, CL = Cindy Leong, CS = Charlotte Staples

P: Damian Frisch is a German lawyer specialising in medical negligence cases.

DF: I don't want to be accused of causing panic. I myself have had dental work done in Poland and it was excellent. However, anyone thinking of going abroad for treatment needs to know they are taking a risk. You have to be very careful and do extensive research before making a decision. Otherwise, you are gambling with your health as well as your money. Fraudulent claims and dishonest money-making schemes are commonplace and are on the increase – and the regulatory environment in many places is not as rigorous as it should be. In addition to this, many treatments are still experimental and all too often there is no after-care as patients return to their home countries. My advice would be it's better to be safe than sorry – and if something sounds too good to be true, then it probably is.

P: Cindy Leong, the CEO of a hospital in Kuala Lumpur that's particularly popular with foreigners, acknowledges that there are some opportunistic practitioners, but that this should not detract from the reality of the change that is happening.

CL: The old stereotypes of Asia as some kind of impoverished Third World are now very outdated. We boast some of the best doctors in the world and have a wide array of ultra-modern hospitals. On top of that, a few of the operations we offer now are so hi-tech that they are actually only found in Malaysia!

In addition, we offer all-inclusive packages for visitors: we can arrange visas and flights, offer a range of special menus, look after patients' companions, even book holiday resorts for post-surgery recuperation – and all at very reasonable prices. At the same time, of course, 90% of our patients are still local – and they all benefit from our innovations. Furthermore, we ensure that a portion of our profits go towards providing at least a basic level of health care for the poor, so everyone stands to benefit.

P: Certainly, that's how Charlotte Staples, a bank clerk from Rotherham, England, feels.

CS: I had a hip replacement operation in Jordan last year and I can't speak highly enough of the place. I'd been on the waiting list in England for almost a year and I reached the point where I was becoming a very impatient patient! If I'd gone private here, it would've cost me something in the region of ten thousand pounds. As it was, I got my flight, a ten-day stay in hospital, a pioneering new surgical technique *and* a two-week holiday afterwards for just over five thousand. Sun, sand, surgery *and* savings!'

▶ TRACK 65

A <u>man</u> goes to a <u>doctor</u> // and <u>says</u> // 'Doc, // I <u>think</u> there's something <u>wrong</u> with me // <u>Every</u> time I <u>poke</u> myself // it <u>hurts</u>. // <u>Look</u>!' // And he starts <u>poking</u> himself. // He <u>pokes</u> himself in the <u>leg</u>. // 'Ouch!' // He <u>pokes</u> himself // in the <u>ribs</u> // '<u>Aagh</u>!' // He <u>pokes</u> himself // in the <u>head</u> // and he literally <u>screams</u> in agony. // '<u>Aaaaagh</u>! // You <u>see</u> what I <u>mean</u>, Doc?// You <u>see</u> how <u>bad</u> it is? // What's <u>happening</u> to me?'// And the <u>doctor</u> re<u>plies</u> // '<u>Yes</u>. // You <u>seem</u> to have <u>broken</u> your <u>finger</u>!'

REVIEW 6

▶ TRACK 66

1 We've had far fewer problems with it than we were expecting.
2 I don't want to cause you any trouble.
3 What I found strange was that there were so few people there.
4 It shouldn't be that hard to find accommodation.
5 I'm supposed to be going out later, but I don't really feel like it.
6 I doubt anyone will even notice it's gone.

UNIT 13

▶ TRACK 67

1 When I found out I'd won, I was speechless. I just couldn't believe it.
2 Apparently, they discovered she'd been stealing money from them for months.
3 I suddenly realised I'd left the fire on, and by the time I got back to the house, the whole place was in flames.
4 She'd been suffering from the illness for some time, but she hadn't told anyone about it.
5 We finally realised we'd missed the turning and we'd been going in the wrong direction for half an hour!

▶ TRACK 68

Conversation 1

A: Have you read that interview with Taylor Fox in there?
B: No. I was just having a quick flick through. Why?
A: Oh, I just thought it was interesting. Did you know she's got two adopted kids from Malawi?

B: I did, yeah. From what I've heard, she couldn't have kids of her own.
A: No, actually, as I understand it, she'd already had a son with Scott Blake.
B: She's married to Scott Blake!
A: *Was*. They got divorced a while back. She's with Cody Lescott now.
B: Of course! I was going to say. So, how come she split up with Scott Blake? He seems really nice.
A: That's the image, but it turns out he's a bit of a jerk. He'd been leading a bit of a double life. He was very popular with the ladies and she decided she just couldn't trust him! That's why they called it a day.
B: You're joking! He comes across as so clean-cut and pleasant.
A: Well, apparently not. It seems – how shall I put it – that he likes to spread the love a lot!
B: Well, that's changed my opinion of him! She's better off without him in that case, then.
A: Absolutely. You should read the interview. She had quite an interesting upbringing. She just sounds very down-to-earth.

Conversation 2

C: Have you seen Ollie recently?
D: No, not for ages. Have you?
C: Yeah, I saw him last week. We went for a drink.
D: Right. How is he?
C: Oh, he's good. Really good, actually. You know he left his job at Byflix?
D: No! Really? I was told he was doing well there.
C: He was, he was, but he'd actually been thinking about leaving for a while – basically ever since he started going out with Leila.
D: Who's Leila?
C: When was the last time you saw him?
D: It must've been about a year ago. As far as I know, he wasn't seeing anyone then.
C: Oh, maybe. Well, anyway, she's Finnish. They met on holiday. She lives in Helsinki. They were commuting between here and there more or less every two weeks, but in the end, he decided to quit his job and move there.
D: You're joking!
C: No. Apparently, she's got a really good job so they can both afford to live off her salary.
D: So he's just going to be a house husband, then!
C: Yeah, well, he said he'd sent CVs to a couple of companies, but if that came to nothing he was going to retrain as an English teacher.
D: Really? Well, that's a change for the better!

▶ TRACK 69

1

I went to a wedding in Sweden last year. It wasn't so different to weddings I've seen, but the odd thing was: firstly, there was a lot of singing during the reception, which I joined in even though I'm tone deaf! Then there were lots of speeches. Anyone could make a toast and speak. And when the groom left the room for whatever reason, male guests would leap up and kiss the bride.

Another thing I discovered is that when the couple exchange vows, the person who says 'I do' loudest is supposed to be the one who'll wear the trousers in their marriage.

2

Here in Japan, the second Monday in January is called Seijin No Hi – Coming-of-Age Day. Everyone who turns twenty that year is invited to a big reception organised by the local authority to mark the fact they're now legally adults. The girls wear traditional Japanese outfits, worth thousands of pounds, which is why most girls just hire them for the day. The guys usually wear suits, but some do dress more traditionally too. At the reception there's a lengthy speech by the local mayor to congratulate them and remind them of their new responsibilities and small gifts are handed out to everyone. Family and friends usually gather outside the town hall to take photos. Then we go out and party the night away.

3

People here find death an awkward subject. In Puerto Rico, I think we have a healthier, more open attitude. When someone dies, the funeral company usually preserves the body so it can be displayed in a coffin. However, recently there's been a trend to dress the bodies and place them in a themed setting, such as sitting on their motorbike. The body's on display at least two days so everybody – friends, family, neighbours, children and adults – can pay their respects and take photos with the body before it is buried. This is all part of celebrating their life and the photo is an important record of the event. It's part of a person's history and honouring the dead is very important, which is why we also visit the graves of loved ones every year.

4

I have just had my first baby, Aadit. Family is core to the Hindu faith so there are several rites connected to birth and children. Right after the birth, the baby is washed and then the father brushes a mixture of honey and butter on the baby's lips. He then whispers special holy words in the baby's right ear as a blessing for his future life. I had quite a difficult labour but seeing my husband do that was so beautiful, I immediately forgot all the pain and exhaustion. We didn't actually name the baby till ten days after the birth, because a priest consults an astrological chart to find the position of the stars and choose the initials of the name. Later in the year we'll mark other events like the baby's first trip outside and the first time he has solid food.

UNIT 14

▶ TRACK 70

Conversation 1

A: Hi. I'd like to open a bank account, please.

B: Certainly. Do you have some form of identification with you?

A: Yes, I've got my passport here. Is that OK?

B: Yes, that's fine, but we also need proof of your current address. Do you have a utility bill – a gas bill or electricity bill or anything – with you?

A: No, I don't, I'm afraid. You see, I'm not directly paying bills at the moment. I'm living in a shared house, a student house, and I just pay a fixed amount every month.

B: OK. Well, do you have any proof of income or a National Insurance number at all?

A: No. No, I don't. I told you. I'm a student. I'm not working. I have my passport, my driving licence from back home, three cheques I want to deposit and this letter from my uni.

B: Oh, can I just have a quick look at that? Ah. OK, I see. Right, well this should be fine. What kind of account were you after?

A: Just a normal current account.

B: OK. Well, what we can do is give you a three-month trial period on a current account, which will cost you £10 a month, and if you do decide to stay with us after that, the £30 will be refunded.

A: OK. Well I guess that's fair enough.

B: Great, so if you could just fill out these forms …

Conversation 2

C: Hi. I'm flying to Caracas and I need to get hold of some Venezuelan currency. I'm not sure what it's called, I'm afraid.

D: No problem. I'll just check for you. Yes, there we are. It's the bolivar. How much are you looking for?

C: I'm after about £500 worth, please.

D: I'm not sure if we actually keep that currency in stock. Let's see. I'm awfully sorry, Madam, but I'm afraid you're out of luck.

C: Oh, OK, that's a bit annoying.

D: We do have reserves of the less popular currencies from time to time, but more often we tend to order them in.

C: Right – yeah, I won't have time.

D: I'm terribly sorry. Would US dollars do? As I understand it, they're often accepted instead of the local currency. Otherwise, I'm sure you can just change money once you arrive or make a withdrawal from a cashpoint there.

C: In theory, yes, but I've been caught out before thinking that. Maybe I'll get some dollars just to be on the safe side.

D: Of course. How much would you like?

C: I'll take 300, please.

D: OK. That'll be £206.75.

C: Really? What's the exchange rate?

D: We're currently selling at 1.48 to the pound and then there's 2% commission on all transactions.

C: Right. Well, that's slightly more than I was expecting, I must say. Can I pay by Visa?

D: Yeah, of course. Just pop the card in there. And just enter your PIN number. Thanks.

▶ TRACK 71

1 I'll look into the matter at once.
2 The computers are being very slow today.
3 There must've been some kind of mix-up.
4 I'm afraid our system is down at the moment.
5 I'm afraid there's absolutely nothing we can do.
6 I'm afraid I'm not authorised to make that decision.
7 I'll have a word with my manager and see what I can do.

▶ TRACK 72

The husband bought bricks and hired builders. Before too long, the pile of silver was almost gone, but their mansion remained unfinished. The husband decided to see if the moneybag would produce more silver, so without his wife's knowledge, he opened the bag for a second time that day. Instantly, another lump of silver rolled out. He opened it a third time and received a third lump.

He thought to himself, 'If I go on like this, I can get the house finished in no time!' He completely forgot the old man's warning. However, when he opened the bag a fourth time, it was empty. This time not one bit of silver fell out. It was just an old cloth bag. When he turned to look at his unfinished house, that was gone as well. There before him was his old hut with its leaking roof.

The poor man fell to his knees in despair, crying 'How I wish I'd never opened that bag! Now everything is lost.' His wife came over to comfort him, saying, 'Not all is lost. We still have each other. Let's go back to the mountain and cut firewood like we did before. That's a more reliable way of earning a living.'

And from that day on, that's exactly what they did.

1 28 pence out of every pound
2 the sixteen hundreds
3 370.9 million

▶ TRACK 74

1 three point seven million
   three million seven hundred thousand
2 fifteen hundred
   one and a half thousand
3 nought point nought two
   two hundredths
4 two thirds
   two out of three
5 forty percent
   two fifths
6 minus ten degrees
   ten below zero

▶ TRACK 75

1 The exact odds of winning the lottery are 1 in 13,983,816 when there are 49 numbers to choose from.
2 In Italy, food accounts for just under one fifth of a family's budget.
3 In the UK last year, 1.4 million people paid over £500 in bank charges – for example, for exceeding overdraft limits.
4 On average, families spend just 0.015% of their income on books.
5 Over three quarters of all women worry about how they'll pay off credit card bills and loans – far more than men.
6 Only about one in ten men know their current level of debt.

▶ TRACK 76

Zak: Here's an offer. If you give me one dollar each week, I promise to give you $2.6 million at some point in the future. There's just one catch, when I say 'at some point in the future', I mean at any point within the next quarter of a million years! Tempted? I bet you aren't. So why is it that so many people gamble on lotteries when the odds are nearly one in fourteen million? Probably because the whole marketing of lotteries downplays the odds against winning and emphasises the dream, the ease of getting money, and the 'good causes' that are funded by the profits lotteries make. But I don't see subsidising things like opera and Olympic sportsmen as a good cause. And it's not good when profits simply go to the government or the company that runs the lottery.

Not only does the advertising of lotteries tend to obscure this tiny chance, it also sends this subtle message – people don't need to work hard or get a good education to become wealthy; all you have to do is choose six numbers and your dreams will come true. And then also consider what those dreams are. Are they for a better society and health care? Peace and understanding? *No!* It's a mansion and a Ferrari for me! These are values – anti-educational, money-driven and selfish – that go against society. No doubt Stacy will argue that in fact it's all innocent fun and that the stakes are small, but not only do lotteries damage society in this way, they also bring pain to individuals. Take these words from John, a gambling addict from Sydney, for example: 'I sometimes gambled away my whole paycheck and had nothing left with which to pay the mortgage or feed the family. In the end, I'd bet on anything – horse races, rugby, roulette, even what the weather would be like – but it all started with lottery tickets. I wish I'd never seen one.'

There's more at stake than we imagine. Gambling destroys people's lives and nine times out of ten it starts with lotteries. They're a tax on the poor and benefit the rich and they undermine social values. They really should be banned.

▶ TRACK 77

Stacy: Well, that really was a sad story that Zak finished with there, wasn't it? Sad – but, sadly for him, also rather misleading in this particular debate. Of course, compulsive gambling is not something that we should approve of. It not only causes pain to the gambler, but also hurts their family and friends. However, addictive behaviour can take many forms: if it wasn't gambling, it might well be drugs or shopping or work. Banning lotteries won't reduce addictive behaviour – even if it were true that nine out of ten gambling addictions started with the lottery. By the way, I'd be interested to hear the source of that figure – dubiousstatistics.com, I'd imagine. But just for a moment, say it was true, nine out of ten gambling addicts start with lotteries, should we also consider banning cigarettes on the basis that heroin addicts started by smoking? Or prohibit credit cards because some people go on to be shopaholics and run up huge debts? No. In the end, I actually agree with Zak – we should take responsibility for our future wealth. It's just that where he suggests we do that by banning the lottery and investing in education, I believe that people should do it by learning self-control.

Which brings me to his point that the lottery somehow goes against hard work and education. With the greatest respect – that's complete rubbish! People don't spend money on the lottery instead of studying and working hard – it's on top of it. Similarly, lottery dreams don't replace friendship, they add to it. The real equivalent of spending money on a lottery ticket is buying, say, an ice cream. Neither are necessary for living – they provide pleasure. Let's face it, gambling in one form or another has featured in human society since time began, because it's fun! The only difference is that, unlike ice cream, the lottery ticket, however remote the chance is, might just possibly bring you the additional benefit of riches.

From that standpoint, it's a sound investment. Now Zak may not find lotteries exciting or wish that he had a Ferrari, but I do – and I can't see that there is anything anti-social in that or anything worth banning.

REVIEW 7

▶ TRACK 78

1 She found out he'd been lying to her for ages.
2 I wish he wouldn't shout at me so often.
3 He was arrested and charged with murder.
4 They said it'd already been delivered, but I haven't received it yet.
5 I wish I could've been there to see it.
6 I wish I'd never said anything about it now!

UNIT 15

▶ TRACK 79

A: Mmmm, this is delicious!
B: Thanks.
A: What's in it? It's got a bit of a lemony taste.
B: Yeah, that's the lemongrass.
A: Lemongrass?

B: Yeah, it's this … actually I don't know what you call it – a herb or spice. It looks sort of like a spring onion, you know. It's like a greyish-white stick. Anyway, you drop it in the sauce while it's cooking and it gives it a kind of citrusy flavour.

A: You don't eat it then?

B: No. It's got kind of a woody texture – it's pretty tough – so you just pick it out at the end.

A: Right – and the orangey colour … is that from carrots?

B: No. It's pumpkin and red lentils.

A: Pumpkin?

B: You know, like a big orange squash – like a melon or something – but rounder and the flesh is harder.

A: Oh yes, of course. Pumpkin – I know this word.

B: Yeah, so you use that or sometimes I use sweet potato instead.

A: Right. So how do you make it?

B: Oh, it's dead easy. You get a large onion and a couple of cloves of garlic and ginger and you chop them all really finely. I actually sometimes use a food processor. Then you put some oil in a pan and heat it up and you just throw everything into the oil, with a couple of bits of lemongrass, and I sometimes put in a whole chilli as well – just to spice things up a bit – you know, like to flavour the oil.

A: Right.

B: And then you cook it quite quickly, but you have to keep stirring 'cos you don't want it to burn. Otherwise, it can be a bit bitter.

A: OK.

B: Then you throw in the pumpkin. Oh, I should've said you have to cut stuff into cubes.

A: How big?

B: I don't know – about an inch – a couple of centimetres? It doesn't matter that much – you blend it all in the end.

A: I meant how big should the pumpkin be?

B: Oh sorry! Yeah, I don't know – they vary so much in size. Biggish, I guess, but not like the huge ones.

A: OK, and then what? You just add water and boil it?

B: Yeah, more or less. You add lentils – roughly a cupful – and a tin of coconut milk.

A: Oh right. Coconut milk.

B: Yeah, actually I often use less, because I find it a bit much otherwise. And then I add about a litre or so of chicken stock and, as you say, bring it to the boil and then once it's boiling, you reduce the heat and leave it for fifteen minutes or so – till the pumpkin's soft, anyway – and then just blend it till it's smooth.

A: So when do you take out the lemongrass?

B: Oh right, yeah. Sorry. Basically after it's simmered – at the end. It sort of floats to the surface. You just get it out with a spoon.

A: And the green herbs?

B: Well, you can use different things. I usually sprinkle a bit of chopped parsley, but basil's nice as well. And obviously a pinch or two of salt, although personally I got out of the habit of using too much because my dad's got a heart condition and he can't have too much.

A: Right. Well, it's great.

B: Yeah, I like it. Actually I sometimes do it as a sauce – just everything in reduced quantities – and I cook pieces of cod or chicken in it.

A: Mmm. Sounds great.

▶ **TRACK 80**

1

Consumer groups are today calling for firm action following recent revelations that food sold by supermarkets as beef has on occasion been found to contain traces of horse meat. This has been blamed on organised criminal gangs substituting the cheaper meat at some stage of the complex, multi-national food production cycle. In response, the government is promising to carry out a full investigation in an attempt to uncover any illegal activity in the food chain and to restore public faith in the food industry. Sales of frozen beef burgers have dropped by almost 50% since the initial findings, while sales of frozen ready meals have dropped by over 10%.

2

One of Johannesburg's most persistent – and successful – fraudsters has finally been arrested and is due to appear in court today accused of defrauding restaurants, a charge which carries a maximum penalty of nine months in prison and a 100,000 rand fine. For over a year, Wouter Gunning, aged 54, has been eating out on a regular basis in many of the city's most exclusive restaurants – and all completely free of charge. Gunning is accused of habitually introducing a cockroach into his food as he neared the end of his meals – safe in the knowledge that high-end establishments would be so sensitive to the damage that any negative publicity could cause that they would invariably waive any charge.

Remarkably, the scam only came to light following a chance conversation between two waiters from different restaurants. Mr Gunning denies all charges against him and will be pleading not guilty on the basis of temporary insanity.

3

The world's population is expected to reach nine billion by 2050, and it is estimated that food production will have to increase by 70% in the next 35 years to prevent widespread hunger. Many experts recommend using technology and data analysis to help improve the situation. Scientists claim that the analysis of large volumes of data collected from fields, warehouses, trucks and even animals' stomachs may be the key to developing more efficient farming techniques. For example, innovations in the way data is collected from cattle have the potential to transform dairy and beef production. Cows can now be fed an e-pill that will sit in their stomachs and transmit information about the animals, including heart rate, temperature, and so on. It is hoped that this will alert farmers to any animals in need of attention and ensure swift medical treatment, thus helping to reduce the $60 billion lost each year from animal sickness and death.

4

A new report urges shoppers to abandon weekly supermarket visits and instead to shop little and often, as new findings show that the cost of wasted food to UK households now exceeds £12 billion a year. The average household throws out over £450 worth of good food per year, while the average family with children squanders around £700.

Researchers also found that more than half the good food thrown out has been bought and then simply left unused. Each day 24 million whole slices of bread, 1.5 million sausages and 440,000 ready meals are simply discarded. In response to the report, the environment minister voiced her dismay:

'These findings are shocking – and at a time when global food shortages are in the headlines this kind of wastefulness becomes even more appalling. This is costing consumers three times over. Not only are they paying hard-earned money for food they're not eating, there's also the cost of dealing with the waste this creates. And then there are the climate change costs of growing, processing, packaging, transporting, and refrigerating food – just for it all to end up in the rubbish bin.'

1 The government is promising to carry out a full investigation.
2 Gunning is accused of habitually introducing a cockroach into his food as he neared the end of his meals.
3 Many experts recommend using technology and data analysis to help improve the situation.
4 A new report urges shoppers to abandon weekly supermarket visits.

UNIT 16

► TRACK 82

I = Ian, C = Claudia

C: Hello. Claudia Hellmann speaking.
I: Oh, hi, Claudia. This is Ian calling, from Madrid.
C: Oh hi, Ian. How're things?
I: Pretty good, thanks. A bit hectic – as usual for this time of year – but, you know, hectic is good. Anyway, listen, I'm just calling, really, to try to arrange a good time to talk through the sales strategy ahead of the coming season.
C: Yeah, that sounds good. When were you thinking of?
I: Well, to be honest, the sooner, the better. Would next week be good for you at all?
C: Well, if you wouldn´t mind, I´d rather wait till the week after. I'll be visiting Spain for a trade fair so I could fit in a day with you then.
I: Oh, is that the one in Valencia?
C: Yeah, that's right. Are you going?
I: No, I'm afraid not.
C: That's OK, I can easily come to head office. What day would work best for you?
I: The Tuesday would suit me best. That's the 24th, preferably.
C: OK, great. I can make any time after ten.
I: OK. I'll pencil it in. Perhaps I could actually get Piotr from Warsaw to come over too. Face-to-face is always better and it'd be good to have input from another market.

► TRACK 83

C = Customer Services Operator, F = Fabio

C: Hello, Customer Services.
F: Hi. I wonder if you can help me. I'm phoning to chase up an order I placed with your company some time ago – and that I still haven't received.
C: I'm sorry to hear that. Let's see what we can do. Would you happen to have the order number there?
F: Yeah, I do. It's EIA-290-3969.
C: Right. I'm just checking that now and I can't actually see any record of the transaction. When was the order placed?
F: The 29th of August, so that's over a month ago now. It should be under my name – Fabio Baldassari.
C: Ah, OK. I've got it now. I'm afraid there must've been some kind of mix-up in the system because it doesn't appear to have been sent out yet. I do apologise. I'll get that off to you ASAP.
F: OK. Well, at least that explains that, then!
C: Again, I'm really sorry about that again, Mr Baldassari.
F: It's OK. These things happen.
C: Thanks for being so understanding. I've just put that through and it'll be going out today by special delivery, so it should be with you first thing tomorrow. That's at no extra charge, of course.
F: Great. Thanks. Would you mind just emailing me confirmation of that?

C: No, of course not. Can I just take your email address?
F: Sure. It's baldassari – that's B-A-L-D-A-double S-A-R-I underscore f at meccanica dot com. That's meccanica with a double c.
C: Got it. OK. I'll send that through in a minute.

► TRACK 84

1 at
2 forward slash
3 underscore
4 dot
5 hyphen (you can also say 'dash')

► TRACK 85

1 postmaster at claes geller brink – that's c-l-a-e-s-g-e-double l-e-r-b-r-i-n-k dot com
2 w-w-w dot study tefl – that's t-e-f-l, dot co dot u-k
3 zip dot oh nine eight dot k-d at mail dot r-u
4 do or die, that's all one word, underscore ninety-nine at sez-nam – that's s-e-z-n-a-m dot c-z
5 u-c-y-l-j-e-double-h – that's 'double', the word and then h – not double h – at u-c-l dot a-c dot u-k
6 h-t-t-p colon and then two forward slashes, w-w-w dot xoomer – that's x-double o-m-e-r, dot alice, dot i-t forward slash, sweet floral albion – that's all one word – forward slash, capital s, capital f, capital a, dot h-t-m

► TRACK 86

P = Presenter, KT = Kevin Thomas, DE = Damien Evans

P: *Dragon's Den* is soon to enter a new series, with prospective entrepreneurs trying to raise money by pitching their ideas to five self-made millionaires who provide capital and business expertise in return for a stake in their companies. The show, which originates from a Japanese programme called *The Money Tigers*, has become an enormous success, with many other countries adopting similar formats. One of those countries, which may surprise some people, is Afghanistan. Kevin Thomas reports.

KT: In a country which has been devastated by war and where the average income is less than $500 a year, starting up a company is a risky business. Yet if Afghanistan, which still heavily depends on foreign aid, is ever going to sustain itself, then it's a risk more investors are going to have to take, according to Damien Evans, a development economist:

DE: Small and medium-sized businesses are easily the biggest employers and if employment there is going to rise as it needs to, then it's these kinds of businesses which will have to be encouraged, developed and expanded. The problem at the moment is not just instability, but a lack of skills such as financial planning and marketing strategies among business people. These are still relatively new concepts for many people there.

KT: Which is where *Fikr wa Talash* comes in. 'Dream and Achieve', as the programme is translated in English, is loosely based on business programmes such as *Dragon's Den*. The show aims to provide just that sort of basic business education as struggling entrepreneurs present their businesses and plans for expansion, which then come under scrutiny from local experts. Unlike the British version though, there are just two cash prizes and the proposed businesses also directly reflect the rather different needs of the Afghan economy. Investors in Britain have backed things such as software that allows you to create a personalised doll with the face of your choice, a men's style magazine aimed at the super-rich, and a website that searches the internet and alerts users to special offers for online gambling. In contrast, the Afghan programme included proposals to set up a dairy and a jam-making factory.

The winner of the first series was Faizulhaq Moshkani, a father of nine who had been running a plastic recycling plant in Kandahar until high fuel costs ultimately forced him to close down. The first prize of $20,000 has enabled him to build a mini-hydroelectric plant to power a new factory. The benefit for the country is that it'll soon be able to produce its own plastic rather than having to import it all from abroad.

But 'Dream and Achieve' is not simply about education and development, it's also entertainment. It is one of numerous reality TV shows which have found success in the country, including the hugely popular singing contest *Afghan Star*. TV producer Farzad Amini:

'Reality TV is popular all around the world because it's overwhelmingly positive. It gives ordinary people a chance to succeed and this brings hope to the viewers.'

Second place in 'Dream and Achieve' went to a 25-year-old mother of five. Just two decades ago, as a woman, she wouldn't have been able to work, let alone run a business. Another character featured was an ex-warlord who had rejected violence in favour of milk production. Not the kind of background you'd find people having on the British programme and sure signs of a complex and changing society.

P: That was Kevin Thomas reporting.

▶ TRACK 87

1   *Dragon's Den* is soon to enter a new series, with prospective entrepreneurs trying to raise money
2   millionaires who provide capital and business expertise in return for a stake in their companies
3   Afghanistan still heavily depends on foreign aid
4   Small and medium-sized businesses are easily the biggest employers
5   The problem at the moment is a lack of skills such as financial planning
6   plans for expansion come under scrutiny from local experts
7   high fuel costs ultimately forced him to close down
8   the hugely popular singing contest *Afghan Star*

REVIEW 8

▶ TRACK 88

1   Once you've finished that, come and tell me.
2   It'll allow us to check stock levels more efficiently.
3   I'll be seeing him later, so I can ask him if you want.
4   Would you consider branching out into other areas?
5   After the riots, they're threatening to ban public protests.
6   I used to be good at it, but I can't really do it anymore.

**Outcomes Upper Intermediate
Student's Book**

Hugh Dellar and Andrew Walkley

Publisher: Gavin McLean

Publishing Consultant: Karen Spiller

Development Editor: Stephanie Parker

Head of Strategic Marketing ELT: Charlotte Ellis

Project Editor: Nicholas Ventullo

Production Controller: Elaine Willis

Cover design: emc design

Text design: Alex Dull

Compositor: emc design

National Geographic Liaison:
   Wesley Della Volla / Leila Hishmeh

Audio: Tom, Dick and Debbie Ltd.

DVD: Tom, Dick and Debbie Ltd.

ISBN: 978-1-305-09338-6

National Geographic Learning
Cheriton House
North Way
Andover
UK
SP10 5BE

Cengage Learning is a leading provider of customised learning solutions with office locations around the globe, including Singapore, the United Kingdom, Australia, Mexico, Brazil and Japan. Locate our local office at **international.cengage.com/region**

Cengage Learning products are represented in Canada by Nelson Education Ltd.

Visit National Geographic Learning online at **ngl.cengage.com**
Visit our corporate website at **www.cengage.com**

CREDITS

Although every effort has been made to contact copyright holders before publication, this has not always been possible. If contacted, the publisher will undertake to rectify any errors or omissions at the earliest opportunity.

Printed in Greece by Bakis SA
Print Number: 01   Print Year: 2014

Photos

The publishers would like to thank the following teachers who provided the feedback and user insights on the first edition of Outcomes that has helped us develop this new edition:

Helen Tooke, Università Commerciale Luigi Bocconi, Milan, Italy; Jessica Lynton, Università Commerciale Luigi Bocconi, Milan, Italy; Abigail Fulbrook, Chiba, Japan; Hilary Irving, Central School of English, London, UK; Karen Corne; UK; Izabela Michalak; Poland; James Grant, Japan; Jeanine Hack; English Language Coach.com, London, UK; Dylan Gates, Granada, Spain; Claire Hart, ELT teacher, Germany; Matthew Ellman, British Council, Malaysia; Carla Stroulger, American Language Academy, Madrid, Spain; Richard Willmsen, British Study Centres, London, UK; Chloe Turner, St Giles Schools of Languages, London Central, UK; Jo Faith, St Giles Schools of Languages, London Central, UK; Sheila Vine, Javelin Communication, Germany; Hugh Podmore, St Giles Schools of Languages, London Central, UK; Simon Thomas, St Giles, UK; Various teachers at English Studio Academic management, UK; Isabel Andrés, EOI Valdemoro, Madrid, Spain; Isidro Almendariz, Universidad Complutense, Madrid, Spain; Simon Thorley, British Council, Madrid, Spain; Blanca Gozalo, EOI Fuenlabrada, Madrid, Spain; Ana Salvador, EOI Fuenlabrada, Madrid, Spain; Virginia Ron, EOI Rivas, Madrid, Spain; Nara Carlini, Università Cattolica, Milan, Italy; Coletto Russo, British Institutes, Milan, Italy; Lucia Luciani, Centro di Formaziones Casati, Milan, Italy; Rosetta d'Agostino, New English Teaching, Milan, Italy; James Rock, Università Cattolica, Milan, Italy; Olga Smolenskaya, Russia, Adam Scott, St Giles College, Brighton, UK